Note for the Reader

Due to the extensive restoration work that was required following the 1997 earthquake, the interiors of many historic buildings have been transformed and allocated for other uses. It is not possible to write a new edition of the guidebook at this time, as many works have yet to be completed and others are still in the planning phase. The general layout of the guidebook is still valid, but we feel it is important to inform our readers of the most significant changes that have been made so far.

1) The Pinacoteca Comunale, or municipal art gallery, was formerly located in Piazza del Comune (p. 109) but is now on Via San Francesco, on the ground floor of Palazzo Giacobetti (p. 85). Though this is not its permanent venue, it will nevertheless be located in this building.
2) Plate glass has been installed in the flooring in the Cathedral of San Rufino to show the ancient layout of the church founded by Bishop Hugo.
3) The crypt of the Basilica of Santa Chiara has undergone radical transformation. The alabaster cladding has been removed and the entry route has been changed extensively.
4) Palazzo Giampè now houses the court. The important remains of a richly frescoed Roman villa have been found beneath it, but they are not open at this time because excavation work is still underway.
5) The Post Office was moved outside Borgo Aretino past Porta Nuova (p. 159); the old Post Office (p. 106) now houses the Territorial Tourism Service.
6) The Palazzo del Capitano del Popolo in Piazza del Comune (p. 106) now houses the UNESCO Archives, the International Society for Franciscan Studies and the Accademia Properziana del Subasio.
7) The interior of the Palazzo Comunale has undergone radical changes, and part of its old architectural layout has been restored.

Thank you for choosing our guidebook

Soc. Ed. Minerva Assisi

P.M. Della Porta – E. Genovesi – E. Lunghi

Guide
to
ASSISI
History and Art

Coop. Editrice Minerva – Assisi

Note:
1. – In English, the terms CONVENT and MONASTERY refer to buildings for religious communities of nuns and monks respectively. In Italian, however, the distinction between the terms CONVENTO and MONASTERO is based on different criteria. A CONVENTO is the residence of either friars or nuns who adhere to the rules of the mendicant orders (e.g., Franciscans, Dominicans, and the orders derived from these). A MONASTERO is the residence of monks or nuns who adhere to the Benedictine rule or to other rules derived from it (e.g., Benedictines, Cistercians, Carthusians, etc.).
In this guide, these terms are left in the original Italian. The accepted English equivalent is added in parentheses whenever necessary.
2. – When referring to names of places, the original Italian names are not translated into English. For example, the Basilica of St. Francis is left as the « Basilica di San Francesco » or « The Basilica of San Francesco ».

The authors are particularly indebted to the following:
Don Elmo Antonini, responsible for the Archivio Capitolare di Assisi; Francesco Bastianini, Marino Bigaroni O.F.M., Director of the Library of the Chiesa Nuova; Don Aldo Brunacci; Luciano Canonici O.F.M., responsible for the Archivio of the Basilica patriarcale di Santa Maria degli Angeli; Francesco Guarino, Director of the Sezione di Archivio di Stato di Assisi; heirs of Laurenzio Laurenzi; Pro Civitate Christiana; Francesco Passeri; Giancarlo Ronci; Gerhard Ruf O.F.M.C.; Viviana Sonno, Director of the Biblioteca Comunale di Assisi, Gino Zanotti O.F.M.C., Director of the Biblioteca del Sacro Convento.

Photographs have been supplied by the following:
Azienda di Promozione Turistica di Assisi; Pro Civitate Christiana; Editrice Minerva Assisi; Edizioni Zubboli; Pino Antonelli; Andrea De Giovanni; Marcello Fedeli; Francesco Paolo Paci.

Editors:
Pier Maurizio Della Porta, Maurizio Zubboli.

Graphic Project:
Burcini–Sawada Design

Translation:
Mary O'Bringer: *First, Fourth, Fifth, Sixth, Seventh and Eighth Itinerary*

Julia Perry: *The Environment, The History, Religious Ceremonies and Folklore, Second and Third Itinerary*

INDICE

Cipriano Piccolpasso, Assisi (1579)

Laurenzio Laurenzi, Le Cittadelle (Fortresses) (1926)

THE ENVIRONMENT

« Assisi is situated on the side of a mountain, although she encircles it all with walls on the northern side. The steep cliffs on which she was founded make her impregnable. From this side, you can see the Tescio River, which I would call a stream since it barely flows in the winter and carries great numbers of stones, and at other times it is often dry and there is not even a drop of water. This river is within gunshot of the city and it is born in its territory about six miles away. Above its banks is the road that goes to Nocera, which is about six miles from this city, and in this distance one can also see the spring of St. Francis. This side of the mountain is unfertile and full of nothing but fire and building wood, which is quite abundant. The other hills nearby are full and are adorned with delicate fruit trees; they have a great quantity of olive trees, beautiful vineyards and excellent and plentiful pastures of its mountains. Everything it owns in the valley is perfect and very fruitful ».
(C. Piccolpasso, *The First Book of Plans and Portraits of the Cities and the Lands of Umbria under the Government of Perugia*, 1578–79).
Cipriano Piccolpasso's description still suits the city. In fact, Assisi rises on a

mountainous branch of the Subasio group and its highest point, where La Rocca Maggiore is located, is 505 meters above sea level. The valley and the sloping lands are quite fertile and are cultivated with wheat, forage, corn and, more recently, sunflowers, whose dramatic blossoms create an even more colorful and characteristic panorama that can be seen from the city.

The cultivation of vineyards is also important. These vineyards are becoming more and more refined and selective, producing good table wines such as Rosso d'Assisi, Grechetto, Trebbiano and Sagrantino.

Vast olive groves cover the rugged terrain, especially on the soutwestern sides of Mount Subasio between Assisi and Spello.

Normally, the entire mountain group is defined as Mount Subasio, and this group includes the Subasio itself (1290 m above sea level), as well as Mount Civetelle (1261 m), Mount Sermolla (1192 m) Colle San Rufino (1192 m) and Mount Pietrolungo (914 m).

Assisi's geographic position gives its wind currents particular characteristics. Because the Subasio mountain group is isolated with respect to the Appenine chain, their slopes are buffeted by seasonal winds. Despite the nearby depression of the Spoletine Valley, the city is cooled by the soft breezes that blow throughout the day, even in summer. During the winter, however, the climate is dry and cold and the night temperature often falls below zero especially during January and February.

From a morphological and geographical viewpoint, the Subasio mountains have many characteristics in common with the other Appenines, such as their rounded summmits and steep mountainsides, the eastern slopes usually being the steepest. There are deep ravines on the western side – Fosso delle Carceri, Fosso Rosceto and Fosso Renaro – and here the outcroppings of calcareous formations of the marine sedimentary series, in which many fossils can be found, are more evident. In fact, because of the red ammonite outcroppings found near the Eremo delle Carceri and the Abbey of San Benedetto, ammonite can be bought in Assisi's souvenir shops. Belemnite is found in both the « majolica » area and in the rock quarry between Mount Sermolla and Fosso Renaro.

Massive limestone, cornelian and red ammonite outcroppings are found on the west side of the Subasio, whereas the more widespread and stratigraphically distinct white, pink and red limestone formations are present on both the east and west sides as well as on the higher slopes of the mountain. For centuries, these stones have provided building material for Assisi. There are vast karst formations on top of the mountain. Noteworthy examples include the Mortaro Grande, Mortaiolo and Mortaro delle Trosce, which are large funnel–shaped depressions, some of which are 50 meters deep, that were once incorrectly believed to be volcanic craters.

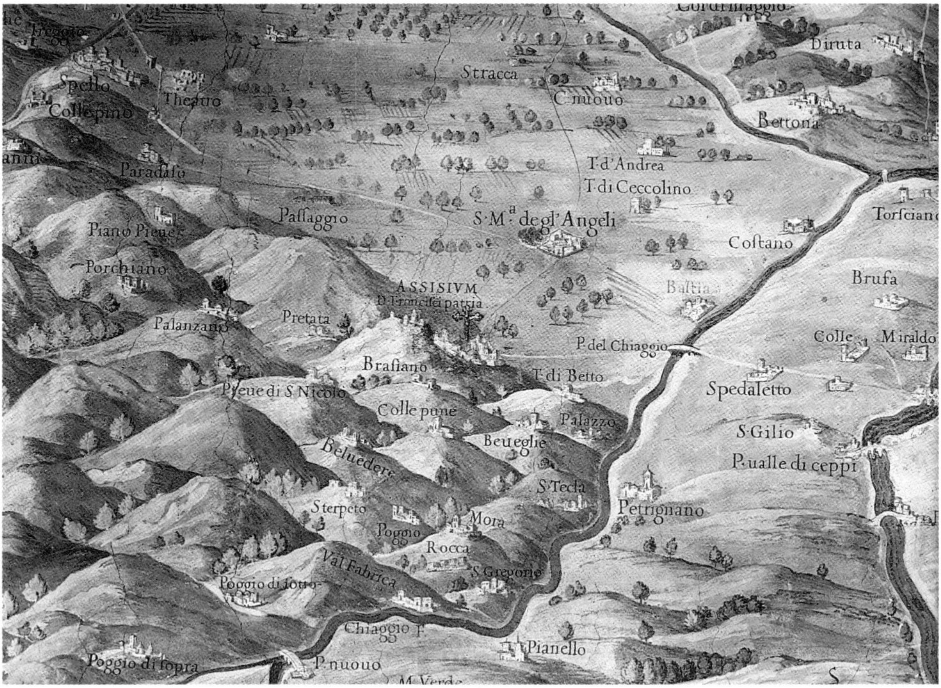

Ignazio Danti, Perugian Countryside, Assisi, and Surrounding Area (detail), Vatican, Galleria delle Carte Geografiche (1580–83)

The type of vegetation on Mount Subasio depends on the climatic conditions of its slopes and the diverse morphology and geology of the soil. The first area, up to an altitude of about 500 or 600 m is made up of olive groves. The second area is covered with patchy woods of large–leaf trees, mainly turkey oak, black hornbeam, oakwood, ash and mountain maple. Beechwood can be found on the northern side. In some areas on the western side, there are groves of holm–oaks. The Sasso Rosso woods and the holm–oak grove of the Carceri are particularly important. The latter offers an example of what the spontaneous vegetation of this area must have looked like. Human intervention has upset this vegetation almost completely, not only because of the age–old practice of deforestation but also because of the reforestation interventions, most of which took place during this century. These techniques introduced species, particularly conifers, that were alien to the native flora. Some examples include black pine, pseudotsuga, larch pine and atlantic cedar.

From an altitude of 900 m up to the summit of Mount Subasio, there are grassy fields of that offer nourishing pasture lands to the numerous herds of sheep, cattle and horses that graze there in the summer.

As far as the fauna is concerned, during the past few decades, some species such as the royal eagle, the partridge and the grey partridge have disappeared, whereas badgers, weasels, foxes, wildcats, jack rabbits, squirrels and hedgehogs are still present. While robins, nightingales and jays are seen frequently, it is also possible to find woodpeckers and buzzards as well as nocturnal birds such as horn owls, tawny owls and barn owls. In the near future, a project will be carried out for the repopulation of the deer and roe–deer that were once abundant on Mount Subasio, as documented by medieval and Renaissance records.

THE HISTORY

From the origins to the birth of the Commune

The oldest traces of human habitation in the territory later known as Assisi go back to the early Bronze Age (1900–1800 B.C.) and consist of objects that are now part of the Bellucci Collection in the Museo Archeologico in Perugia. Other archeological findings also reveal the presence of human dwellings at later times. While a group of small votive bronzes, dating to the 5th century B.C., indicate the location of a religious gathering place on the summit of Mount Subasio, in the actual town of Assisi there is no evidence of such an early human presence. An excavation near Via Arco dei Priori yielded fragments of vases and other votive materials dating to the 6th century B.C. Rather than proving the establishment of an actual town, these findings seem to indicate the location of a sanctuary that did not develop into a permanent settlement until the Hellenistic Age.

Information regarding pre–Roman and Roman Assisi is available from epigraphic and archeological sources rather than from other historical documents. The first mention of Assisi by name was found in the Latin elegy of Propertius (*scandentisque Asis consurgit vertice murus/murus ab ingenio notior ille tuo*, Propertius IV, I, 125 and foll.) Pliny refers to the inhabitants of Assisi as members of the Umbrian population and the name of the city is found in the Greek writings of Ptolemy and Procopius.

Umbrian Assisi was politically influenced by nearby Perugia, a powerful and prosperous Etruscan city. Like the other Umbrian cities, Assisi became part of the Roman Confederation in 89 B.C. and was formally made a Roman *municipium* by the *lex Julia de civitate*. Epigraphic documentation indicates that this political change developed gradually. In fact, the Umbrian magistracy, known as marones, as well as the Umbrian language (written using the Latin alphabet) were conserved.

As Assisi grew, it became a prosperous city whose physical development followed an organic pattern. It was surrounded by mighty walls; terraces built to conform to the terrain were also supported by powerful substructures. The monumental remains of this era have allowed the reconstruction of the pattern of the walls and of the urban structure. The probable time of construction of the city walls is thought to fall between the end of the 2nd century and the middle of the 1st century B.C., or in other words, between the end of the Umbrian period and the beginning of the municipium period. The city wall, 2500 m long, encircles a surface area of approximately 600,000 square meters. Of all the doors and gates that marked the openings in the wall, only one, porta urbica, remains. Today it is part of the Palazzo Fiumi–Roncalli. The view from the valley could shown an urban landscape of broad steps leading upward to the sacred monuments, whose focal point was the Temple of Minerva and the space below it, which was believed to be the Forum. It is possible that the city Forum was located in the vast terraced area situated somewhere between the present–day Piazza San Rufino and Piazza Nuova. This was also the site of the Circus, where the Amphitheater was also built, presumably around the middle of the 1st century A.D. The hypothesis that Assisi developed from its origins as a religious gathering place is an interesting one, and the idea that is was a sacred place persists in its history. Archeological findings and historical documents testify to a tradition of devotion to many divinities: Hercules, Aretei, Bonus Eventus, Ianipater, Jupiter, Paganicus, Minerva and the Dioscuri, Castor and Pollux, to whom were dedicated the statues placed in the tetrastyle aedicula in front of the Temple of Minerva. These images and their association with the water and health cults are reflected in the abundance of fountains and cisterns throughout Assisi. This tendency and the presence of the aedicula in the central terrace of the temple has caused many to theorize that this sacred building may, in fact, have been dedicated to the Dioscuri.

Life in the *Roman municipium* must have reached a high economic, social and cultural level, judging from archeological remains of its monuments and the decoration of private buildings (see the so called « house of Propertius »). It should be remembered that most scholars retain that the great Latin poet, Sextus Propertius, was from Assisi.

According to tradition, the 3rd century marked the transition of Assisi from a pagan to a Christian city when San Rufino, its first bishop, was martyred by drowning in the Chiascio River in 238 A.D. For a long period after the 3rd century, references to Assisi are rare. After the fall of the Roman Empire, *Assisium* was damaged by barbarian invasions. After the Belisario's conquest of the Gothic fortification held by Theodoric, it fell under Byzantine domination. Later, despite strong resistance from the Byzantine garrison led by Sisifro, it was captured by Totila. This episode in the military history of Assisi is described by Procopius in *De bello gotico*. After it was invaded by Alboino in 568, Assisi fell under Lombard domination and became part of the Duchy of Spoleto. The armies of Charlemagne also occupied the town and destroyed the city walls, which were later rebuilt. Writings concerning life in Assisi during this period are scarce and thus little is known of its urban changes. It is assumed that there was a long period of decline that persisted until the end of the 11th century.

The diffusion of Benedictine monasteries created numerous monastic centers near Assisi (see San Benedetto on Mount Subasio). Eleventh–century documents indicate the construction of new buildings in the town center as well as the appropriation of other buildings by religious groups.

Further evidence of this renewal occurred when Bishop Ugone of Assisi built a new church, dedicated to San Rufino, on the site of a more modest one that had

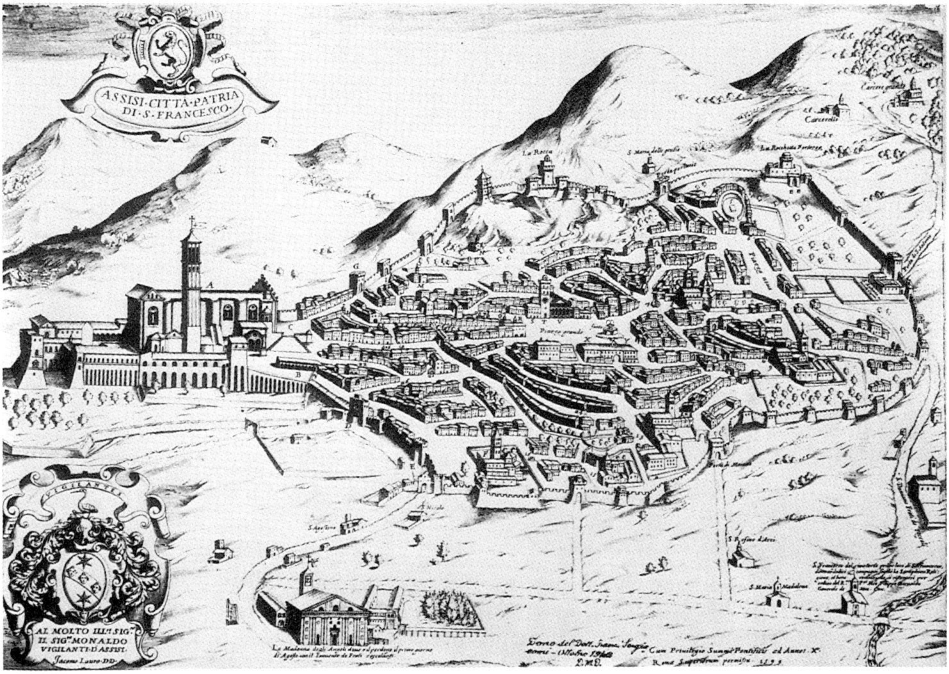

Giacomo Lauro, Assisi, the Home of St. Francis (1599)

been built earlier in the 7th century. This new church later became the cathedral. In addition, this was a time of economic and demographic growth but also the beginning of political and territorial controversies. These controversies led to wars between Assisi and Perugia which continued for many years.

From the 11th century until the 14th century, there were many different settlements in the Assisi area. In 1160, a decree issued by Frederick Barbarossa established its borders and put its jurisdiction under the control of his empire. After a revolt against this imperial power, Assisi was conquered in 1174 by Christian, Archbishop of Magonza. Three years later, authority to govern Assisi was given to Conrad of Urslingen, who resided in the same fortress that the emperor himself had visited many times. The changes in the political and social conditions galvanized the forces that would later give birth to the formation of the free « comune » of Assisi.

In 1198, a crisis of imperial power developed when the church claimed that it had the right to control the territories of the Duchy of Spoleto. Taking advantage of the general situation, the *homines populi* of Assisi rose up against Conrad, Duke of Spoleto and Count of Assisi, by destroying the fortress and the homes of the noblemen who had sustained the imperial power. The new Comune found it had to fight for its rights against many antagonistic factors: the demands of papal power,

the antipathy of the territory's feudal nobles and the expansionistic goals of the Commune of Perugia, against whom Assisi had fought to establish its boundaries. This conflict ended in 1202 with the terrible defeat of the armies of Assisi near Collestrada. Within Assisi, however, conflict continued between the *boni homines* or nobles and the *homines populi*, who represented the emerging middle class of merchants and artisans who, having gained political and economic strength, claimed the right to govern the town.
The military defeat also represented the defeat of the middle class. The nobles, who had been exiled and had found refuge in Perugia after the defeat of 1202, returned to Assisi strengthened in their determination to become the governing class once again. In 1203, a document sanctioned peace between the two factions but with the practical victory of the *boni homines*. Things continued to develop, however; the *homines populi* gradually reacquired land so that a document of 1210 indicates that a better balance had developed between the two groups of citizens in the Commune and its residents' liberation from feudal ties was thus sanctioned, although *sub condicione.*

Saint Francis and the first Franciscan institution

The son of Monna Pica and Pietro di Bernardone, destined to become the most famous citizen of Assisi, was born towards the end of the 12th century. There are few facts regarding his birth and childhood. Although he was named Giovanni at birth, it is traditionally said that his merchant father decided to call him Francesco to celebrate the wealth he had amassed through his French contacts who supplied him with their goods, the so–called « panni franceschi » (French clothes) that filled his storeroom. According to the Franciscan *legendae*, it was during one of these trips that this long–awaited son was born. These hagiographic accounts say that he was born in a stable, between a donkey and an ox, in order to show that the figure of Francis was an *alter Christus* from the very beginning. His birthdate, which was determined by calculating backwards on the basis of the saint's age when he died, has been placed between 1181 and 1182.
The first biographers – Thomas of Celano, the « Three Companions » – describe Francis as the courteous and generous son of a prosperous merchant family. He was well–placed in the social life of Assisi and was always willing to share his wealth with his companions.
Although he worked in his father's business, Francis dreamed instead of a life of adventure and investiture as a knight. In fact, he fought in the Battle of Collestrada in 1202 and was taken prisoner. Upon his release, he returned to Assisi. He grew restless and after a while he left for Apulia to fight with Gualtiero di Brienne who was preparing a crusade. During his journey, Francis became seriously ill and after meditating at length and receiving miraculous visions that revealed his true

vocation to him, he returned to Assisi. Renouncing his dream of military glory and becoming more and more detached from his worldly way of life, he dedicated himself to works of charity. According to the Franciscan legends, while on a pilgrimage to Rome, Francis met « Lady Poverty » for the first time: she was to be his beloved bride for the rest of his life. He exchanged his fine clothes for a beggar's rags and, giving away his remaining possessions, he begged for alms. Thus, he experienced that perfect joy which was to sustain him during a life of suffering and voluntary privation that ended when, lying on the naked ground, he met « sister death ». Francis' encounter with the leper and the miracle of the Crucifix of San Damiano that spoke to him, saying, « Go and repair my house », convinced Francis that he wanted to live in poverty to serve the Lord. Francis abandoned his fine clothes and began to live as a « penitent », wearing a hermit's robe and boots and carrying a walking stick. In fact, just like one of the « penitents » who volunteer their help to construct new churches or to restore old churches, he began to rebuild the little church of San Damiano, taking the words of the Crucified Christ literally. However, Francis' path to sainthood was not over yet. While listening the Gospel, he became convinced that to strive for perfection, one must not only live in absolute poverty and purity but also preach the word of God. Francis then exchanged his hermit's garb and boots for a homespun habit cut in the form of a cross and belted with a funiculum (cord) and he began to carry out his vocation by bringing the Gospel message to the people. He quickly attracted companions in his work and they were offered refuge at the Porziuncola, which had been granted to Francis by the Benedictine monks. These first Franciscans went to Rome between 1209 and 1210 to ask the Pope to confirm their way of religious life.

They were met with mistrust by the Holy See, since at that time, the Church was facing the problem of lay movements that, in some cases, had given way to decidedly unorthodox positions. Innocent III was pope at that time and with great determination, he had put into effect two different lines of conduct, so that if on the one hand he was repressing any groups whose beliefs were deemed to be heretical, on the other hand he maintained papal control over movements that conformed to Catholic orthodoxy. The friars of Assisi obtained papal consent and returned first to Rivotorto and then to Santa Maria degli Angeli to begin their mission.

Between 1211 and 1212, Chiara di Favarone d'Offreduccio followed Francis'example, leaving her home against her family's wishes. She fled to the Porziuncola, where St. Francis cut her hair to confirm her choice of a life of poverty and penitence. Clare and her early followers established their residence at the church of San Damiano.

In a short time, Francis' followers became very numerous. Duing the chapter held at the Porziuncola in 1217, the Friars Minor decided to extend their preaching activities to the regions across the Alps. The friars attracted followers wherever they went. Since the number and political consistency of the movement were now in-

From the book by William Brockedon, Assisi (1842)

creasing, the first problems began to arise between the friars who wished to remain strictly faithful to the Franciscan rule and those who wished to respect its ideals without adhering to it rigidly, especially as far as the interpretation of the concept of poverty was concerned. When he heard the news of the problems that had arisen within his movement, Francis hurried back from Palestine. Both the birth of the Order as well as its clericalization were approved definitively by Pope Honorius III, initially with the *Regula non bullata* (Rule without the papal seal) in 1221. Then in 1223, he assigned to the Order of the Friars Minor a text containing Francis' principles in the form that had been drawn up by the jurists of the Papal Curia. This rule was called the *Regula bullata* (Rule with the papal seal).
As early as 1220, however, Brother Francis had resigned the leadership of his order to dedicate himself even more fervently to preaching, prayer and penance. Two years before his death, while he was praying on Mount La Verna, Francis received the most meaningful sign of his sanctity when his body was marked with the Stigmata. This episode reinforced the parallel drawn between the life of St. Francis and the life of Christ. His principles of faith and of religious life were set down in the *Canticle of the Creatures* and in his *Testament*, in which the principles of his choice of religious life were strictly confirmed.
Francis died in 1226, surrounded by his brothers. The citizens of Assisi triumphantly carried his body to the crypt of the Church of San Giorgio, which is now the Chap-

el of the Sacrament in the Church of Santa Chiara. This is the place in which Francis was initially buried and Pope Gregory IX celebrated his solemn canonization ceremony here on July 16, 1228.
Clare lived on for many years after Francis' death and it was not until shortly before death in 1253 that she received for her own Order Pope Innocent IV's approval of the rule that conformed to the *Regula bullata* of the Friars Minor.
St. Francis is certainly one of the most fascinating figures of the Christian world. Literature, music and the figurative arts have been inspired by the saint, whom Dante compares to the sun, and by his message, still valid even today, that preaches peace, love and respect for all creation, together with the noble feeling of joyous gratitude for being part of this creation.
A vast amount of literature has been written about the life of the saint. The early biographies handed down to us by his followers, Thomas of Celano and the « three companions », and writings inspired by Franciscan mysticism – *The Little Flowers and Mirror of Perfection* – are not only proof of the great mark left by Francis on his own contemporaries but they also offer insight as to the life and customs of the times.

From the 13th to the 16th century

The period between the 13th and the 16th centuries brought prosperity to Assisi. Political and social tranquillity permitted the Commune to extend its domain. Large country land–holders divided their properties into smaller areas as many land–owners preferred to live in the city. The population increase caused by this move to the city resulted in increased construction activity. Assisi then developed the elongated shape it has now. Large buildings for religious use defined the urban pattern of the town. The Basilicas of San Francesco and Santa Chiara were placed at the ends of streets that cross the main square (Piazza del Comune), where the city councilors established the political and administrative centers of the community.
In 1212, they asked the Benedictines for the small building of San Donato, formerly the Temple of Minerva, which became the seat of the Podestà (city magistrate). By 1228, the square was enlarged to allow the construction of many palaces over the course of the next century, as homes for the magistrates. The city walls were enlarged for the first time in 1260 to include the Basilica and Convent of Santa Chiara. A new and final addition to the walls was made in 1316 during a period of urban organization and planned construction activity.
In 1237, Pope Gregory IX granted the people of Assisi the privilege of freely electing the Podestà as well as their other magistrates. The office of « Capitano del Popolo » (Captain of the People), which local historians believe was instituted in 1230, is first documented in 1262, and the magistracy of the Priori is mentioned as early as 1330. Assisi's economy seems to have flourished during this period, and

artisans' products and consumer goods appear to have been sold mostly on the local market.
The strength of the Franciscan presence in Assisi was emphasized by the enormous Basilica of San Francesco, which was large and out of proportion with respect to the size of the city during the 13th century. Its presence reflected such religious, cultural and political power that no new religious order was established there. After the death and canonization of St. Francis, large crowds of pilgrims came to Assisi, especially for the « Assisi Pardon ». Furthermore, the construction of the basilica also attracted many great artists such as Giunta Pisano, Cimabue, the Roman painters and Giotto. They were followed by the fourteenth–century Sienese masters, Pietro Lorenzetti and Simone Martini. The development of other religious institutions born after the Franciscan movement changed the cultural and urban environment. These churches and hospitals of charitable associations and the buildings of lay confraternities that arose between the 14th and 15th centuries provided a financial base for the further development of the city's artistic heritage. Within this ambience, the literary genre of the laud, both lyric and dramatic, was created. By this time, the Church gave its complete trust to the Guelph–dominated city, so that the Basilica essentially became a fortified papal residence and Pope Innocent IX gave the friars custody of the papal treasury. The second decade of the 14th century saw political conflicts within Assisi when in September of 1319, the Ghibelline Muzio di Francesco overthrew the Guelphs. The Guelphs became allied with Perugia and brought war against Assisi. Muzio di Francesco, in desperate need of money, sacked the treasury of the basilica, thus bringing upon himself the anger of Pope John XXII, who excommunicated him and the entire city.
The war ended with the city's submission to Perugia and caused much damage throughout the city, including damage to the city walls, whose reconstruction was forbidden by the Perugian magistrates.
After the period of the papal residence in Avignon, Assisi came under the control of the Spanish Cardinal Egidio Albornoz, who led it back to papal affiliation, thus setting the city free of Perugia's domination. He also began urban reconstruction, including the city walls and the fortress. Peace did not last long, however, and friction developed between two factions, the *Parte de Sopra* (« Part from Above »), led by the Guelph Nepis family, and the *Parte de Sotto* (« Part from Below »), led by the Ghibelline Guglielmo di Carlo, nephew of Muzio di Francesco. Fighting for domination of the city, the Ghibellines prevailed and Guglielmo di Carlo ruled the town until 1385.
Conflict between the factions resumed and so until the first half of the 16th century, Assisi suffered sacking and destruction by many armies. Having fallen into the hands of Broglia di Trino, who was at the service of Pope Boniface IX, Assisi found itself under the domination of Giangaleazzo Visconti in 1400. After Visconti's death, the Ghibelline Francesco Fiumi of the *Parte de Sotto*, helped by

Cimabue, St. Francis, detail

the dukes of Montefeltro, conquered the city but he only remained in power for one year, because Assisi's Ghibellines were defeated by the Guelph troops led by the Perugian, Malatesta Baglioni. The command of the city was then given to a captain of fortune, Braccio Fortebraccio. In 1419, an attempt to revolt against the Perugians failed and this was soon followed by a period of harsh repression. Following Braccio's death, the city returned to papal domination. In 1438, Francesco Sforza, to whom Pope Martin V had already given authority over Assisi, was attacked by the troops of Francesco Piccinino, who was in the service of Perugia. The worst sack of the city occurred following its conquest in 1442 by the troops of Niccolò Piccinino, who destroyed part of the city walls, profaned the convents, pillaged many buildings and burned the documents of the city's *armarium.*

Assisi was too weakened by these attacks to find the strength to continue its internal conflicts. Nevertheless, factional hatred was rekindled because of the conflict that broke out in 1488 between the Oddi family and the Baglioni family in Perugia. In Assisi, the Nepis family sided with the former and the Fiumi family with the latter, thus involving the factions they headed in a period of renewed violence and destruction.

Then in 1503, the city underwent yet another violent sacking, this time by Cesare Borgia's troops.

Assisi, now under complete papal domination, finally saw the end of the fratricidal fighting that had ravaged it for almost two centuries. In 1542, the Pope sent a new governor, Giovanni Andrea Cruciani, to proclaim the new law that the city would no longer be divided into five districts or « Porte » but into three and that « *... each one of these thirds, upper and lower simultaneously, be united and that they never again mention the upper and lower or Guelph and Ghibelline parts, under the penalty of forfeiting their offices ...* ».

This period of war and pestilence certainly created an unfavorable environment for the city, its art and its culture. In spite of the interest that several popes had expressed in the city – for example, the work commissioned by Pius II and Sixtus IV for the restoration and enlargement of the Rocca Maggiore as well as the work commissioned by the latter in the Basilica and Convent of San Francesco – most of the work was required to repair the damages of war and was done by workmen from other areas, especially the Lombard masters.

Among the important artists associated with Assisi during the late 15th and early 16th centuries were Andrea d'Assisi, known as l'Ingegno or Giovanni di Pietro Spagna, Tiberio d'Assisi and Dono Doni.

The first stone was laid for the Basilica of Santa Maria degli Angeli in 1569. The basilica was designed by Galeazzo Alessi, a Perugian whose work can also be seen in the Basilica of San Francesco. He also restored the structures of the Cathedral of San Rufino, an unfortunate event in our opinion, since he concealed its Romanesque architecture forever.

During this period, the « Accademia del Monte » was established in Assisi. Its name was changed to « Accademia dei Desiosi » and was changed yet again in 1656 to « Accademia degli Eccitati ». Its members worked on religious or moral dissertations and composed and presented pastoral fables and plays. Today it is known as the « Accademia Properziana del Subasio ».
During the 16th and 17th centuries, a great deal of musical activity was also carried out by the choirs of the Basilica of San Francesco and in the Cathedral of San Rufino.
Nevertheless, at this time Assisi was far removed from the intellectual and artistic vitality that had given rise to the most important monuments of the city during the 13th and 14th centuries. In fact, after the Albornoz era, Assisi experienced slow yet continuous cultural and economic decline in spite of the fertility of the surrounding territory. Descriptions of the city offered by sixteenth–century authors such as Leandro Alberti, give us an image of desolate abandon. According to Cipriano Piccolpasso, who described the city in *The First Book of Plans and Potraits of the Cities and Lands of Umbria under the Government of Perugia* (1578–79), « *It is a poorly arranged city where one sees many abandoned and ruined houses next to inhabited ones, so that it seems to be the remains of a city rather than a complete city. I believe it has been reduced to this by time or by war* ». When he discusses its residents, Piccolpasso says that some of them are famous doctors or soldiers *even though they are an idle people ... They are unpleasant people, not very courteous to foreigners nor even to each other.*

From the 17th century to the Unification of Italy

By now, Assisi had been absorbed completely into the domain governed by the papacy, and an oligarchy of noblemen and merchants reemerged. They built new buildings, almost always using older structures. These constructions changed the appearance of the city and they weighed down the urban structure with imposing architecture that was not compatible with the medieval scale of the earlier buildings. Some examples of this are Palazzi Bernabei, Giacobetti, Fiumi –Roncalli, Bini and Locatelli.
Much of the construction was also religious in nature, one of the most important being the Chiesa Nuova, which was built in 1615. The work of artists such as Giorgetti, Marinelli, Martelli and Cesare Sermei, all of whom had also worked in the Basilica of San Francesco, can be seen here.
Oddly juxtaposed with these pretentious buildings were the ruins of the houses that were abandoned as the population declined. The agricultural economy was essentially based on the exploitation of the lands toward the valley, whose landscape was changed by new settlements and by the drainage of the wetlands through the diversion of the water channels. At this time, sharecropping became widespread

and in the area around Assisi it has remained the most common juridical relationship between farmers and landowners until just recently.

Assisi also declined in importance as a religious center. In fact, after the Council of Trent (1545–1563), theologians and intellectuals reflected renewed interest in the original Church and in its early martyrs. They considered the Middle Ages a period of spiritual decadence and thus the movements that arose during that time were thought to be less deserving of attention. This attitude prevailed until the beginning of the 19th century and foreign travelers in Italy showed little interest in Assisi except for its Roman ruins. Johann Wolfgang Goethe came to Assisi in 1786 only to admire the Temple of Minerva. In *Italian Journey* he said, *« with a strong wind I went into Assisi as I wanted to take a walk through that world that seemed so solitary. I left behind with great distaste the enormous constructions of the babelich overlapping of churches in which Saint Francis lies »*. Other writers were more interested in the basilica for its artistic treasures than for its sacredness. Even the cartography of the period gave scant attention to the city. The maps of Assisi made in the 17th and 18th centuries were based on sixteenth–century models. They emphasized the imposing buildings of the Franciscan communities while neglecting to represent the civilian structures. Based on this, it could be deduced that most of these map–makers had no direct knowledge of the city.

Plagues and earthquakes again brought torment to Assisi between the 17th and 19th centuries. Few inhabitants remained within the city walls and then Assisi fell into cultural and economic decline. Not even the Enlightenment or the French occupation between 1797 and 1798 could shake the city from its torpor.

Napoleon's descent into Italy damaged the city even further. In 1808, the French troops sacked the churches for works of art and once again, precious treasures were stolen from the Basilica of San Francesco.

The earthquakes of 1832 and 1833 caused such severe damage that the Basilica of Santa Maria degli Angeli had to be rebuilt almost completely. Many citizens, lacking the money necessary to rebuild their homes, resorted to selling the stones and roofing tiles from abandoned houses.

In 1848, following the statute granted by Pius IX, there was a certain intellectual reawakening in the city. A citizens' group favoring the vision of national unity according to the federalist theory of Vincenzo Gioberti was established. Garibaldi's presence was of little consequence and in fact, the Republicans ruled for just a short time from February to June, 1849. After this, Assisi returned under pontifical protection. On September 29, 1860, the Piedmont army swept through Assisi without meeting any resistance and the city was annexed to the kingdom of Italy.

From the discovery of the remains of St. Francis and St. Clare until the Fascist period

Once again, it is Assisi's role as a holy city that influences its destiny. The discovery of the remains of St. Francis in 1818 and those of St. Clare in 1850 resulted in solemn ceremonies that attracted crowds of pilgrims to Assisi.

Because of these events, as well as the Romantics' interest in the Middle Ages, Assisi once again attracted not only pilgrims but also intellectuals from many different countries. Although these intellectuals described the city as poor, they made it into a spiritual temple of culture and art. In the second half of the 19th century, the French historian Ernest Renan wrote, « *The city is even older than its monuments. It is completely medieval; whole streets that have been abandoned have remained, stone for stone, what they were in the fourteenth century.... The profusion of art goes beyond all imagination. The outside, the inside, the doors, the windows, the beams, the chimneys: all the parts of the houses are painted and sculpted* ».

The work carried out by the historian Antonio Cristofani during this period deserves mention. In 1886, he published a work that continues to be fundamental for anyone studying the city's past: *History of the city of Assisi.*

However, more than anyone else between the end of the last century and the beginning of the 20th century, Paul Sabatier, Johannes Jorgensen, Eduard Schneider, and G.K. Chesterton revived the Franciscan message and spread their knowledge of Assisi's charm. The « Società Internazionale di Studi Francescani », a society that still has its headquarters in the city, was founded thanks to Paul Sabatier, who was assisted by the Assisi scholar Francesco Pennacchi.

The influx of pilgrims and tourists provoked an increase in the cash assets of the private sector. The city's urban structure was altered by a resumption in construction activity that followed a moderate population increase.

In 1866, the construction of the railway encouraged more visitors and the road system was modified to facilitate connections between the city and the station.

Inadequate lodging facilities prompted far–seeing private investors to build new hotels. The first to be opened was Hotel Subasio, built in 1868 by Andrea Rossi. Main arteries were created inside the city walls, thus resulting in the demolition of ancient buildings and profoundly changing the look of the city.

The abolition of the religious societies, authorized by the provisional goverment of Marquis Gioacchino Napoleone Pepoli with his decree of December 11, 1860, had already changed the face of the city, damaging its artistic heritage. Some ecclesiastical buildings that were confiscated by the state were stripped of their furnishing and their architectural structure was modified as well. However, the rearrangement of the street patterns and the medieval revival that took place for the Franciscan Year that was proclaimed in 1926 had even more dire consequences. The piazza, which had already been disfigured in 1881 by the demolition of the building on the east side to make way for the entrance to the modern–day Via San Gabriele dell'Addolorata, was further ruined by the demolition of the Church of San Niccolò, which was replaced with the neo–Gothic Post Office. The Fascist era encouraged the rise of these false architectural styles, as seen in the Convitto Nazionale

Principe di Napoli in Piazza Matteotti and in the Istituto Serafico per sordomuti e ciechi (Institute for the Blind, Deaf and Dumb) built in 1940 in the lower part of the city. Also practiced during this period was the removal of the external plaster from the buildings in order to recreate a « medieval city of stone », thus presenting – at just a cursory glance, in any case – a confusion of ancient walls, seventeeth– and eighteenth–century constructions and modern fakes.

The city in our times

Because of tourism, starting at the end of the 19th century, hotels, cafés and stores were built and there developed various local artisan traditions geared towards the production of artifacts to be sold to tourists.Ceramics, wrought iron and embroidery continue to be typical products of the local artisans.
Thus, there was progressive economic revival and population growth, even if the ensuing uncontrolled building activity unfortunately caused the negative results discussed earlier. World War II brought this economic rebirth to a standstill.
The « city of stone » suffered little physical damage during the war. In fact, Assisi was declared a hospital city through the mediation of the Holy See following the proposal of the podestà, and thanks also to the commander of the German occupation, Colonel Müller, a man who was sensitive not only to the beauty and richness of the city's artistic treasures but also to its role as the birthplace of St. Francis. Observing its mission of charity, Assisi also welcomed war refugees, thus vastly incresing its number of poor resident.
Recovery from the economic consequences of World War II was certainly not easy, but once again, the city's sacredness played a role in its revival. The proclamation of the Holy Year of 1950 relaunched tourist activity and breathed new life into tourism–related businesses. In fact, whereas before the war there had been an elite type of tourism, during the Holy Year, given the importance of the devotional practice of visiting the Franciscan shrines, a great number of tourists chose to visit Assisi. This was the beginning of mass tourism and the city had to prepare for it by building adequate structures. Fortunately, during the fifties, Assisi was included in a group of historically important cities that were required to devise a town planning scheme (1956). This became the basis of Giovanni Astengo's project for the preservation and development of the urban center and its surrounding territory.
We should also mention the activity of Arnaldo Fortini, who with his in–depth studies on the history of Assisi and on Franciscanism, both during the Fascist era and later, contributed to keeping alive devotional and intellectual interest in the cultural heritage of the city and in the emblematic significance that the city, as the birthplace of St. Francis, has assumed all over the world.
Currently, Assisi's economic activity is tied mainly to tourism, which seems to increase year by year. Thousands of people visit Assisi each year. They are attracted not only by its role as a city of peace and of prayer, by its works of art and by its

still well–preserved natural environment, but also by the hospitality that its tourist facilities can offer. Unfortunately, this has caused residents to move out of the city center, since people have found it preferable to restore houses and stores to make them into hotels,pensions and various types of stores. In the valley below Assisi, in addition to tourist facilities, small and middle–size industries in various areas of production have developed. Consequently, the depopulation of the city center has been accompanied by a sharp increase in the population of these suburban areas.
The Franciscan message has been incorporated by various peace and environmental movements. It has been used, and perhaps abused, by political parties and by various organizations for propaganda purposes. Nevertheless, anything of any validity is always destined to become the banner for many different groups, while still maintaining its own integrity and commitment to goodness and justice.
The « World Day of Peace » was celebrated in Assisi on October 27, 1986. Invited by Pope John Paul II, representatives of all races and religions were united for the first time in history to pray for one thing: world peace. Because the Franciscan message is universal, Assisi was granted the privilege and responsibility of showing to world the positive feelings experienced by all religions for brotherhood among people and for respect for the earth.

RELIGIOUS CEREMONIES AND FOLKLORE

Holy Week

The religious ceremonies held during Easter week are particularly fascinating and touching.

At sunset on each Friday during Lent, the ceremony of the **Corda pia** (cord of piety) is celebrated in the Basilica of San Francesco. Wearing cords around their necks, the friars walk in procession to the Chapel of the Crucifix and then, on their knees and with their arms outstretched, they recite the invocations and antiphons of the liturgy. The name given to this ceremony is derived from the first words of the refrain of the Latin hymn sung for the occasion: *Corda pia enflammantur dum Francisci venerantur stigmata insigna.*

On Holy Thursday, in the Cathedral of San Rufino, the **Deposition from the Cross** is commemorated after the *Missa in coena Domini*. As the ancient *laudes* are sung, a 15th century Crucified is taken from the cross, placed on a bier and venerated by the faithful. At the conclusion of this liturgy, « sepulchers » are arranged on the main altars of all the churches in the city.

On the morning of Good Friday, the **Procession of the Dead Christ** is held. A bier bearing a statue of Christ is carried in a procession to the Basilica of San Francesco, stopping at the cloistered convents along the way. The procession is very dramatic because of the penitents who, wearing hooded habits, bear crowns of thorns on their heads. Barefooted, they follow the procession carrying heavy wooden crosses on their shoulders.

In the evening, another procession leaves from San Rufino. This honors the *Virgin of Sorrow*, who is symbolized by the seven swords piercing her heart. This statue is accompanied by the confraternities and the penitents as it is brought to the Basilica of San Francesco to join the procession of the « dead Christ ». On this occasion, the city is illuminated only by torchlight. The long line of clerics, penitents and confreres, the flickering light of the torches and the « death rolls » of the drums make this devotional practice very touching and dramatic. This ceremony evokes a dramatic laud, the Laud of the Passion, which is described in the fourteenth–century statutes of Assisi's confraternities. Ever since that time, this ceremony has marked one of the devotional duties of the confreres.

Calendimaggio

During the early days of May, a unique festival is celebrated in Assisi. For the three days of Calendimaggio, the city is divided into the two factions that fought to rule the city from the Middle Ages up to the Renaissance, causing much destruc-

Assisi, Good Friday procession

tion and bloodshed. These factions are the *Parte de Sopra* (Part from Above) and the *Parte de Sotto* (Part from Below).

During Calendimaggio, these two groups challenge each other to a courtly duel composed of music, reconstruction of the city's medieval life and ancient popular games. At the end, a prize is awarded.

Even a simple walk through the city is astounding, as during this period, the streets of Assisi seemed to have gone back through time. The look of the city, the banners, the citizens – almost all of whom are in costume, the taverns and the very air itself allow us relive a fantastic medieval dream.

Ascension Day

It is customary to go up on Mount Subasio to spend the night on the eve of this feastday. On Ascension Day, Mass is celebrated at the « Stazi », or mountain shelters. Afterwards, popular games are organized. In the past, sticks and staffs were decorated with flowers from Mount Subasio to recall the ancient customs of the shepherds, who celebrated the advent of good weather and their return to the mountain pastures. Today, however, laws protecting the environment prohibit this tradition in order to preserve the floral species that grow on the mountain.

Pentecost Monday

From the loggia of the Upper Church of the Basilica of San Francesco, people are blessed with the Holy Veil of the Virgin. It was brought to Assisi from the Orient by Tommaso Orsini, who then donated it to the city.
On this occasion, an evocative procession goes from the Lower Church to the lawn in front of the Upper Church.

Corpus Christi

The procession held on the eighth day of Corpus Christi is very particular. This procession, known as the **Procession of the fleas**, crosses the upper part of the city, going along some of the oldest and most characteristic alleys, which are traditionally « carpeted » with flowers.

Feast of the Vow

On June 22nd, there is a commemoration of Assisi's liberation from the Saracens, which took place through the intervention of St. Clare. On the eve of this feast, the city is illuminated with torches to recreate the vigil of prayer that St. Clare and her sisters dedicated to this intention.
On the morning of June 22nd, the mayor and an entourage of pages and trumpeters participate in a procession from the Cathedral to the Piazza del Comune. The procession then continues on toward San Damiano, where votive candles are lit during a religious ceremony.

The Assisi Pardon

This ceremony, celebrated from July 31st to August 2nd, extends the plenary indulgence, granted directly to St. Francis by Pope Honorius III, to all the faithful who assemble in the Porziuncola after they have made their confessions and received Holy Communion.
Numerous pilgrims, mostly from southern Italy, flock to participate in the solemn

religious ceremonies that are celebrated during this period in the Basilica of Santa Maria degli Angeli.
The Assisi Pardon is one of the most important indulgences in the Christian world because it offers the faithful who participate the special privilege of total remission from sin.

Feasts of San Rufino and St. Clare

According to the Statutes of the Commune and of the city's confraternities that date to the 14th and 15th centuries, on the feast of San Rufino (patron saint of Assisi) and on the feast days of the other saints who protect the city (St. Francis and St. Clare), the city authorities were required to go to the churches dedicated to these saints to offer votive candles.
This still takes place during the solemn religious rites held on the occasion of these two important festivities, which are celebrated on August 10th and 11th, respectively. Cultural events such as concerts and plays are also held on these two days.

The Ride of Satriano

The Ride of Satriano is held on the first Sunday in September to reenact St. Francis' final return to Assisi, an episode recounted in Thomas of Celano's *Second Life*. This horseback ride is held in commemoration of the knights of the Commune, who rode out not only to meet their saint but above all, to protect him. A sort of procession on horseback goes from Assisi to Nocera Umbra and back. It goes through the streets of the city, stopping in Piazza del Comune, and it is preceded by a relic of St. Francis.

Feast of St. Francis

On October 3rd and 4th, the feast of St. Francis is celebrated. Religious, civil and military authorities preside over the feast. Ever since the saint was named the patron of Italy, each year one of regions offers oil for the votive lamp placed before the saint's tomb. On the evening of October 3rd, St. Francis' death is commemorated in the Basilica of Santa Maria degli Angeli, whereas the solemn offering of the oil takes place in the Assisi basilica on October 4th. During these days, there are special folklore events given by the region donating the oil.

Christmas festivities

To recreate the Franciscan story of the crib of Greccio, Christmas creches are set up along the streets and squares of Assisi as well as in its churches. Some of these creches have great artistic value. Popular Christmas plays are performed in the outlying towns.

Lower Basilica of San Francesco, porch

First Itinerary

THE BASILICA DI SAN FRANCESCO AND THE SACRO CONVENTO

Upon the death of St. Francis, which occurred near the Porziuncola on October 3, 1226, his body was carried from the chapel in the woods of the valley to the Chiesa di San Giorgio (St. George), near Assisi, to avoid possible attempts of theft by rival Perugia. On March 29, 1228, Simone di Pucciarello, citizen of Assisi, donated to Brother Elia, both in the name of and on behalf of Pope Gregory IX, a tract of land in the hamlet of *Colle dell'Inferno* (*Hell Hill*). This area was once used for executions and is located at the bottom of the hill where the slope ends abruptly in the direction of the Tescio River Valley. On April 29 Gregory IX announced that he wished to build an *ecclesia specialis (special church*) which would function both as a tomb for the saint and a *caput et mater* (*head and mother*) for the Minor Order, granting indulgence to all who would help with the construction of the Basilica. Brother Elia was assigned to collect donations for the construction of a church and Convento for the religious. On July 17, the day after the canonization of St. Francis, Gregory IX laid the first stone of the new church. According to the original plan, the building should have been very plain, inspired by the ideals of poverty of the early Franciscan movement. The construction proceeded rapidly and, on May 25, 1230, the body was entombed in a cell which had been prepared for it under the main altar. After the appointment of Brother Elia as head of the Order (1232–39) the idea changed to that of making the monument a visible proof of the extraordinary influence of the Franciscan movement. The part which had already been built was turned into an enormous crypt which, due to the steep slope of the site, became the base for a second church and served as a classroom for the monastery, a church for preaching, and a papal chapel. The original trussed ceiling was replaced with massive cross vaults with large ribs in the Lombard Romanesque style. Franciscan sources give the credit for the construction to Brother Elia, who personally supervised the construction of the cross vaults.
When Brother Elia fell out of favor, after being excommunicated by Gregory IX in 1240 for the friendship which linked him with Emperor Frederick II, the Englishman Hymen of Faversham became the new head of the Order. It was probably due to his influence that workers from the North were called to Assisi, bringing with them the slender and elegant forms used in the luminous hall of the Upper Church, forms which are comparable to examples from the Anjou Gothic. The names of the architects who designed the project are not known. Giorgio Vasari attributes the project to one *Jacopo Todesco*, father of Arnolfo di Cambio. Nineteenth century German historiography praises the role of Filippo da Campello who, however, seems to have been more an administrator than an architect. Another hypothesis attributes the project to master Paolo Luprandi, cited as a witness in a document of 1239. Finally, still another source identifies the architect as Brother Giovanni da Penna, who in 1238 built the aqueduct which brought water to the Convento. The construction of the Basilica was brought to completion within a period of 20 years. It must have already been finished in 1253, when Innocent IV solemnly consecrated the altars and appointed Filippo da Campello in charge of the decoration, with permission to use as funds the donations left by the pilgrims.

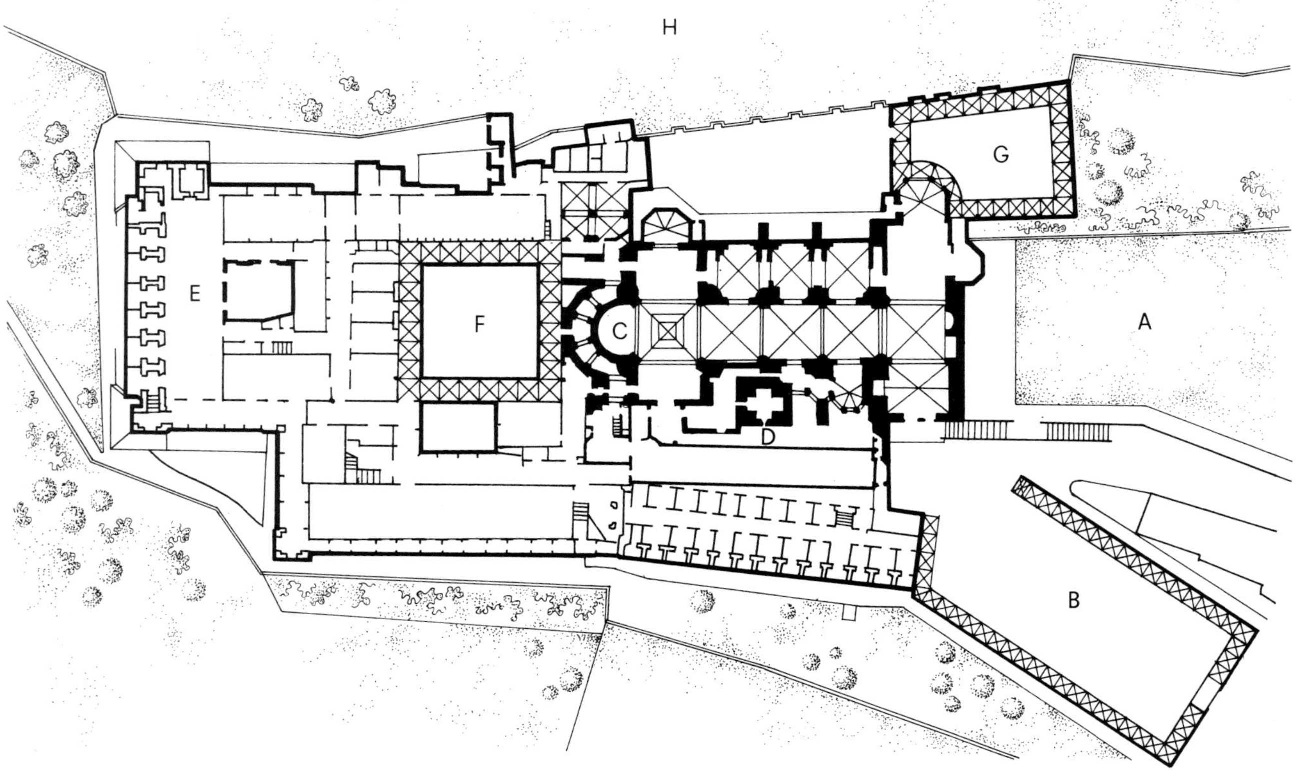

BASILICA DI S. FRANCESCO AND SACRO CONVENTO

A Upper piazza
B Lower piazza
C Basilica
D Bell Tower
E Sacro convento
F Cloister of Pope Sixtus IV
G Cemetery
H Selva (Wood)

In addition to the church, Gregory IX promoted the construction of a papal palace and a Convento, used as early as 1230 by a community of friars. The papal palace was finished before 1239; Brother Elia was living there, greatly scandalizing his fellow brothers. The Convento was enlarged several times between the 14th and 15th century, and assumed its final form during the reign of Sixtus IV (1471–1484) who ordered the construction of the cloister and the great scarp wall facing Perugia, on which a very large portrait of him was placed. After the expropriation of the ecclesiastical estates following Italian unification, the Convento became the property of the State, which used it as a boarding school for orphans. In 1929 it again became the possession of the monastic community.
Externally, the Basilica consists of two independent churches, one superimposed upon the other. Each church has a single nave and transept, but they are not identical, for the transept of the Lower Church juts out further than that of the Upper Church. The entire complex of Church and Convento was designed so as to be seen in a foreshortened view from the lower piazza, due to the steeply sloping terrain which also prevented the construction of the façade of the Lower Church, accessible only from a side entrance. The Upper Church has a simple gable façade. It is constructed entirely of white limestone, with the exception of the enormous pink stone buttresses, six on each side: *These turrets are said to have been made in honor of the twelve apostles. They are in pink stone in memory of their martyrdom and the shedding of their blood for the sake of Christ*. (Brother Ludovico da Pietralunga, about 1570). The unusually high apse is divided into two parts by a cornice. The lower part is semicircular in form and is supported by sturdy, flying buttresses. The upper part is polygonal and has three large windows. On the left side is the also unusually high Romanesque **bell tower**, built at the same time as the church and perhaps already finished when a bell was cast for it in 1239. It is divided into three levels by cornices of small hanging arches divided by pilasters and ends with a belfry opened by three arches. The belfry was topped by a cusp which was torn down in 1530.

As one arrives from Perugia, one's view of the church can be confused by the Convento, composed of many structures added over the centuries. To the west, is a large rectangular construction, the infirmary, supported by the enormous scarp wall. Its long southern façade is scanned by a double row of arches. A vast area in front of the Upper Basilica was donated to the friars by the Commune in 1246. The terracing and support walls date from 1278. The lower piazza, which even in antiquity was already crowded by shops during the annual celebrations of the Feasts of the Pardon and of the Saint's death, was not surrounded by porticos until 1474. The great stairway with its two flights of stairs which connects the two piazzas was reconstructed in 1731.

The entrance to the **Lower Church** is protected by a Renaissance porch built by the sculptor Francesco di Bartolomeo da Pietrasanta (1486–1487), during the period in which the head of the Order was Francesco Nani, nicknamed Sansone (Samson). It consists of a large arch supported by two columns, and an attic decorated by friezes with festoons. An *Annunciation* is sculpted on the sides of the arch. Written on the frieze of the archivolt are the words: *FRATER FRANCISCUS SANSON GENERALIS MINORUM FIERI FECIT, 1487.*
The beautiful Gothic portal, a true masterpiece of plastic ornamentation, was finished just before 1271, at which time one *domina Berta* left five poplars from her farm for doors to be built in memory of St. Francis. The portal has two three–lobed

openings divided by a columned trumeau with capitals decorated with human heads and a rose window with richly–latticed, small, spiral columns. On each side of these columns are two smaller windows with lobate lattices. Under the rose window is a small mosaic with *St. Francis Conferring His Blessing* against a gold background, done in a style similar to that of the Maestro di San Francesco. The cornice has an ogival outline and is divided into concentric bands, which are decorated with carvings of plants and with marble inlay. Around it are written the words: *INDULGENTIA PLENARIA QUOTIDIANA PERPETUA.* The ancient shutters were replaced upon the reception of a legacy from the minorite Ottaviano Preconi da Messina, bishop of Monopoli and Palermo. Each is divided into five panels, alternately large and small, which are decorated in the grotesque manner and with figures in relief. The shutter on the left was inlaid in 1550 by Niccolò di Ugolinuccio da Cagli, perhaps following a design by Dono Doni. Beginning from the top, the scenes depicted are: *The Ascension, St. Francis and St. Clare, St. Francis and the Wolf of Gubbio, St. Clare Driving Back the Saracens*. There is a record of one Pompeo Scarcione da Foligno having been paid in 1573 for work done on the shutter on the right. Beginning at the top, the scenes depicted are: *Glory of St. Francis, St. Ludwig in Bishop's Habit and St. Anthony of Padua with the Child, St. Ludwig Riding to Rome, St. Anthony of Padua Healing a Child.* On the wall next to the entrance is the tomb of Francesco Cicholi da Assisi († 1336). Slightly above are two memorial stones. One commemorates the 7th centennial of the death of Brother Elia in 1953. The other is a bust of Benedict XIV, dated 1754, in memory of the benefits he granted to the Basilica. The lunette under the porch is decorated with an *Enthroned Madonna Surrounded by St. Francis, St. Anthony and Two Other Saints*, by an anonymous painter of the end of the 16th century.

The **interior** of the Lower Church has a floor plan in the shape of a Tau, or Egyptian cross, which was a symbol dear to St. Francis. The original plan called for a nave, without aisles, divided into four bays and covered by a cross vault with square sectioned ribs in a strongly Romanesque style. The third bay was partitioned by an iconostasis, with a pulpit from which the mass was celebrated. The presbytery has a transept covered by a barrel vault and cap–shaped apse. During the construction work the entrance hall was added, perhaps replacing a hall leading to the papal palace. The date for the extension is uncertain, but it must certainly have preceded the completion of the Upper Church, which is supported by its walls. The cross vault has polygonal ribs of an already Gothic form. At the end of the 13th century the chapels within the walls of the nave were opened. Those to the right were connected by intermediate passageways to satisfy the increasing request for the burial of nobles, and for the purpose of forming a kind of lateral aisle to ease the flow of pilgrims. The same modification was made with the head of the transept. At that time the one–light mullioned windows which illuminated the nave were closed and the altar tables were removed from against the walls. Their former presence is indicated by chisel marks in the curtain–wall.
The entrance bay, or **narthex**, was already decorated at the end of the 13th century. The various bands of plants along the ribs and the starred sky of the vaults are what

Lower Basilica, narthex, Ottaviano Nelli, Maestà, (1422)

remains of the decorations of this period. The frescoes on the walls were done between 1646 and 1647 by Cesare Sermei and Girolamo Martelli. In the counterfaçade are two *Angels Holding a Curtain*; on the left wall is an *Adoration of the Shepherds* and, in two ovals, the *Annunciation*. On the right wall is *Announcement by a Pilgrim of the Birth of St. Francis*; above the arch is *The Glory of St. Francis Adored by Popes Sixtus V and Paul V*; on the underside of the arch are the busts of popes who were the protectors of the Franciscan Order: *Honorius III, Gregory IX, Alexander V, Sixtus IV* and, finally, *Clement XIV*, whose bust was added in the 18th century. On the left is the very small **Cappella di San Sebastiano** (1), already in existence in 1542, at which time it belonged to the Maestri Comacini (Masters of Como). The pictorial decoration was done by Girolamo Martelli (1646) who was commissioned by Ortensia and Valerio Paci. At the altar is a painting of *Madonna with Child and St. Sebastian*; on the left is *St. Sebastian Healed by Irene*; on the right is *St. Sebastian before Diocletian*; on the vault is *Angels with Implements from the Passion*; on the underside of the arch is *Allegory of Faith and Fortitude*.

Next to the chapel is the *Madonna of Health* painted by Ottaviano Nelli from Gubbio, portraying an *Enthroned Madonna and SS. Anthony the Abbot, Francis, Rufino, and Veronica*. It was commissioned thanks to a documented legacy dated April 14, 1422. The *St. Christopher* which is frescoed on the column above the holy water font was done by an anonymous Perugian master from the end of the 14th century.

Against the opposite wall is a sepulchral monument (2) from the end of the 13th century, which has the form of a three–lobed shrine supported by five corbels. In-

side it is buried a member of the Florentine Cerchi family, to which belong the coats of arms on the coffin. The large porphyry vase was used in antiquity as a holy water font. According to a legend it was donated by the Queen of Cyprus for completion of the church. Under the monument is the tomb of the lawyer Andrea Gabrielli († 1638) with his portrait by Cesare Sermei.
The back wall of the narthex is occupied by a niche used for the **choir** (3). Constructed in 1458 by the Nepis family of Assisi, it bears the inscription: *A.D. MCCCCLVIII A FAMILIA DE NEPIS ASSISINATE ERECTUM*. With the exception of one wooden panel which functions as a door, the choir is decorated by panels in pink stone which are trimmed with red and white marble inlay and framed with puttos in majolica, most of which have been lost. Above is a balustrade in marble and stuccos, redone in 1667. It bears the inscription *A.D. MDCLXVII DOMINIS DE NEPIS ANNUENTIBUS ORNATUM* and the engraved texts of three papal bulls containing the privileges granted to the Church by Gregory IX, Alexander IV, and Clement IV. From the balustrade the relic of the Veil of the Madonna was presented to the public. The frescoes in the lunette, *The Coronation of the Vergin* and *God* (1646), were done by Girolamo Martelli.
Next to the choir is the **Sepulchral Monument of John of Brienne** (4), King of Jerusalem and Emperor of Constantinople, Franciscan Tertiary, and personal friend of St. Francis. He was present in 1228 at the canonization of the Saint and brought expensive gifts, such as the tapestries used in the ceremony. The monument is a three-lobed shrine supported by a base with small pillars and decorated with six of the Apostles and the family coat of arms.
Above the coffin are two angels opening the curtains of a funeral parlor in which a body is lying. Further up are two asymmetrical groups consisting of a standing *Virgin with Child* and a marching *Lion Carrying a Crowned Figure* who is sitting upon a faldstool with his legs crossed. The tomb was sculpted at the end of the 13th century by an Umbrian master who is identified by some, based on his style, as the author of a bronze architrave of the Cathedral of Orvieto which bears the signature of Rubeo. The present position of the tomb is not the original one. During its transfer, various frescoes from the 13th century were destroyed, and only a few of their fragments remain on the wall.
The frescoes at the back of the narthex were done by Cesare Sermei (inscription: *ANNO DOMINI MDCXXXXV DIE VERO PRIMA MENSIS MARTII*), and cover an earlier decoration by Andrea da Bologna, which is partly uncovered at the entrance of the Cappella di Santa Caterina. In the vault is a half–figure of *God with Two Angels Supporting the World*. On the back wall are *Christ at the Pillar* and *Ecce Homo*; in two ovals are *St. Francis* and *St. Anthony of Padua*. On the right wall are *The Way to Calvary, Zachary, The Preparation of the Cross* and *Isaiah*. On the left wall are *The Crucifixion, The Virgin Fainting, Jeremiah, The Resurrection of Christ* and *David.*
To the right of the narthex is the **Cappella di Sant'Antonio Abate** (5), recently turned into a Sacramental Chapel. It was finished before 1360 by Francesco di Vagnuccio di Assisi, who had it decorated. The frescoes by Pace di Bartolo have been lost due to the humidity of the surroundings. In two monuments are buried the Duke of Spoleto Blasco Fernandez di Belviso and his son Garcia, who were treach-

erously murdered in the Castle of Piediluco in 1367. The two arcosolium tombs, with the statue of the deceased supported above each sarchophagus by small lions, were commissioned in 1373 by the Duke's widow, Sancia de' Cortinis.

Through a door on the left side of the narthex one enters the **Cemetery** (6), a small cloister with a trapezoidal floor plan enclosed by two series of loggias. It was constructed by the Lombard masters Pietro and Ambrogio between 1492 and 1493, while Francesco Sansone was head of the Order. At the center are cypress trees and a terra–cotta statue of *St. Francis* by Luigi Sapia. On the floor of the portico and on the walls are numerous tombstones from local brotherhoods, and the noble families of Assisi and other towns. The oldest is dated 1295. By passing through a gate one enters a garden which faces the outside wall of the church.

Lower Basilica, Cappella di Santa Caterina, Andrea de'Bartoli, Dispute of St. Catherine (1368), detail

At the head of the narthex is located the **Cappella di Santa Caterina** (7), constructed before 1343 when it was used by Franciscan Tertiary nuns. Temporarily buried inside was Egidio Albornoz, the powerful Spanish cardinal sent to Italy by Innocent VI in 1353 to subject to the Church the Patrimonial cities which had rebelled when the Holy See was transferred to Avignon. He died at Viterbo on August 23, 1367 and was buried in Assisi in 1368. The preparation of the funeral chapel was done by Matteo di Giovannello di Gattapone of Gubbio, who designed the beautiful stone facing. The cardinal's coffin was moved in 1372 to Toledo, Spain.

On the walls are frescoes with stories of St. Catherine by Andrea de' Bartoli from Bologna, who received 450 florins in 1368 from the heirs of Cardinal Albornoz. On the right wall, from the bottom, are *The Conversion of St. Catherine* and *St. Catherine before Emperor Maxentius*. On the left are *St. Catherine's Dispute* and *Martyrdom of the Philosophers*. On the inside of the entrance arch, on the right, are: *St. Biagio, St. Eugene, St. Ludwig; Conversion of Empress Faustina in Prison; Faustina's Martyrdom*. On the left are: *St. Sabino with Cardinal Albornoz Kneeling at His Feet, St. Clement, St. Francis; Martyrdom of St. Catherine; Death and Angelic Apotheosis of the Saint*. In the window splays are figures of saints alternated with the Albornoz coats of arms.

Above the altar is a multicolored wooden *Crucifix* from the end of the 15th century, formerly located in the Cappella di San Giovanni. The stained glass of the three two–light windows is dated around 1320. The window in the center is attributed to

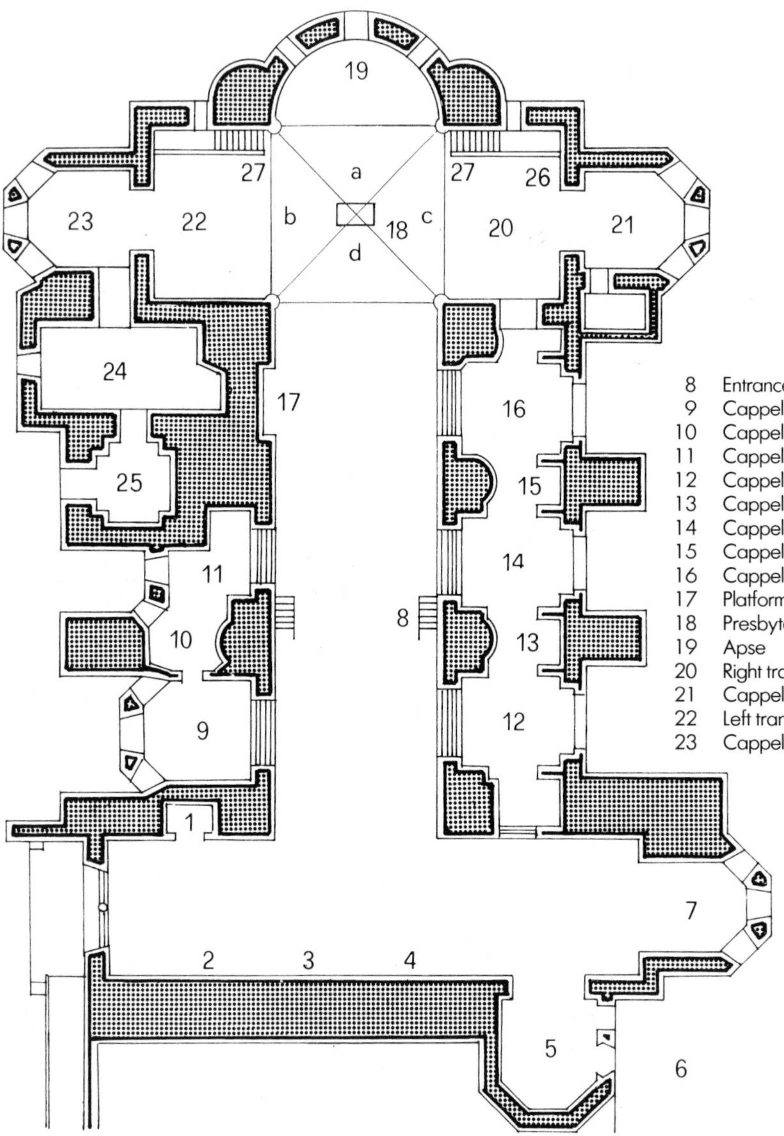

8 Entrance to the Crypt
9 Cappella di San Martino
10 Cappella Fontana
11 Cappella di Sant'Andrea
12 Cappella di Santo Stefano
13 Cappella di San Lorenzo
14 Cappella di Sant'Antonio da Pado
15 Cappella di San Valentino
16 Cappella di Maria Maddalena
17 Platform of St. Stanislas
18 Presbytery
19 Apse
20 Right transept
21 Cappella di San Nicola
22 Left transept
23 Cappella di San Giovanni Battista

LOWER CHURCH

1 Cappella di San Sebastiano
2 Sepulchral monument of the Cerchi family
3 Choir
4 Sepulchral monument of Jonh of Brienne
5 Cappella di Sant'Antonio Abate
6 Cemetery
7 Cappella di Santa Caterina

24 Lower sacristy
25 Hidden sacristy
26 Chapter room
27 Stairs to the Cloister

a Glory of St. Francis
b Allegory of Obedience
c Allegory of Castity
d Allegory of Poverty

Giovanni di Bonino of Assisi, also known as the Maestro di Figline. The two on the sides were done by collaborators, thought by some to be Angeletto and Pietro da Gubbio. The decoration consists of isolated figures of saints. In the central two-light window, from above left, are: *Madonna Holding Child; St. Catherine; St. Agnes; St. Lucia; St. Francis; St. Clare*. In the left two–light window, from above left, are: *St. Cecilia; One of the Marys; St. Thecla; St. Margaret; St. Anthony of Padua; St. Petronilla*. In the right two–light window are: *Mary Magdalen and a Saint; a Saint; St. Agatha; a Crowned Saint; St. Ludwig of Toulouse*.

On the walls of the **nave** can be seen the fragmentary remains of a fresco decoration, partially destroyed a few decades after completion by the opening of the chapel arches. These are the oldest decorations in the church, done around 1253 by a great Umbrian painter known as the Maestro di San Francesco. There is a beautiful variety of ornamental motifs on the ribs and on the vault, where the illusion of a starry sky is accentuated by the use of small mirrors concealed within the plaster. The choice of episodes was inspired by the desire of St. Francis to conform as much as possible with the life of Christ.

On the right wall are episodes from the Passion of Christ. On the first bay are *Christ Stripped of His Clothing and Preparation of the Cross* and *Crucifixion*; on the second bay are *The Deposition of the Cross* and *Lamentation Over the Body of Christ;* on the third bay is *Apparition of Christ in Emmaus*. Under this latter episode is a very deteriorated fresco of a *Madonna with Child and an Angel* which decorated the tomb of Cardinal Pietro di Barro († 1252). On the left wall are stories of St. Francis, inspired by the *Vita Secunda* by Tommaso da Celano. On the first bay are *St. Francis Removes His Clothes and Returns Them to His Father* and *The Dream of Innocent III*; on the second bay are *The Sermon to the Birds* and *The Stigmata of St. Francis*; on the third bay is *Funeral Rites of the Saint with Recognition of the Stigmata.*

Halfway into the nave are two ramps (8) descending to the **Crypt**, which was excavated following the discovery of the tomb of St. Francis on December 12, 1818, and which required 52 nights of work. Conforming with the preferences of the times, the crypt was constructed in the neoclassic style by the Assisan architect Giuseppe Brizi (1822–1824). The severe neo–Romanesque appearance is the result of a restoration by Ugo Tarchi (1925–32). Behind the altar, protected by a grate, is the stone urn in which the body of the Saint was originally placed. In 1932 the remains of Blessed Rufino, Angelo, Masseo, and Leone, the four companions of St. Francis, were placed in the niches at the corners of the crypt. At the entrance to the crypt, where the entrance stairs meet, is the tomb of the Blessed Jacopa de' Settesoli. Above the railing is a wrought iron lamp designed by Ugo Tarchi (1939) which burns votive oil offered in turns by Italian cities.

A few small stairs away, in the first bay on the left, is the **Cappella di San Martino** (9), built on a higher level, as were all the other chapels in the nave, to avoid weakening the slab of bedrock on which the church rests.

The chapel was built for Gentile Partino da Montefiore, cardinal bearing the San Martino ai Monti title. In March 1312 the powerful Franciscan prelate was returning from a delicate mission in Hungary, where he had negotiated the ascent to the throne of Caroberto of Anjou, when he stopped in Assisi to leave expensive gifts

Lower Basilica, Cappella di San Martino, Simone Martini, Investiture of St. Martin (1312–15)

sent to the tomb of the Saint by King Caroberto and Queen Mary and to remove the pontifical treasures kept in the Upper Sacristy on behalf of Clement V. On this occasion he left the friars of the Sacro Convento the conspicuous sum of 600 florins *for a chapel which he orders to be made in the Basilica of St. Francis*. Having left Assisi for France, he stopped in Siena, where he probably came in contact with Simone Martini, who was then at work on a *Maestà* in the Palazzo Pubblico and who was to become the artist of the cycle on the chapel walls.

The chapel is a projection consisting of a barrel vault and a pentagonal, rib vaulted hall and has ribs with splendid leaved capitals painted in blue and gold. The lower part of the walls is covered with red and white stone inlay. In the back wall are three pairs of windows. The entire surface of the chapel was decorated between 1312 and 1315 by Simone Martini of Siena with stories of St. Martin which are narrated in the form of a fable, conforming with the style of the French sagas of chivalry. The courtly spirit of the scenes is perhaps attributable to the intervention of Robert of Anjou, King of Naples, brother of Caroberto, and to St. Ludwig of Toulouse in the capacity of executor of the will of Cardinal Gentile.

The cycle is read from the lower register. Beginning on the left are: *St. Martin Gives His Cloak to a Poor Man at the Door of Amiens; Christ Appears to Him in a Dream Holding the Donated Cloak; He is Knighted by Emperor Julian; He Renounces His Weapons and Confronts the Enemy Armed only with a Cross*. In the second register from the left are: *St. Martin Brings Back to Life a Young Girl in Chartres; The Saint, Deep in Meditation, Is Shaken by an Altar Boy for the Celebration of the Mass; The Angels, while He Celebrates Mass in Albenga, Return to Him a Tunic Given to a Beggar; The Emperor Valentinian Pays Homage to Him by Dropping to His Feet* . At the top of the vault are: *Death of the Saint; The Funeral Rites in the Presence of St. Ambrose*. On the counterfaçade, above the entrance arch is *Cardinal Gentile da Montefiore Kneeling before St. Martin*. On the underside of the entrance arch, from below, on the left are: *SS. Clare and Elizabeth; SS. Louis IX, King of France, and Ludwig of Toulouse*. On the right are: *SS. Mary Magdalen and Catherine; SS. Anthony of Padua and Francis*. On the splays of the three two–light windows are 18 busts of saints.

Lower Basilica, Cappella di Santo Stefano, Giacomo Giorgetti, Allegory of Charity, (mid 17th century)

The stained glass of the windows, which is contemporary with the frescoes, is attributed to Giovanni di Bonino, perhaps with the participation of Simone Martini. The panes on the left are, from top to bottom: *Busts of Archangels; St. Gregory the Great and St. Martin; St. Francis and St. Nicholas; St. Rufino and St. Stephen*. The central panes are: *Busts of Archangels; Jesus Christ and the Virgin Mary; St. Martin and St. Peter; Cardinal Gentile Pertino da Montefiore in Franciscan Habit and St. Martin Pope*. The panes on the right are: *Busts of Archangels; St. Jerome and St. Paul; St. Damian and St. Martin; St. Anthony of Padua and St. Lawrence*.

From the Cappella di San Martino one enters the **Cappella Fontana** (10), a narrow, irregular room with rough walls which is located between the pillar and the pylon of the buttress. In a tabernacle is a multicolored wooden statue of the *Madonna* (17th century) dedicated to the memory of St. Giuseppe da Copertino. From the Cappella Fontana one enters the **Cappella di Sant'Andrea** (11), located next to the bell tower. The chapel once belonged to the Aromatari family of Assisi and bears their coat of arms, a mortar and pestle. On the walls are twenty–two bronze gilded panels with *Episodes from the Life of Christ* (1988), by Tommaso Gismondi.

By means of stairs to the right of the first bay, one enters the **Cappella di Santo Stefano** (12), which was once dedicated to St. Ludwig of Toulouse and was built about the end of the 13th century. At one time Cardinal Gentile Partino da Montefiore was buried in a niche located in the back wall destroyed due to the changes made on the altar in 1763. In 1535 the chapel was given to the members of the Brotherhood of St. Stephen and St. Gregory. Displayed in the chapel was the so called *Banner of the Pestilence* (about 1470), by Niccolò di Liberatore da Foligno, now preserved in the Priesterhaus of Kevelaer. This banner was carried in procession by the Brotherhood in times of calamity. The chapel has a quadrangular floor plan, is covered by a cross vault, and has a large window divided into four sections. Two passages located behind the cylindrical buttresses connect it with the Cappella di Sant'Antonio and with the narthex.

On the walls is a series of frescoes with stories of St. Stephen, painted by the mannerist Dono Doni of Assisi and commissioned by the Brotherhood of St. Stephen for the sum of 400 scudi. The master began work in 1574, but died on June 17, 1575 before bringing it to completion. In each web of the vault are represented a prophet and a sybil accompanied by angels with placards. On the vault section above the entrance is a *Jeremiah and the Sibyl of Tivoli*; on the left is *Micha and the Sibyl of Persia*; on the vault section by the window is *Daniel and the Sibyl of Eritrea*; on the right is *David and the Sibyl of Cumae*. In the lunette on the right is *St. Stephen's Debate in the Synagogue*; in the counterfaçade are *St. Stephen Driven from Jerusalem* and *Allegory of Charity and Prudence*; on the left is *Stoning to Death of St. Stephen*. The *Allegories of Faith and Charity*, present under the entrance arch, were added by Giacomo Giorgetti (mid 17th century). Above the altar is an embossed copper tryptych by Tommaso Gismondi (1990) representing the *Parables of the Prodigal Son, the Lost Drachma, and the Lost Sheep*.

The stained glass of the four–light window was commissioned by Cardinal Gentile Partino da Montefiore, who had his coat of arms and portrait (post 1312) placed there. The cartoon has traditionally been attributed to Angeletto da Gubbio, who collaborated with Giovanni di Bonino, considered to be the Maestro delle Vele.

From above left in the first pane are: *Symbol of Matthew the Evangelist; St. Ludwig with the Bishop's Insignia; Angel with Crown; St. Ludwig Kneeling in Civilian Clothing.* In the second pane are: *Symbol of John the Evangelist; Christ Conferring His Blessing; Angel with a Vase; St. Francis*. In the third pane are: *Symbol of Luke the Evangelist; The Virgin Mary; Angel with a Vase; St. Anthony of Padua*. In the fourth pane are: *Symbol of Mark the Evangelist; St. Ludwig, King; Angel with Cardinal's Hat; Cardinal Gentile Partino Kneeling.*

In the narrow passage between the Cappella di Santo Stefano and that of Sant'Antonio is the **Cappella di San Lorenzo** (13), decorated with frescoes by Andrea de' Bartoli (about 1368). In the vault is *Christ within a Lozenge Carried by Angels*; on the curved surface of the turret is the *Martyrdom of St. Lawrence*; on the walls are the *Sermon in the Garden* and the *Capture of Christ*.

From the second bay of the nave one enters the **Cappella di Sant'Antonio da Padova** (14). This chapel was built before 1300, since at that date it appears in a testament. In the 14th century it belonged to the Lelli family of Assisi, which placed its coat of arms there. In the early 15th century it passed to Gentile di Bernardo Fiumi, and then in 1429 to Count Guidantonio da Montefeltro.

The chapel is identical to that of St. Stephen, except for the rounded profile of the ribs which were redone in 1487. On the floor is the tombstone of Bishop Tegrimio Tegrimi († 1632). On the walls are stories of St. Anthony of Padua, painted by Cesare Sermei in 1610 by order of Iacopo Vanzini, keeper of the Holy Convento. On the webs of the cross vault are: *St. Francis; St. Ludwig of Toulouse; St. Clare; St. Bonaventure da Bagnoregio*. In the lunette on the left wall is *St. Anthony Preaching before Gregory IX*. Below the lunette are *St. Anthony Performing a Miracle on a Pregnant Woman* and *Apparition of St. Anthony to the Money Lenders*. In the lunette on the right wall is *Miracle of the Mule*. Below the lunette are *St. Anthony Returning a Man to Life* and *St. Anthony and Brother Elia Before Gregory IX*. On the counterfaçade is *St. Anthony Returning a Young Man to Life and Saving a Shipwreck Victim*. The window splays, and the undersides of the arches which connect the chapel with those adjoining it, are decorated by numerous *Busts of Saints*. On the entrance arch are the *Busts of Franciscans*.

The stained glass of the four–light window illustrates episodes from the life of St. Anthony and is attributed to Giovanni di Bonino of Assisi. It was perhaps executed before 1317, due to the presence in the group of Franciscan bishop Ludwig of Toulouse without a saint's halo. Each story occupies two adjacent panes. From above left are: *Busts of Angels; Martyrdom of the Franciscans at Ceuta; St. Anthony Taking the Franciscan Habit; Sermon to the Fish*. From above right are: *Busts of Angels; Temptation of St. Anthony,* (the pane on the right is modern and replaces a pane of the *Assumption of the Virgin*, preserved in a Convento storehouse); *Sermon of St. Anthony; Apparition of St. Francis at the Arles Chapter*. In the rosette are the busts of 12 companions of St. Francis.

In a passage which connects the Cappella di Sant'Antonio and that of Maria Maddalena is the **Cappella di San Valentino** (15). This chapel already existed in 1388 and was dedicated to Blessed Valentino da Narni, who died at the Carceri sul Monte Subasio in 1378 and whose image is painted on a pillar. On the ground is the

Lower Basilica, Cappella di Maria Maddalena, Giotto, The Raising of Lazarus (1305–10)

tombstone of Brother Hugo of Hertlepool († 1302), engraved with his reposing figure. In the wall, protected by a grating, is a niche with *St. Peter Enthroned Between St. Francis and a Friar (?) at Prayer* (early 14th century). The chapel once belonged to the Counts Fiumi di Sterpeto and bears their 16th century coat of arms painted on the vault. From the third bay one enters the **Cappella di Maria Maddalena** (16), the appearance of which is identical to that of the previous chapels except for the back wall, in which there are several marble slabs decorated with mosaics taken from the iconostasis in the nave. The chapel is connected to the right transept by a passageway. The pictorial decoration is inspired by the life of St. Mary Magdalen. It was commissioned by the Franciscan Teobaldo Pontano da Todi, bishop of Assisi from 1296 to 1329, and cost 600 gold florins. The prelate had himself represented twice, once as a simple friar at the feet of Mary Magdalen, and then as bishop at the feet of St. Rufino. The work has been unanimously attributed by experts to Giotto and was done immediately after the completion of the frescoes of the Cappella degli Scrovegni in Padua (1305), from which it resumes the composition of two episodes, *Raising of Lazarus* and *Noli Me Tangere*. The master was assisted by numerous collaborators, two of whom were Stefano Fiorentino and the Maestro delle Vele, who also worked on the walls of the presbytery.

The story begins with the lower register and continues in the lunettes. On the left wall are *The Supper in the House of the Pharisee* and *Raising of Lazarus*. On the right wall are *Noli Me Tangere* and *Journey to Marseilles by Mary Magdalen and Miracle of the Princess Found Alive with her Newborn on a Reef in the Middle of the Sea*. In the right lunette is *Mary Magdalen Speaking with the Angels*. In the lunette on the counterfaçade is *Mary Magdalen Receiving the Vestments from the Hermit Zosimus*. In the left lunette is *Mary Magdalen Receiving Communion from St. Maximinus.* On the vault, against a blue background with stars, are four circles with the figures of the *Redeemer Conferring His Blessing, Mary Magdalen, Lazarus* and *St. Martha*. On the sides of the connecting passages and on the back walls are painted isolated figures of saints. On the left are *Bishop Pontano and St. Rufino* and *Penitent Saint*. On the right are half–length *Portrait of a Saint*, perhaps one of the pious women, and *Bishop Pontano and Mary Magdalen*. On the altar wall, on the left, are *Mary, Sister of Moses* and *Penitent Mary Magdalen (?)*. On the right are *St. Helen* and *Martyred Saint*.

On the window splay are eight more half–figures of saints, not identifiable. On the underside of the entrance arch, from the lower right are: *Two Saints; St. Augustine and another Saint; Sts. Paul and David; Sts. Peter and Matthew; The Good Thief and St. Longinus; Two Saints*.

The four–light mullioned window is illustrated with episodes from the life of Mary Magdalen. It preceded the decoration of the walls and was done following the sketches by a 13th century master, probably of local origin and with a style similar to that of the Maestro del Farneto. The sequence begins with the light on the right. In the first pane, from below are: *Supper in the House of a Pharisee; Encounter at the Gates of Bethany; Raising of Lazarus; Supper in the House of Mary Magdalen*. In the second pane, from below are: *Apparition of Christ to the Marys; Jesus Defending Mary Magdalen from the Accusations of Martha; Apparition to Mary Magdalen of Christ as Gardener; Noli Me Tangere*. In the third pane, from the top are: *Madonna with Child; Magdalen in the Desert; Mary Magdalen Receiving Vestments from an Angel; Burial of Mary Magdalen*. In the fourth pane, from the top are: *Redeemer; Mary Magdalen; Mary of Cleophe; Mary of Salome*.

To the left of the third bay is the **Platform of St. Stanislas** (17), dedicated to the archbishop of Cracow who was killed by order of King Boleslav and canonized in Assisi in 1253 by Innocent IV. An altar built by the Chapter of the Cracow Cathedral and dedicated to the Saint was already existent in the church in 1256. Following the opening of the chapels, a new altar was built in an arch dug into the wall, and was covered with marble slabs decorated in the style of the Cosmati family. These slabs were removed from the iconostasis which had once existed between the presbytery and the nave and which was torn down around 1300, when access to the presbytery was conceded to the laity. From the iconostasis hung a cross painted by Giunta Pisano for Brother Elia (1236), who had himself represented adoring the Crucifix. The mass was celebrated from here, as is demonstrated by the two niches in the wall of the last bay, used for the holy objects. The original arrangement can be reconstructed by using as a guide the episode of the *Nativity of Greccio* painted by Giotto.

The decoration of the platform, commissioned by the Soldani family of Assisi, was done by Puccio Capanna (about 1337). On the back wall is the *Coronation of the Virgin*, unfinished. On the intrados are *St. Stanislas Bringing Back to Life a Dead Man so that He May Testify to His Innocence* and *Martyrdom of the Saint*. The small

Lower Basilica, Giotto's workshop, Allegory of Chastity (1305–10), detail

Crucifixion was done by a disciple. At the base of the platform is a 17th century fresco depicting *The Blessed Jacopa de' Settesoli Holding a Tunic of Ashen Cloth*. At the center of the **Presbytery** (18), at the top of four steps, is the Gothic papal altar in which there is a *fenestella confessionis* which opens onto the tomb of St. Francis. It was consecrated by Innocent IV in 1253. The altar is a large marble monolith donated to the Basilica by Emperor of Constantinople John of Brienne. It rests on four large slabs of pink Subasian stone and has twenty small columns done in differing styles and separated by small trilobed arches decorated with mosaics. Under the altar on the choir side is a small fluted column containing a relic of St. John the Baptist donated by Innocent IV.

The walls of the presbytery are entirely covered with pictorial decoration, which due to its symbolic significance has been carefully preserved by the religious community. The *Glory of St. Francis* and the *Franciscan Virtues* frescoed in the cross vault above the altar are paragoned with the *Stories from the Childhood of Christ* and the *Passion of Christ* in the two transepts, thus emphasizing the similarity of the Saint's life with that of Christ within a kind of apocalyptical framework. The complex program of cycles is concluded in the apse vault (19) with the representation of the mission entrusted by the Saint to the Minorites. Of the scene, destroyed in the 17th century, there remains an accurate description by Giorgio Vasari and Brother Ludovico da Pietralunga.

The frescoes replace an older decoration done by the Maestro di San Francesco and Cimabue. The new decoration began with the head of the right transept, painted by the Maestro di San Nicola (Master of St. Nicholas) at the end of the 13th century. In the first decade of the 14th century the job was taken over by Giotto's Florentine studio, which left the work incomplete at the level of the apse platform. After a brief interruption, the left transept was entrusted to Pietro Lorenzetti of Siena, who brought it to completion within the second decade of the 14th century, perhaps before the explosive disorder in Assisi during the Ghibelline rule of Muzio di Francesco (1319) and the war with Perugia (1320).

The conceptual culmination of the program is expressed in the four vault sections, where there can be seen against a golden background the *Glory of St. Francis* and the three monastic vows. In the keystone is an *Apocalyptic Christ* holding in His hand a hammer and a Bible, and in His mouth a double–edged sword. The allegorical figures on the ribs were inspired by the Apocalypse by St. John. On the arch which opens onto the nave are the busts of the first ten companions of the Saint. The execution of the frescoes is the result of the collaboration of two distinguished masters. The first, characterized by an elegant and precious naturalism, is a strict Tuscan disciple of Giotto, identified as Stefano Fiorentino. The second is the author of *Gloriosus Franciscus*, in which there appears a more expressive realism typical of the Umbrian disciples of Giotto, and is identified as Angeletto da Gubbio, known as the Maestro delle Vele.

In the web on the apse side is the **Glory of St. Francis (a).** The saint, sitting on a throne surmounted by a flag with the cross and seven stars, is carried to heaven by angels singing hosanna. This is a theme inspired by the *Legenda Maior* by St. Bonaventure, in which Francis is interpreted as the angel of the sixth seal of the Apocalypse.

In the web on the left is the **Allegory of Obedience (b).** Within an arcade sits Obedience, depicted as an old friar with wings who imposes a yoke on another kneeling friar while being assisted by a double–faced Prudence and by Humility holding a candle. On the left an angel introduces two devouts, while on the right another chases away Haughtiness, symbolized by a centaur. The sides are crowded with hosts of adoring angels. Above, St. Francis between two kneeling angels is taken for the yoke by two hands descending from heaven.

In the web on the right is the **Allegory of Chastity (c).** Chastity is enclosed in a castle tower where she is served by two angels who bring her a crown and a palm. From the terraces Purity and Fortitude appear to assist four angels purifying a youth. Outside, the castle is guarded by nine bearded knights. On the left, St. Francis, accompanied by two angels, welcomes a friar, a Poor Clare and a layman, to symbolize the three Franciscan orders. On the right, Penitence and three angels drive away into an abyss the figure of Profane Love, a naked youth blindfolded and with the claws of a bird of prey, ahead of whom fall Death and Indecency.

In the web toward the nave is the **Allegory of Poverty (d).** On top of a rock, Christ unites in matrimony St. Francis and Poverty, a woman with ragged clothes at whom a child is throwing stones while another brings her thorns. Present for the matrimony are the personifications of Hope and Charity, intermingled with hosts of angels. On the left an angel summons a youth who is giving his cloak to a poor man, while on the right another points to three people who, by leaving the scene, symbolize Av-

Lower Basilica, right transept, Giotto's workshop, Crucifixion (1305–10)

arice. Above, two angels carry to heaven the worldly goods renounced by the Saint, which are represented by precious clothes and a palace.
In the apse vault is a gloomy *Last Judgement* (1623), painted by Cesare Sermei to replace the *Heavenly Glory* by Stefano Fiorentino, once praised by Lorenzo Ghiberti and Giorgio Vasari. The three one–light windows have modern stained glass by Lodovico and Rosa Caselli and portray *St. Francis* between *St. Clare* and *St. Elizabeth*. The beautiful choir was commissioned in 1467 to Paolino di Giovanni d'Ascoli and, upon his death, was brought to completion by Apollonio da Ripatransone (1471). It is composed of two rows of choir stalls, with 29 seats in the upper row and 18 in the lower row. On the smooth, back panels of the chairs are either carved leaves or inlaid flowered vases, and on the arms are fanciful figures. The right head of the choir bears the words: *OPUS APOLLONII DE RIPATRANSONE COMPLETUM DE MENSE APRELIS 1471.*
The vault of the right wing of the transept (20) is decorated with eight large **Stories from the Childhood of Christ**. These were painted by the same disciples of Giotto as those who worked under the direction of the master in the webs of the cross vault. We find ourselves before one of the greatest masterpieces of Italian 14th century painting for the beauty of the colors, the variety in design, and the bold solutions to perspective which anticipate Rennaissance innovations. The sequence is introduced by the *Annunciation*, which is located at the head of the transept and was done by the Maestro di San Nicola. The sequence continues into the vault with: *The Visitation; The Nativity; The Adoration of the Magi; Presentation of Jesus at the Tem-*

1.

2.

3.

4.

5.

6.

7.

8.

9.

10.

11.

ple; The Flight to Egypt; The Slaughter of the Innocents; Jesus Debating with the Learned Men; The Return of Jesus to Bethlehem after the Debate. The scenes are divided by ornamental bands with the *busts of saints and prophets*. On the walls of the transept are various *post mortem* miracles of St. Francis which continue the sequence of the Franciscan Legend of the Upper Basilica. Along the walls are: *Miracle of the Girl Fallen from the Balcony; Death and Raising from the Dead of the Boy of Suessa*, divided into two episodes by the entrance arch of the Cappella di San Nicola; *St. Francis and Death Crowned*. On the right wall is a *Crucifixion* attributed to Giotto, with St. Francis accompanied by friars at the foot of the cross. In the vault above the stairs leading to the cloister, in a roundel, is *Christ Conferring His Blessing*. On the right wall is a *Virgin Mary in Maestà with Child, Four Angels and St. Francis*, an important fresco by Cimabue (about 1280), saved during the renovations of the 14th century with the exception of the figure which served as a twin on the left, destroyed by the opening of a doorway leading to the Cappella di Maria Maddalena. The portrait of St. Francis is striking in its harsh realisim and fedelity to the accounts by hagiographical sources. *He was a most eloquent man, with a jovial appearance and kind expression, and was never lazy and never haughty. He was small in stature, slender and straight shouldered. His legs were thin and his feet small. He had thin hands with long fingers and protruding fingernails, and his skin was delicate. His head was round and regular, with a slightly oval and protuding face and a small, flat forehead. He had dark eyes which were normal in size and all simplicity in expression. His hair was also dark, his eyebrows were straight and his nose was thin, straight and regular. He had regular, straight, white teeth, thin lips, and a sparse, black beard. His speech was mild but burning and penetrating, and his voice was strong, sweet, clear and resonant. He wore rough clothing, was a short sleeper, and was most open–handed.*

(Tommaso da Celano, *Vita* I, 83)

Next to the entrance to the Cappella di San Nicola, next to an ancient altar dedicated to St. Elizabeth of Hungary, are the half–figures of five saints painted by Simone Martini. From the left they are: *St. Francis, St. Ludwig of Toulouse, St. Elizabeth of Hungary, St. Margaret, St. Henry of Hungary* (the last two being traditionally mistaken for St. Clare and St. Louis King of France). By the same painter are the *Madonna with Child between St. Stephen and St. Ladislaus* on the wall in the corner. The frescoes were paid for with the generous donations sent to the Basilica by King Caroberto of Hungary.

Near the door communicating with the Cappella di Maria Maddalena was the tomb of the Blessed Giovanni Anglico († 1232), portrayed on the wall by an unknown painter about the middle of the 14th century. Behind an iron grating and below the *Maestà* by Cimabue are buried *Five Holy Friars*, represented on a nearby wall in half–figure by Pietro Lorenzetti.

At the head of the transept is the entrance to the **Cappella di San Nicola** (21). This was built by Cardinal Napoleone Orsini for his brother Giovanni Gaetano, who died during the conclave of Perugia in 1292–94. The decoration was done before 1306, when the chapel was already in use. It is polygonal with a short avant-corps covered by a barrel vault and a pentagonal rib vaulted hall with elaborate capitals.

In the back walls are three two–light windows. The imprints of the Orsini coat of arms are the originals. In a niche above the altar is the funeral monument with a youth in deacon's vestments lying on a bed while two angels raise the curtains of the alcove. The work of an Umbrian master educated in French statuary, it anticipates the style of the Duomo of Orvieto.
The vault and the walls of the chapel are decorated with a series of stories of St. Nicholas and with other saints. Recently, these frescoes have been attributed to Giotto, who was engaged in work on the last stories of the Franciscan Legend. The master, however, appears to have limited himself to painting several busts of saints on the splays and the tryptych on the altar. The rest he assigned to at least two disciples known as the Maestro di San Nicola, painter of the stories of the Saint and of the *Annunciation* in the exterior, and the Maestro Espressionista di Santa Chiara.
On an imitation tryptych above the tomb is *Madonna with Child between St. Nicholas and St. Francis*. On the window splays are the half–figures of 28 saints alternated with the Orsini coats of arms. On the barrel vault, from top to bottom, on the right are: *St. Nicholas Throwing the Three Gold Balls to the Girls of Panthera; St. Nicholas Saving the Sailors from a Storm; St. Nicholas Receiving Three Roman Horsemen at Myra; Two Apostles*. On the left are: *St. Nicholas Saving Three Innocents from Decapitation*; *The Sailors Pouring the Oil of Diana into the Sea; St. Nicholas Appearing to Constantine in a Dream; Two Apostles*. On the lateral wall on the right are: *St. Nicholas Bringing a Child back to Life; St. Nicholas Freeing Adeodatus; St. Nicholas Returning Adeodatus to His Parents; St. Peter; St. Andrew; An Apostle*. On the left wall is *An Elderly Jew Striking the Image of the Saint*. The two scenes below have been lost. On the counterfaçade is *The Redeemer Conferring His Blessing from a Shrine*. To the left is *St. Francis Introducing Napoleone Orsini and Three Cardinals*. To the right is *St. Nicholas Introducing Giovanni Gaetano Orsini and Three Cardinals*. Below, on the right, are *St. John the Baptist* and *An Apostle*. On the left are *St. Mary Magdalen* and *An Apostle*. On the underside of the entrance arch, from below right, are: *SS. Agnes and Cecilia; SS. Adrian and George; SS. Anthony and Francis*. From below left are *SS. Clare and Elizabeth; SS. Savino and Vittorino; SS. Rufino and Nicholas*.
The panes of the three windows are contemporary with the decorations, and were perhaps done from cartoons by the Maestro di San Nicola. In the left pane, from the top, are: *St. Vincent; St. Francis; St. Augustine; St. Ambrose; St. Vittorino; St. Rufino; Orsini Coats of Arms*. In the central pane are: *St. Francis Introducing Giovanni Gaetano Orsini; The Redeemer; Cardinal Napoleone Orsini; St. Nicholas; Orsini Coats of Arms*. In the right pane are: *St. Stephen; St. Lawrence; St. Francis; St. Anthony; St. Gregory; St. Jerome; Orsini Coats of Arms*.
The left wing of the transept (22) is decorated by a series of **Stories of the Passion of Christ** painted with lyric intensity and chromatic variety by Pietro Lorenzetti of Siena in the second decade of the 14th century. The famous *Crucifixion*, with its circle of horsemen crowded around the giant crucifix, was mutilated at the bottom from the placement on an altar (1604) torn down in 1870. At the same time the busts of four companions of St. Francis were destroyed.
The stories are divided by an ornamental band with *busts of saints and prophets* in-

Lower Basilica, left transept, Pietro Lorenzetti, Deposition (1315–20)

side medallions. The series begins on the right, from the top of the vault, with: *Entry into Jerusalem; The Last Supper; Washing of the Feet; Capture of Christ in the Garden; The Flogging; The Carrying of the Cross; Crucifixion; Judah's Suicide; Stigmata of St. Francis*. On the bottom wall are: *Deposition from the Cross; Deposition in the Sepulcher; Descent of Christ to Limbo; Resurrection*. Beside a door is a bust of *St. Vittorino*. Further to the right, where once there was an altar dedicated to St. John the Evangelist, is the *Madonna with Child Between St. John the Evangelist and St. Francis*. It is popularly called the *Madonna dei Tramonti (Madonna of the Sunsets*) due to the sunlight which illuminates it at sunset as it filters through the doorway which leads to the cloister. Underneath is *Crucifix, Coats of Arms, and Portrait of the Donor at Prayer*. In a feigned niche is *Still Life with Book, and Two Cruets with Water and Wine for the Mass*. On the back wall are: *Busts of St. Nicholas; St. Catherine; St. Clare; St. Thecla*. Below is *Fake Chair with Painted Shadow*. On the vault of the stairway leading to the cloister, in a roundel, is *St. Francis Conferring a Blessing.*
At the head of the transept is the entrance to the **Cappella di San Giovanni Battista** (23). This was built at the end of the 13th century for Cardinal Napoleone Orsini, to whom belong the numerous coats of arms on the stone walls. The cardinal died at Avignon, thus leaving the sepulchre above the altar empty. In 1926 a bronze cupboard, designed by Father Bonaventura Marinangeli and decorated with *Stories of the Virgin Mary*, was placed there to contain the relic of what is known as the *Veil of the Madonna*. The shape of the chapel is identical to that of the Cappella di San Nicola facing it. Of the original decoration there remains the frescoed trip-

tych above the sepulcher, representing the *Madonna with Child between St. John the Baptist and St. Francis*, done by Pietro Lorenzetti. Of the three two–light windows, only the middle one preserves its original panes, the design of which has been recently attributed to the Roman Jacopo Torriti. The panes are, from the top: *Two Angels; Annunciation by the Angel to Zachary; St. John the Baptist Encountering Jesus; Orsini Coats of Arms*. The panes of the side windows were done following ancient models by the Tolleri firm of Florence.

From the St. John Chapel one enters the **Lower Sacristy** (24). Documented only from 1341, it was built at the end of the 13th century to replace a chapel which preceded it. It has an L–shaped floor plan with a narrow passage and a large room covered by a barrel vault. The stonework structure and the 14th century decoration in fake marble were discovered after a fire which broke out on the night of June 12, 1952. This was followed by the discovery of an important fresco by the Maestro di Figline, a *Madonna with Child, Angels, St. Francis and St. Clare* (14th century), in a niche high in the wall of the bell tower, corresponding with a room used in antiquity to gather the tithes collected in the Dioceses of the Duchy of Spoleto. In 1952, several *Stories of the Virgin Mary and the Four Virtues* (1646–48), painted by Giacomo Giorgetti, were destroyed by fire. That which remains is a roundel with *Charity and an Angel Holding a Curtain*. Also surviving the fire was a fresco by Cesare Sermei, *St. Francis Received in Paradise* (1630), painted on a vault which divided the room in half and now in the Convento in Rivotorto. On the wall is a detached fresco by Tiberio D'Assisi, *Madonna with Child, St. Anne and Madonna with Child and St. Joseph, St. Sebastian and St. Bernardino*, brought from the external chapel of the Chiesa di San Bernardino.

At the base of the bell tower is the entrance to a *Hidden Sacristy* (25) with very valuable wooden cupboards carved by one Mastro Stefano.

Through a door in the right wing of the transept a stairway leads to an ambulatory which surrounds the choir of the Lower Church, beside which there is a rampant vault. From here it is possible to enter the ancient **Chapter Room** (26), part of the papal palace built by express order of Gregory IX in 1228 and dating from between 1230 and 1240. The hall has a quadrangular floor plan and cross vaults without ribs supported by a massive pillar in the center of the hall. In a lunette is a grandiose but unfinished fresco by Puccio Capanna, representing the *Crucifixion and SS. Ludwig of Toulouse, Paul, the Virgin Mary, Francis, Clare, John the Evangelist, Peter, and Anthony of Padua* (about 1340). It is a masterpiece of 14th century Italian painting for the composure of its figures, solid and monumental as in the best Giotto.

In several glass showcases on the wall important Franciscan relics are displayed. From the entrance, clockwise, they are: *Chalice and Paten of St. Francis*, in embossed and engraved silver, gift of the Abbot of St. Benedetto al Subasio; *Two Veils in embroidered Linen*, once having belonged to Jacopa de'Settesoli and used as sudarium during the agony of St. Francis; *Hair Shirt of St. Francis; Horn and Sticks of St. Francis*, used to call the crowds to sermon and to impose silence, gift of Egyptian Sultan Melek–el–Kamil, mounted on silver by Giovanni di Niccoluccio of Siena in the first half of the 14th century; *Solet Annuere*, containing the sealed rules of the

Basilica di San Francesco, view of the apse

Franciscan Order sent to St. Francis by Honorius III in 1223; *Stone* on which the Saint's head rested in the tomb; *Coins* and other objects found in the Saint's urn opened in 1818; *Tunic, felt Boots, Hood and Belt of St. Francis*; *White flannel Clothing* worn by the saint during his final illness; *Felt Boots*, made by St. Clare for the stigmatized saint; *Ostensory* containing a small piece of suede the Saint habitually kept on the wound in his side; 17th century silver *Reliquary*, with the *Chartula fratris Leonis*, a sheet of parchment paper written on by St. Francis and sent to Brother Leone. On this parchment is written the *Laudes Dei Atissimi* composed on Mt. Verna, and the blessing to Brother Leone with the symbol of the Greek letter Tau.

By climbing the steep staircases (27) at the sides of the apse, one exits to a terrace which opens onto the large cloister. From here can be seen the apse portion of the two superimposed churches. The lower apse is semicircular, the upper is polygonal with large windows and is flanked by two cylindrical piers. The **cloister** was built in 1476 according to the wishes of the Franciscan Sixtus IV della Rovere, to whom belong the coats of arms with the keys of the Church. Giorgio Vasari attributes the design to the Florentine Baccio Pontelli. Data in the archives attribute its execution to workers from Como. The cloister has two superimposed arcades, the lower having six arches on each side, and a well for a cistern in the center. The lunettes are frescoed with very poorly preserved *Stories of St. Francis* in green clay, painted by the local mannerist Dono Doni between 1564 and 1570.

From the terrace one enters the **Museo del Tesoro**, which holds a collection of paintings and various relics connected with the history of the Basilica. Although it has been sacked many times – by Ghibelline Muzio di Francesco in 1320, by Giampaolo Baglioni in 1492, by Jacopo Fiumi in 1497 and, finally, by the French troops between 1798 and 1810 – the collection preserves important sacred vestments and items in gold, given to the Basilica by illustrious individuals devoted to the Saint. Some of the pieces exhibited are to be considered among the masterpieces of French goldsmithery of the 13th century. The collection is exhibited in the so-called Sala Gotica in glass reliquaries complete with explanations and relevant photos.

On the right entrance wall is a large Flemish tapestry representing the *Franciscan Tree*, donated by Sixtus IV in 1479. Opposite are *Four choir stalls* (1467–71) by Apollonio de Giovanni da Ripatransone, brought from the choir of the Lower Basilica. Just beyond the ticket office are: *Dossal in embroidered yellow silk*, made in Palermo the first quarter of the 13th century, gift of Emperor of Constantinople John of Brienne; *The Prophet Isaiah* (about 1280) by the Maestro di San Francesco, panel of a large polyptych with two faces, already displayed on the main altar of the Chiesa di San Francesco al Prato in Perugia; *Face of God*, by Iacopo Torriti, sinopite of the fresco with the *Creation of the World* in the first bay of the Upper Basilica; *Processional Cross* made of gilt, embossed, and engraved copper, Umbrian school of the end of the 12th century; *Madonna with Child*, wooden sculpture of the Umbrian school of the second half of the 13th century, brought from a church in the city; *Cross* painted on both sides by an Umbrian disciple of the Maestro di San Francesco, called the *Blue Crucifix Master* for his preference for blue, from an altar

Museo del Tesoro, Flemish made, Franciscan Tree (1479)

in the Lower Basilica; *Reliquary for the finger of St. Andrew*, made of engraved and inscribed gold–plated silver, quartz and rubies, Roman made in the 13th century, donated by Nicholas IV in 1288; another *Dossal in red silk*, made in Palermo during the first quarter of the 13th century and donated by John of Brienne; *Crucifix with the Virgin Mary, St. John, Mary Magdalen, Mary Mother of James and, above, the Ascension*, by an Umbrian master active from 1220 to 1240, brought from the castle of Porziano near Assisi; antependium representing *St. Francis and Four of His Miracles, Miracle of the Girl with Head Attached to Her Shoulder, St. Francis Healing Bartolomeo da Narni, Miracle of the Possessed Woman, Miracle of a Crippled Man*, by an Umbrian painter from the middle of the 13th century, called the Maestro del Tesoro (Master of the Treasure), from the Lower Basilica.

The collection continues with: *St. Martin Sharing His Cloak with a Beggar* (about 1315), by Simone Martini, sinopite of the fresco with the same name in the Cappella di San Martino; *Tabernacle* (1570), in embossed copper, executed by Giulio Danti according to a design by Galeazzo Alessi for the main altar of the Lower Basilica; showcase with numerous medieval *ceramics* (13th–14th centuries) found in 1968 under the floor of the main refectory of the Convento. On a low podium in the middle of the room are: *Reliquary of the Veste Inconsutile* (seamless robe), gold-plated silver, made in Paris in the second half of the 13th century, representing on the front a *Resurrected Christ Between St. Clare, St. Francis and Three Worshipping Poor Clares*, and on the back *Nativity and God Conferring His Blessing*, gift of Queen Joan, wife of Philip the Fair, King of France; small ivory statue of a *Madonna with Child*, with traces of polychromy, masterpiece of Parisian sculpture from the end of the 13th century. Inside a removable drawer, is the *Missal of St. Ludwig*, opened to pages 105–106, decorated with a *Crucifixion* and an *Apocalyptic Christ* (1255–60), done by a Parisian miniaturist, perhaps gift of St. Louis IX King of France for liturgical services at the main altar of the Lower Church.

In a reliquary are: *Processional Cross*, quartz crystal, amber and gold–plated copper, Venetian made, from the middle of the 13th century; and *Reliquary of St. Vito*, silver, Venetian school of the 15th–16th century. In another reliquary are: *Relic of the Holy Thorn*, engraved silver, Parisian school 1260–70; and *Pair of Angels* in gold-plated silver, Umbrian school of the 15th century perhaps belonging to a reliquary. Next is the *Reliquary box of St. Orsola*, gold–plated silver, champlevé enamel, gold-plated and inscribed glass, quartz crystal, Umbrian made in the 14th century. The enamels under the base represent *Stories of the Magi* and originate from an older reliquary of the French school; the inscribed glass with the *Stigmata of St. Francis* is by a local painter whose style was that of Puccio Capanna; *Chalice of Nicholas IV* (about 1290), gold–plated, embossed silver, masterpiece by the Sienese goldsmith Guccio di Mannaia, enriched by translucent, illustrated enamels, gift of Nicholas IV. In a showcase are: *Reliquary of St. James*, gold–plated silver, French school of the middle 14th century; *Reliquary of St. Catherine's Hair*, silver, ivory, and pearls, French school of the middle 14th century; *Reliquary of St. Sebastian*, gold–plated copper, Umbrian–Sienese school, 14th century; *Seal from the Sacro Convento* (1427). In a reliquary is a *Jewel box* in the Carthusian style, ivory, wood, and bronze, Embriachi workshop, beginning of the 15th century.

Next is a *Reliquary case*, painted wood, Umbrian school of the middle 15th century, identified with the case which contained the slippers of St. Francis after he received the stigmata. In a reliquary in the middle of the room is a Venetian *Cross* in quartz crystal and gold–plated silver (14th century), decorated by two miniatures with the *Crucifixion* and *Madonna with Child Between St. Catherine and St. Nicholas* (other miniatures with figures of saints appear at the foot and in the arms of the cross); *Pair of candlesticks* (1332), quartz crystal and silver, Venetian school, donated by Galgano della Marra, executioner of Puglia. The miniatures of Franciscan saints at the feet are from the early 17th century. In a showcase are: *St. Francis, St. Anthony the Abbot* (about 1360), disciple of Pace di Bartolo, tablets from a polyptych perhaps originating from the Cappella di Sant'Antonio Abate; *Cross* in engraved olive wood, Byzantine school middle of the 15th century, decorated on the front with the *Crucifixion* and on the back with *Stories of the Virgin*; *Processional Cross*, Umbrian school of the 15th century; four *Chalices* from the 14th century; *Reliquary of the Cross of the Blessed Egidio*, gold-plated copper, Umbrian school of the 15th century; *Processional Standard* printed on both sides with the monogram of St. Bernardino, and on the pedestal *Stigmata of St. Francis*, *Annunciation* (about 1427), attributed to Pellegrino di Giovanni, from the sacristy of the Lower Church. In a showcase are: *Reliquary of St. Rose*, silver and precious stones, French school, middle 15th century, with additions in the 18th century; *Reliquary of St. Biagio*, silver, gold–plated copper and enamel, French school, middle 14th century; *Reliquary of St. Fortunato*, gold–plated copper, quartz crystal, and amber, Umbrian school of the 15th century, rebuilt in 1562; *Processional cross*, silver, made in Lombardy in the 17th century; *Reliquary of St. Feliciano*, gold–plated and enameled copper, Umbrian school, 15th century; *Reliquary of the Stone of the Holy Sepulcher*, silver, gold–plated copper, enamels and nielli, Umbrian school of the 14th century with Venetian addition in the 15th century.

Museo del Tesoro, Parisian school, Madonna with Child (end of the 13th century)

In a reliquary are: *Madonna with Child*, painted by a Venetian–Byzantine master of the end of the 14th century, from the infirmary of the Sacro Convento; *Madonna of Mercy* (16th century), tablet attributed to Dono Doni; *Pair of small bells* in bronze, Roman school, 16th century; three *Chalices* from the 15th century; *Antependium of Sixtus IV* (1476–78), dossal in fabric with embroidered appliqué representing *Sixtus*

IV Kneeling Before St. Francis Raising His Right Hand with the Stigmata and Holding in His Left a Cross, Coat of Arms of the Della Rovere family, band embroidered with the Madonna with Child and twelve saints, Florentine workshop following a design by Antonio del Pollaiolo and Francesco Botticini.
The final glass showcases display Venetian glass from the 17th century and silver objects from the 17th and 18th century. On the back wall are: *Crucifix Amidst Angels and SS. Leonard and Anthony the Abbot, Francis and Clare* (1507) by Tiberio d'Assisi, originally in the Cappella di Sant'Antonio Abate; *Madonna with Child, Worshipping Angels and SS. Catherine of Alexandria, Francis, Elizabeth of Hungary, a Blessed Franciscan, Clare and Louis, King of France* (1516) by Giovanni di Pietro, called lo Spagna, brought from the Cappella di Santa Caterina.

In an adjacent room is displayed **The Perkins Collection**, which once belonged to the American art historian Frederick Mason Perkins and which he left to the Basilica upon his death in 1955. It is composed of a sculpture and 56 paintings by Italian primitive masters, predominantly from Florence and Siena, collected by the scholar in his home in Assisi. The collection was displayed to the public in 1986. No.1, *Enthroned Madonna with Child, St. Catherine and St. Paul*, Tuscan school, middle 14th century; No.2, *Stigmata of St. Francis* (1488), by Antoniazzo Romano; No.3, *Madonna with Child*, workshop of Antoniazzo Romano, end of the 15th century; No.4, *St. Rocco*, by Niccolò di Liberatore, called l'Alunno, end of the 15th century; No.5, portable tryptych with beautifully carved frame, representing in the center a *Madonna with Child and Two Angel Musicians*, and in the wings, *Christ at the Pillar* and *St. John the Baptist*, by Francesco di Gentile, second half of the 15th century; No.6, *Imago Pietatis*, on the back is a *Madonna with Child*, by Domenico Morone, early 16th century; No.7, *Madonna with Child*, by Benvenuto Tisi, called il Garofalo, early 16th century; No.8, *Imago Pietatis*, Emilian school, first half of the 16th century; No.9, *St. Sebastian*, by Giovanni Battista Benvenuti, called l'Ortolano, early 16th century; No.10, roundel with *The Virgin Adoring the Child*, by the Maestro del Tondo (Master of the Roundel) Lathrop (Lucca, early 16th century).
The collection continues with: No.11, *Bust of a Woman*, Venetian school, first half of the 16th century; No. 12, *St. Ranieri*, by Giovanni di Nicola, middle 15th century; No.13, *Madonna with Child*, school of Pisa, second half of the 14th century; No.14, *Nursing Madonna, St. Anthony the Abbot, and St. Nicholas*, Venetian school, last quarter of the 14th century; No.15, *St. Francis of Assisi*, by Zanino di Pietro, early 15th century; No.16, *Madonna with Child*, by the Maestro del Dittico (Master of the Diptych) Sterbini (Venetian–Byzantine area, first half of the 14th century).
Farther along in the collection are: No.17, *Enthroned Madonna with Child and Two Donors* (1404), by Mariotto di Nardo; No.18, *Infant Jesus*, by Pseudo–Pier Francesco Fiorentino (Florence, second half of the 15th century); No.19, *St. Lawrence*, by Gherardo Starnina, early 15th century; No.20, fragment of an altarpiece portraying *St. Peter the Martyr and a Saint*, by Pier Francesco Fiorentino, end of the 15th century; No.21, section of polyptych representing *St. Nicholas of Bari and St. Giovanni Gualberto*, by Lorenzo di Niccolò, early 15th century; No.22, *Ascension of Christ*, by Mariotto di Nardo, early 15th century; No.23, *Episode From the*

Perkins Collection, Florentine school, St. Jerome Penitent (end of the 15th century)

Legend of the Crucifix of Berytus, Bolognese school, first quarter of the 16th century; No.24, *Madonna with Child*, by the Maestro di Sant'Ivo (Florence, end of the 14th century); No.25,*The Virgin Adoring the Child and Donor*, Florentine school, last quarter of the 15th century; No.26, *Madonna of Humility*, by Lorenzo Monaco, early 15th century; No.27, *St. Jerome Penitent*, Florentine school, last quarter of the 15th century; three stained glass windows with *St. Paul, St. Jerome and St. Feliciano* (1458), by Neri da Perugia from a cartoon by a German master, brought from the Duomo in Foligno.

Advancing farther into the collection, one finds: No.28, *Madonna with Child, St. Catherine and St. Anthony the Abbot*, by Bicci di Lorenzo, early 15th century; No.29, *Madonna with Child, St. John the Baptist and St. John the Evangelist*, by Bicci di Lorenzo, third decade of the 15th century; No.30, *Pietà*, Florentine school, last quarter of the 15th century; No.31, *Baptism of Christ*, by the Maestro di Borgo alla Collina (Florence, first quarter of the 15th century); No.32, *St. Francis of Assisi* (about 1430), by Brother Giovanni da Fiesole, called the Beato Angelico; No.33, *Annunciation*, Florentine school, last quarter of the 15th century; No.34, *St. Jerome Penitent*, by Don Pietro Dei, called Bartolomeo della Gatta, end of the 15th century; No.35, *Madonna with Child*, by Masolino da Panicale (?), first half of the 15th century; No.36, *Madonna with Child, St. Sebastian and St. Rocco*, Tuscan school, end of the 15th century; No.37, *Enthroned Madonna with Child Surrounded by Four Saints*, by the Mastro dell'Infanzia (Master of the Infancy), Florence, 3rd quarter of the 14th century.

The collection proceeds with: No.38, portable altarpiece, with *Enthroned Madonna with Child Between Two Angels, St. John the Baptist and St. Peter,* on the doors, *Nativity* and *Crucifixion*, by the Maestro di San Martino alla Palma (Florence, second quarter of the 14th cent.); No.39, marble sculpture representing a *Madonna with Child*, school of Siena, second quarter of the 14th century; No.40, panel of a polyptych with *Saint John the Baptist*, by Segna di Bonaventura, early 14th century, from the Chiesa di Santo Spirito dei Silvestrini in Siena; No.41, *St. James the Greater*, by Giovanni di Paolo, third decade of the 15th century; No.42, *San Bernardino da Siena*, by Giovanni di Paolo, eighth decade of the 15th century; No.43, *San Benedetto da Norcia*, by Taddeo di Bartolo, end of the 14th century; No.44, *St. Elizabeth of Hungary*, by Taddeo di Bartolo, early 15th century.
The remaining items in the collection include: No.45, *St. Christopher*, by Stefano di Giovanni, called il Sassetta, fourth decade of the 15th century; No.46, panel of polyptych representing *St. Paul*, Tuscan school, middle of the 14th century; No.47, *San Bernardino of Siena*, by Sano di Pietro, middle of the 15th century; No.48, relief in carved and painted wood depicting a *Madonna with Child*, by Neroccio di Bartolomeo Landi, third quarter of the 15th century; No.49, *Madonna with Child* (about 1340), by Pietro Lorenzetti; No.50, *Enthroned Madonna with Child, Angels and Saints*, by Pietro Lorenzetti, fourth decade of the 14th century; No.51, section of a ledge representing the *Funeral of a Holy Bishop*, by Pietro Lorenzetti, fourth decade of the 14th century; No.52, *Enthroned Madonna with Child, Angels and Saints*, by a Sienese disciple of Pietro Lorenzetti, second quarter of the 14th century; No.53, panel of polyptych depicting *St. Cecilia*, by Pietro Lorenzetti, fifth decade of the 14th century; No.54, *Nativity Between St. Dominic and St. Catherine of Siena*, by Guidoccio Cozzarelli, last quarter of the 15th century; No.55, *St. Catherine of Siena Receiving the Stigmata*, school of Siena, first quarter of the 16th century; No.56, *Nursing Madonna*, by Andrea di Bartolo, early 15th century; No.57, panel of polyptych depicting *St. Catherine of Alexandria*, by Bartolo di Fredi, end of the 15th century.

Upper Church

The Upper Basilica is entered directly from the lawn in front of it. There could be no greater contrast than that existing between the lively polychromy of the slender gothic forms of the interior of the nave and the severity of the gable façade, constructed in white stone without any hint of color, except for the lost mosaic encrustments of the rose window. The only concession to the modern transalpine style of architecture is the coupled portal with pointed arch, common in French cathedrals, which is decorated with a small, blind rose window and round panels once embellished with mosaics. On the jamb on the left there is a head crowned with grape vines.
The bright façade is divided in half by a stringcourse with a freize of monstrous figures, similar to those which appear on the façade of the Cathedral of San Rufino. In the upper half is a large rose window divided into four concentric circles, in a style typical of the Cosmati family (Roman architects, 12th–14th century). At the sides there are symbols of the Evangelists in relief. In the triangular tympanum is a

Upper Basilica, interior

round window which gives light to the garret. On the left side of the façade, above the buttress, is the loggia of the blessings which is topped by a cupola and was built following a design by Valentino Martelli. From the cupola the Holy Veil of the Madonna was shown to the public.

The interior has a nave, divided into four bays, with transept and polygonal apse. The bays are covered by cross vaults with ogival–shaped ribs which are supported by bundles of slender pillars with crocket capitals. At a certain height the walls recede, forming a gallery which runs the length of the church and passes under the pillars. The Lower Church is forever immersed in half–light due to the closing of the original one–light windows, whereas the airy hall of the Upper Basilica is crossed by bands of colored light originating from the large, lance–shaped, stained glass windows placed in the center of each bay, and from the rose window in the façade. The walls of the apse have been entirely replaced by windows. Two large, four–light windows occupy the head of the transept. This arrangement constitutes an exceptional event, perhaps unique, for the transferral of French Gothic architectural forms to 13th century central Italy.

The Upper Church represents the prototype of monastic Franciscan churches, designed to resemble a covered piazza and used for the liturgy and sermons without the hindrance of lateral aisles. Along with the stained glass windows, characteristic motif of northern architecture, wide use is made of murals, much in the medieval Italian tradition. These once performed the explanatory function entrusted to images since the time of Gregory the Great, and served as both instruction for illiterate pilgrims and as a commentary on the function of the liturgy. Moreover, they answered the symbolic and commemorative needs of an order which was no longer bound to its originally strict poverty and which had become the main ally of the Roman Church.

The interior of the church has been completely covered by a bright polychromy, resulting in the integration of the structures of the walls with feigned architectonic structures. The painted corbels, the fake galleries in the transepts, the illusionistic arcade of the nave are the artifices of a great scenography within which the stories are depicted.

The Upper Basilica is the first place after the end of the late ancient civilization to present an organic, illustrative program articulated in many cycles. It is inspired by a unifying theme centered in the exaltation of St. Francis according to the eschatological interpretation proposed by St. Bonaventure. The key to its reading lies in the clypeate images present in the third cross vault where St. Francis is given the role of intermediary between God and humanity, usually reserved by Christian tradition to the Virgin Mary and John the Baptist.

The program begins in the presbytery, the walls of which are frescoed with stories of the Holy Virgin, The Apocalypse, and the Apostles, which are connected with the dedication of the three altars to the Virgin, to St. Michael the Archangel and to St. Peter. From an iconostasis placed above the main altar, a painted *Cross* once hung facing the nave with which corresponded another two frescoed *Crucifixions* on the side altars, visible only to the clergy. In the upper registers of the nave, facing one another, are the stories of the Old and New Testament which symbolize, in the exegesis of Gioacchino da Fiore, the first two ages of the world, that of the Father and that of the Son. The life of St. Francis, illustrated in the lower portion of the walls, is conceived as a progressive ascent to God. In the words of St. Bonaventure, it is a kind of *Itinerarium Mentis in Deum*, in view of the renewal of the evangelical message brought about by the Saint. His figure appears in the apocalyptic sto-

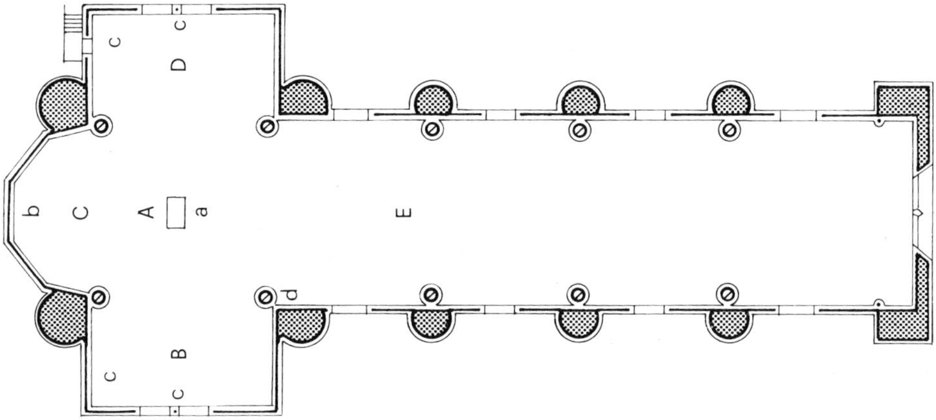

UPPER CHURCH

A Presbytery
B Left transept
C Apse
D Right transept
E Nave

1 Altar
2 Throne
3 Choir
4 Pulpit

ries of the left transept as the Angel of the Sixth Seal, the initiator of the third age, that of the Holy Spirit, as described in the *Legenda Maior.*
This great undertaking was carried out in the last two decades of the 13th century and includes the work of the major artists of central Italy from Cimabue to Jacopo Torriti, to Giotto himself. In Assisi Giotto took the first steps toward a new way of conceiving art, as naturalistic and in perspective, which would point the way to the Italian Renaissance.

It is advisable to begin one's visit from the **Presbytery** (A). The main altar was consecrated in 1253 by Innocent IV. It rests on a three–stepped podium and consists of a large slab of pink stone from Mount Subasio with marble slabs on the sides once bearing decorations done by the Cosmati family which were replaced in 1940. The pictorial decoration, which is characterized by the use of incisive and expressive drawings, was begun in the right transept by the Maestro Oltremontano (Master from beyond the Alps) who was given this title due to his presumed northern origins.
He was replaced by the Florentine Cimabue, who was called from Rome, where his presence in 1272 is documented, by Pope Nicholas III Orsini (1277–80), long–time cardinal protector of the Minorites. The style of the master is directed toward a classicized return to Byzantine models into which are infused a solemn pathos which reaches unequaled heights in the sublime *Crucifixion* of the left transept.
Unfortunately, this impressive collection of paintings has come down to us in a ruinous state due to the oxidation of the white lead extensively used by the painter

UPPER CHURCH - PAINTINGS OF THE TRANSEPT, APSE AND CROSSING

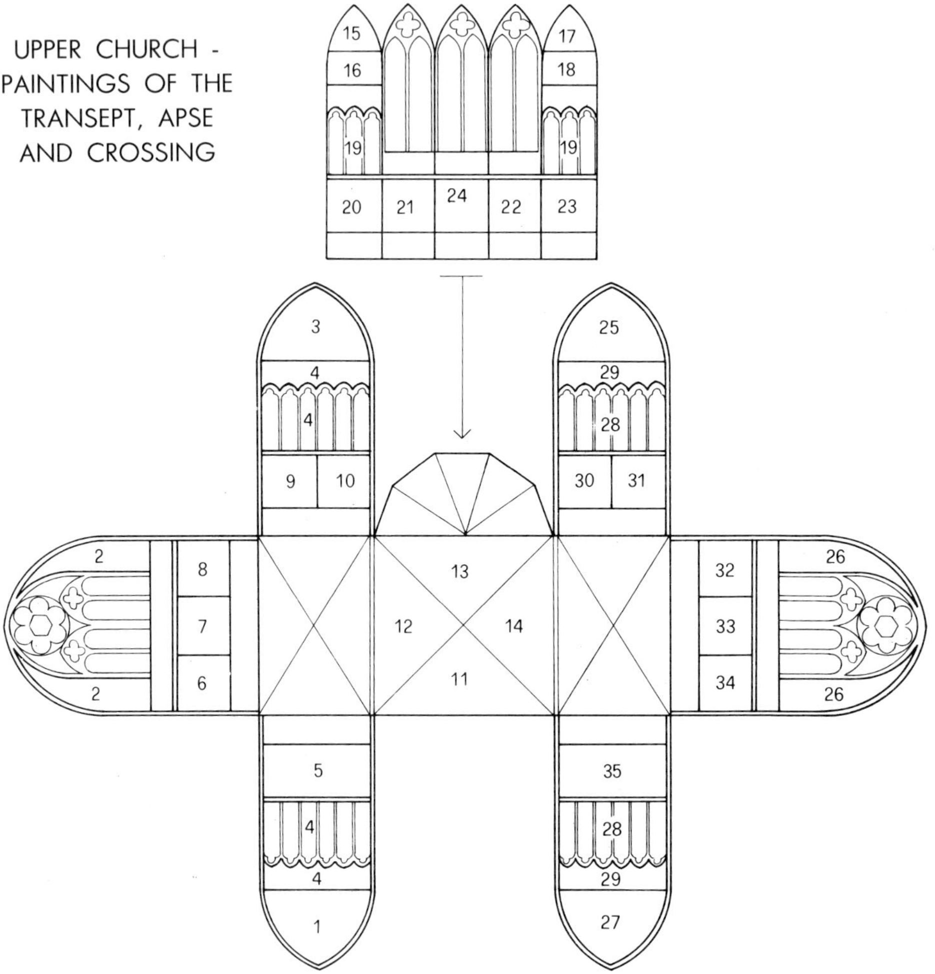

and which upon turning black has caused a general darkening of the painting, resulting in an effect similar to that of a photographic negative.

Left Transept (B)

The entire decoration is attributed to Cimabue, assisted by members of his workshop. In the cross vault is a starry sky. The fresco depicting *Christ in Glory* (1) in the left lunette has been completely lost. On each side of the four–light window there are three *Angels* (2). Still visible in the right lunette is the episode of the *Three Archangels Defeating the Dragon* (3). In the undersides of the arches and in the fake arcades above the triforium are busts of *Angels*. In the triforium are full-length *Angels* (4). The Stories of the Apocalypse of the lower register are separated by bands of plants which support fake corbels.

Crucifixion (5). The scene is dominated by the enormous figure of Christ crucified surrounded by a host of weeping angels. On the left is a group of pious women with St. John turning to the Virgin Mary and taking her hand, and Mary Magdalen throwing her arms open toward the cross while St. Francis embraces it. On the right, Longinus and the Centurion point to Christ while the Pharisees walk away.
The Vision of the Throne and the Book of the Seven Seals (6). Above, within a lozenge, is the Christ Child lying on a throne. On the left is the Book of the Seven Seals. On the sides of the throne are the symbols of the Four Evangelists, surrounded by twenty–four elders and a multitude of angels.
Vision of the Angels at the Four Corners of the Earth (7). The upper half of the scene has almost completely disappeared. Barely distinguishable is the figure of an angel sent by the Lord to save the Chosen and moving among trees and mountains above the walls of a city. Below, four monumental angels hold the winds within horns.
Apocalyptic Christ (8). Within a lozenge is Christ conferring His blessing surrounded by seven angels sounding the trumpets of the Last Judgement. At His feet is an altar, incensed by an angel with a thurible. Below are the Chosen, wearing the Franciscan frock. *The Fall of Babylon* (9). The upper half of the scene has almost disappeared. Barely distinguishable is the angel announcing the fall of Babylon. The buildings of the city fall while the inhabitants and demoniac animals flee through the gates of the city wall. *The Vision of Heavenly Jerusalem* (10). The story has almost completely disappeared. Barely distinguishable is St. John the Evangelist, seated on a rock in the middle of a river, to whom an angel points out the vision of the new Jerusalem, now no longer visible.

Crossing

The decoration is entirely credited to Cimabue. In the webs are *The Four Evangelists* (11–14), accompanied by their respective attributes and a stylized depiction of the lands they converted: Matthew in Judaea; Mark in Italy; Luke in Greece; John in Asia. In the web of Mark the Evangelist is an idealized view of Rome, with its most important monuments and the Orsini coat of arms.

Apse (C)

The decoration was begun by the Maestro Oltremontano and completed by Cimabue. In the lunette above the gallery are represented, on the left, *Announcement to Joachim* (15); *Joachim's Offering at the Temple* (16). On the right are *Birth of the Virgin Mary* (17) and *Wedding of the Virgin Mary* (18). In the fake loggias and in the triforium are the figures of *Angels* (19).
The Virgin Mary Leaving the Apostles (20). The Virgin Mary is lying on a bed around which are seated the twelve apostles and Dionysius Areopagite. Standing, St. John announces the imminence of her death. *The Death of the Virgin Mary* (21). The body of the Virgin is placed on the death bed in the presence of the apostles. Standing behind the bed is Christ, surrounded by angels and patriarchs, taking into His arms the soul of the Virgin.
The Assumption of the Virgin Mary (22). Embraced by Christ, the Virgin is taken to heaven within a lozenge carried by four angels. Below is the empty sepulcher with the apostles in adoration in the presence of patriarchs, martyrs and confessors.
Christ and the Virgin Mary Enthroned (23). On a monumental throne, surrounded by

the angelical hierarchy, saints and patriarchs, are seated the Redeemer and the Virgin Mary, who intercedes for a group of devout Franciscans.
At the center of the apse is a niche with the *Papal throne*, raised on a podium with four steps, probably the work of Roman marble cutters active in the second quarter of the 13th century. The throne is composed of a step, decorated with the sculpted figures of an asp, a basilisk, a lion, and a dragon. The back is decorated with curled leaves in the slopes. There is also a marble choir stall with two lions in pink stone as armrests. The niche is composed of two columns in pink stone with gold leaved capitals, which support an architrave decorated with fake mosaics and a tympanum with a lobed window and rampant curled leaves. Behind, in two shields, are the busts of two popes (24) identified as Gregory IX and Innocent IV.
Right Transept (D)
The decoration was begun by the Maestro Oltremontano, assisted by a Roman master identified as Jacopo Torriti for the figures of the apostles in the small loggia on the right. The apostolic stories are to a large extent the work of collaborators of Cimabue. The webs are decorated with a starry sky, and in the lower corners, by the heads of bearded old men. In the lunette on the left, much damaged, is the *Maiestas Domini* (25) surrounded by the symbols of the Evangelists. At the head of the transept, on the sides of the large window, are the gigantic figures of the prophets *Isaiah and David* (26). In the lunette on the right is *The Transfiguration* (27), where Christ appears inside a lozenge, flanked by Moses and Elias, with the apostles Peter, James and John at His feet. In the gallery of the triforium are painted the full-length figures of *The Twelve Apostles* (28). On the external front, fake cusps alternate with medallions with the *Busts of Angels* (29).
St. Peter Healing a Cripple (30). The Saint, followed by John, takes the hand of the cripple. In the background is the temple of Jerusalem.
St. Peter Healing the Sick and Casting the Devil From the Possessed (31). The Saint, followed by two apostles, blesses a group of sick people sitting on the ground, healing them with his shadow. From the mouth of a possessed man flees a row of demons which cling to the column of a niche, symbol of the portico of Solomon. *The Fall of Simon Magus* (32). Simon Magus balances at the top of a wooden scaffolding, supported by demons. St. Peter blesses him, causing his fall. The story takes place in the presence of Emperor Nero flanked by two soldiers and St. Paul kneeling in prayer. *Martyrdom of St. Peter* (33). The saint is martyred on an upside down cross. The building on the left symbolizes the pyramid of Caius Cestius; that on the right, the *Meta Romuli*.
Martyrdom of St. Paul (34). The lower portion of the scene, with the decapitation of St. Paul, has almost completely disappeared. Above is a rocky countryside with scattered groups of soldiers. *Crucifixion* (35). The scene is dominated by the enormous figure of Christ crucified in the midst of a host of weeping angels. Beside the cross, Longinus holds the lance with which he has pierced Christ's side. Another soldier has a stick with a sponge. On the ground, St. Francis embraces the cross. On the left, the Virgin Mary faints and is supported by the pious women. On the right is a group of Pharisees.
In the semidome of the apse and against the walls of the transept is a splendid

Upper Basilica, Cimabue, St. Mark the Evangelist (1277–80)

wooden choir, commissioned in 1491 by Francesco Sansone to Master Domenico Indovini of San Severino, who completed the work in 1501 with the help of numerous collaborators. In a stall on the left is inscribed: *M.F. SAMSON GENERALIS FIERI CURAVIT. DOMINICUS DE SANCTO SEVERINI ME FECIT MCCCCCI*. The choir is made up of 102 stalls, of which 15 are on each side of the transept and the remaining are situated in two rows in the apse. It is decorated with illusionistic inlays representing perspective compositions, and still lifes of books and musical instruments. On the backs in the second row are repreštented 36 important protagonists of Franciscan history, the Virgin and the Angel of the Annunciation done following cartoons attributed to Lorenzo d'Alessandro of San Severino. On the lectern in the middle of the apse are *The Stigmata of St. Francis* and a *St. Anthony Reading*.
Through a small door in the left transept one enters the **Upper Sacristy**, located between the transept and the bell tower and corresponding with the lower sacristy. The surroundings, bare and unadorned, are covered by a barrel vault. On the walls are four large frescoes with the sketches for various scenes found in the nave. These were recovered following the tearing of a superimposed layer with the *Creation of Eve, Original Sin, Sacrifice of Isaac, Nativity*. There are also various fragments of majolica tiles removed in 1940 from the steps of the main altar. The liturgical vestments are preserved in a polygonal room above the Cappella di San Giovanni.
To the pillar which is located on the corner between the nave and the left transept is attached a stone **pulpit**. This consists of a capital decorated with leaves which supports five panels separated by small twisted columns. Three roughly sculpted faces depict *St. Ludwig of Toulouse, St. Francis, and St. Anthony of Padua*. The pulpit was carved by a local stone–cutter in the second quarter of the 14th century, identified by some as Niccolò da Bettona. In 1347 it was painted blue by one Brother Martino.
Nave (E): **Stories from the Old and New Testament**.
The decoration of the nave is an expansion of a theme already treated in the Lower Basilica, that is the correspondence of the life of St. Francis with the evangelical parable. The *Franciscan Legend* is introduced by two parallel cycles with the stories of the Old (on the right) and the New (on the left) Testaments, which are placed on the walls between the windows on the two superimposed registers. The work was conceived as a result of the election of the first Franciscan pope, Nicholas IV (1288–92, formerly Girolamo Masci da Ascoli), who returned to the friars the use of alms to finance the decoration of the Basilica, a privilege declined in 1281 upon the completion of the transept.
The frescoes were painted by different masters, who probably were inspired by the compositional schemes and the iconography of a cycle existent in the Vatican Basilica. In the fourth bay has been identified the neo–Hellenistic style of the Roman Brother Jacopo Torriti, the painter preferred by Nicholas IV. Following him is a master from the school of Cimabue, probably of local origins, named the Maestro della Cattura (Master of the Capture). The two *Stories of Isaac*, by an anonymous painter, are attributed by some to young Giotto, due to the presence of a plasticity of form and a spacial verity of Roman origin. Also Roman is the painter of the *Stories of Joseph* and the *Pentecost* in the counterfaçade. The last evangelical stories

could be attributed to Giotto, due to the analogies found with the famous Cross in the Chiesa di Santa Maria Novella in Florence.
The stories are read from the wall of the fourth bay to the counterfaçade, from the upper to the lower register. On the undersides of the arches, within frames, are the *busts of saints and prophets*, in large part unidentifiable. The ribs and the surrounding bands are decorated with fake mosaics and plant clusters, and with figures of puttos. In the vault of the third bay, within roundels are: *Redeemer and Angels; Virgin Mary and Angels; St. Francis and Angels; St. John the Baptist and Angels* (Jacopo Torriti and collaborators). In the vault of the first bay are: *St. Gregory the Great; St. Ambrose; St. Jerome; St. Augustine* (Maestro di Isacco and Maestro della Pentecoste). On the right wall, first register (1–8) are: *Creation of the World* (Jacopo Tor-

Upper Basilica, nave, Maestro di Isacco, Isaac Rejecting Esau (1288–92)

UPPER CHURCH – PAINTINGS OF THE NAVE

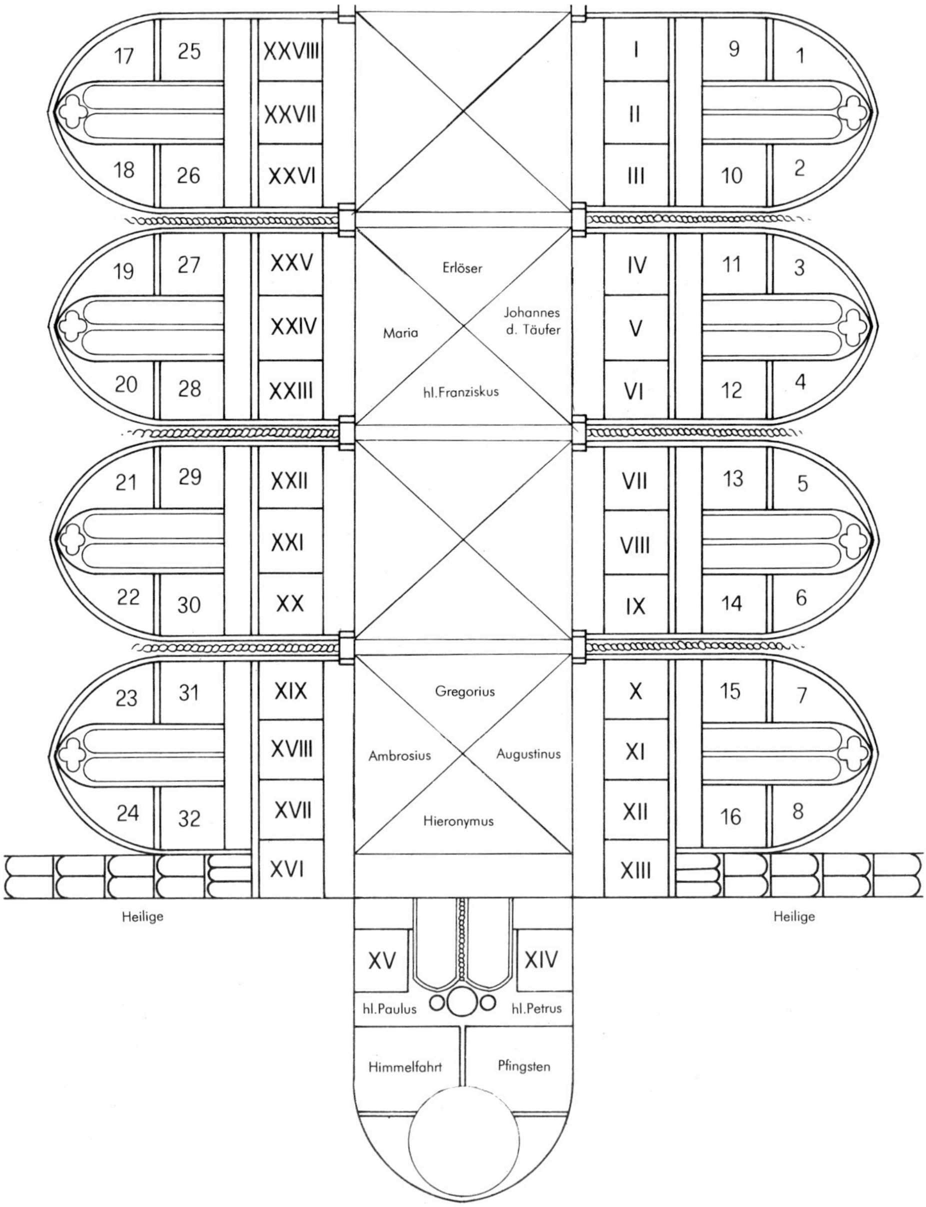

riti); *Creation of Adam* (Jacopo Torriti); *Creation of Eve* (Jacopo Torriti); *Original Sin* (Jacopo Torriti); *Banishment from the Garden of Eden* (Jacopo Torriti ?); *Work of the Progenitors* (destroyed); *The Sacrifice of Cain and Abel* (destroyed); *Murder of Abel* (fragmentary).

In the second register (9–16) are: *The Building of the Ark* (Jacopo Torriti); *Entrance of Noah and the Animals into the Ark* (fragmentary); *Sacrifice of Abraham* (Jacopo Torriti); *The Appearance of the Angels to Abraham* (Jacopo Torriti?); *Isaac Blessing Jacob* (Maestro di Isacco); *Esau Before Isaac* (Maestro di Isacco); *Joseph Lowered into the Pit by His Brothers* (Maestro della Pentecoste); *Joseph Revealing His Identity to His Brothers* (Maestro della Pentecoste).

On the left wall, first register(17–24), are: *Annunciation* (Jacopo Torriti?); *Visitation* (destroyed); *Nativity* (Maestro della Cattura); *Adoration of the Magi* (much deteriorated); *Presentation in the Temple* (Maestro della Cattura); *Flight to Egypt* (fragmentary); *Debate in the Temple* (fragmentary); *Baptism of Christ* (fragmentary).

In the second register (25–32) are: *Wedding in Cana* (Jacopo Torriti?); *Raising of Lazarus* (fragmentary); *Capture of Christ* (Maestro della Cattura); *Christ Before Pilate* (fragmentary); *Ascent to Calvary* (Maestro della Cattura); *Crucifixion* (Tuscan painter?); *Mourning Over Christ's Death* (Giotto ?); *Pious Women at the Sepulcher* (fragmentary).

On the counterfaçade are: *The Pentecost* (Maestro della Pentecoste); *Ascent of Jesus into Heaven* (Maestro di Isacco and collaborator). On the sides of the rose window in two roundels are *St. Peter* and *St. Paul*. In the arch are full–length figures of saints in niches. From the center of the vault, on the right, are: *St. Francis and St. Clare; St. Anthony and St. Benedict; St. Agabito and St. Lawrence; Two Saints*. On the left are: *St. Vittorino and St. Rufino; St. Peter the Martyr and St. Dominic; Two Martyred Saints; Two Martyred Sainted Women*.

Franciscan Legend

In the lower half of the nave are painted twenty–eight stories from the life of St. Francis, the most important part of the decoration of the Upper Church. The narrative cycle is inspired by the *Legenda Maior* of St. Bonaventure, from which are taken the titles placed under the scenes. It is the official illustration of the Saint's life and miracles, desired by the moderates of the Order with the approval of the Roman Curia, for the spreading of the Franciscan message. The episodes narrate a modern story set in a medieval society, in the piazze and countryside of Assisi, with personages taken from real life who, with realistic gestures, express a universal message. The fake portico which frames the episodes, to the contrary, renders the illusionistic effect of a background which continues beyond the walls of the church. The frescoes were begun in the last decade of the 13th century by the Maestro di Isacco, who was responsible for the panels on the right wall from the *Gift of the Cloak* to the *Confirmation of the Rule*, and were completed by Giotto. Vasari maintains that Giotto was called to Assisi by Giovanni da Muro, head of the Order in 1296. The description of the stories is based on the translation from Latin of the title present under each episode.

(I) **St. Francis Is Honored by a Simple Man**

An ordinary citizen of Assisi places his cloak on the ground before Blessed Francis and renders honor to his passage. He affirms, inspired, as is believed, by God, that Francis is worthy of every respect, for he is about to accomplish great things and therefore must be honored by all.

The episode is realistically set in the main piazza of Assisi. In the background is the Temple of Minerva, which is different from the original in the number of columns, five instead of six, and for the presence in the tympanum of a rose window supported by angels, perhaps in remembrance of an original clypeus or of a crown. On the left is the Palazzo del Capitano and the Torre del Popolo. The latter is without the upper floor, not completed until 1305.

(II) **Francis Gives His Cloak to a Poor Man**

When Blessed Francis encountered a noble knight, destitute and poorly dressed, he was moved to compassion by his poverty and immediately took off his cloak and dressed him in it.

The episode takes place in the valley below Assisi, near the Chiesa di San Damiano. On the left are the Asio hill and the city. The door in the foreground with the crossed coats of arms is that of the Basilica of Santa Chiara. On the right is Mt. Subasio with the Monastero di San Benedetto.

(III) **The Vision of the Palace Filled with Arms**

The following night, having fallen asleep, Blessed Francis saw a splendid, large palace filled with arms bearing the sign of the Cross of Christ. Having asked to whom the arms belonged, a heavenly voice replied that they were all destined to him and to his knights.

(IV) **The Prayer in the Chiesa di San Damiano**

While Blessed Francis prayed before the Crucifix, a voice from the cross said to him three times, « Francis, go, repair my house which has fallen into ruin », by this meaning the Church of Rome.

The building in ruin represents the little Chiesa di San Damiano, before the restauration by Francis himself, who built a vault to replace the trussed roof and a transept in place of the presbytery. The Crucifix above the altar copies the ancient iconography of the *Christus Triumphans* of the prodigious cross preserved in the Basilica of Santa Chiara.

(V) **The Renouncement of Worldly Goods**

Blessed Francis returned everything to his father, and leaving his clothing, renounced his paternal and wordly goods saying, « Henceforth I can truly say, "Our Father who art in heaven", for Pietro di Bernardone has disowned me ».

The episode takes place in the piazza in front of the Palazzo Vescovile. St. Francis, having stripped himself naked, is covered by Bishop Guido with his own pallium. On the left, Pietro di Bernardone has on his arm the removed clothing and is held by the wrist while he attempts to strike his son, who is watching the benedictory hand of God.

(VI) **The Dream of Innocent III**

The Pope saw in a dream that the Lateran Basilica was about to collapse, while a small poor man, Blessed Francis, supported it with his shoulder to keep it from falling.

The Pope's alcove is inspired by the architecture in the Stories of Isaac. The Later-

Upper Basilica, nave, Giotto, St. Francis Honored by a Common Man (1292–96), detail

an Basilica is faithfully represented, with mosaics executed at the time of Nicholas IV (1288–92).

(VII) **The Confirmation of the Rule**

The Pope approved the Rule and gave permission to preach penance, and allowed the friars who had accompanied the Saint to receive the tonsure so they might preach the word of God.

The ceremony takes place inside a large hall framed by an arcade in perspective. Recent investigation has demonstrated that in an earlier version the Saint was depicted standing.

(VIII) **The Apparition of the Fiery Chariot**

Blessed Francis was praying in a hovel physically far from his brothers, who were asleep or at prayer in a hovel outside the city. At about midnight, they saw Blessed Francis moving around the house in a bright, fiery chariot, filling the hovel with great light. Those who were awake were amazed; those who were asleep woke up and were terrified.

The hovel frequented by the Saint was in the Cathedral garden, whereas his companions stayed in the hovel in Rivotorto. The apparition is reminiscent of the ascension of the prophet Elijah in a fiery chariot. The two–wheeled chariot and the horses resemble Roman models.

(IX) **The Vision of the Heavenly Thrones**

A friar rapt in ecstasy sees many thrones in heaven, among which there is one more sumptuous and glorious than the others, and he hears a voice saying, « This throne once belonged to a rebellious angel, and it is now reserved for humble Francis ».

(X) **The Devils Are Cast Out of Arezzo**

Blessed Francis saw the demons exultant over the city of Arezzo and said to his companion, « Go, and in the name of God cast out the devils, just as you have been ordained by Our Lord Himself to do, by shouting outside the gates ». As he obeyed shouting, the demons fled, and peace was immediately restored.

On the right is a splendid view of the city of Arezzo, castellated on a hill protected by a sturdy wall. The Gothic church on the left is the Duomo Vecchio, located outside of the city and demolished in 1561 by order of the Duke Cosimo de' Medici.

(XI) **Trial by Fire before the Sultan**

Blessed Francis, to bear witness to the Christian faith, wished to walk into a great fire with the priests of the Sultan of Babylonia; none of them wished to accompany him, but all quickly fled from view.

In the summer of 1219, St. Francis went to the Sultan of Egypt Melek–el–Kamel together with a companion, Brother Illuminato, in the hope of finding martyrdom. Having proved his faith, the Sultan received him benevolently and sent him free with gifts.

(XII) **The Ecstasy of St. Francis**

One day, while Blessed Francis was in fervent prayer, the friars saw his whole body raised above the ground, his arms extended upward; and a bright cloud enveloped him.

(XIII) **The Nativity Scene at Greccio**

Blessed Francis, in memory of the Birth of Christ, ordered a Nativity scene prepared, straw fetched, an ox and an ass brought. He then gave a sermon on the birth of the poor King, and while he preached a knight saw the Infant Jesus in place of the child the Saint had placed there.

The ceremony takes place beside an altar with a ciborium done in a style similar to that of Arnolfo di Cambio, and is almost a sacred representation taken from real life. The church has been identified as the Lower Basilica of San Francesco. In the background can be identified the iconostasis which divided the nave from the presbytery, with the cross by Giunta Pisano facing the nave and viewed from the back, an unconventional and daring representation for its time, and the pulpit from which the mass was celebrated.

(XIV) **The Miracle of the Spring**

Blessed Francis, being in poor health, ascended a mountain on the back of a poor man's donkey, and praying for water in the name of this man, who was dying of thirst, caused water to spring from a rock where there was never any seen before nor afterwards.

« And among others is a most beautiful story in which a thirsty man, in whom can be seen the desire for water, kneeling on the ground, drinks from a spring with a great and truly marvelous effect, so much that he almost seems to be a live person drinking ». (Giorgio Vasari, 1568).

Above the portal, in three roundels, are painted a *Madonna with Child* and *Two Angels*.

(XV) **The Sermon to the Birds**

On the way to Bevagna Blessed Francis preached to many birds; and they were joyful,

Upper Basilica, nave, Giotto, The Dream of Innocent III (1292–96)

outstretching their necks, flapping their wings, opening their beaks and touching his tunic. All this was seen by his companions waiting on the roadside.

« In the Sermon to the Birds there is no drammatic action; there is no scenery, but against the unified blue of the sky the large tree is enough to express the solitude of the entire countryside. The gesture by the accompanying friar follows the Saint with silence and admiration as he cautiously leans over so as not to frighten his gathered audience, while his expression and his whole fragile person seem to be veiled in sweetness ». (Pietro Toesca).

(XVI) **Death of the Knight of Celano**

Blessed Francis implored salvation for the soul of a knight of Celano who had devotedly invited him to dinner and who, after having made his confession and put his affairs in order, while the others were dining, suddenly died and fell asleep in the Lord.

« Everything in the composition contributes to the "catastrophe", to the dramatic "apex". In this sense Giotto was rightly called, more than a naturalist, a great dramatic author ». (Giovanni Previtali).

(XVII) **The Sermon of St.Francis before Pope Honorius III**

Blessed Francis, in the presence of the Pope and the cardinals, prayed so devoutly and effectively that it seemed clear that he spoke not with learned words of human knowledge but by divine inspiration.

« In representing the papal hall, Giotto reproduces the architecture of the times in the same way he reproduces the costumes and the faces of the subjects, that is in the coherent development, within the Assisian cycle, of this 'historical' concept of narration ». (Cesare Gnudi).

(XVIII) **The Apparition of St. Francis at the Arles Chapter**

While Blessed Anthony preached at the Arles Chapter on the subject of the Cross, Blessed Francis, although not bodily present, appeared and, extending his hands, blessed the friars as was witnessed by one Brother Monaldo. The other friars were greatly consoled.

(XIX) **The Saint Receiving the Stigmata on Monte La Verna**

While Blessed Francis prayed on the side of Monte La Verna he saw Christ in the form of a crucified Seraph who imprinted in his hands and feet, as well as his side, the stigmata of the Cross of Our Lord Jesus Christ.

« The episode of the Stigmata which Francis receives on Mt. Verna is felt in the statue–like immobility of the Saint in the midst of solemn natural architecture. Thus something epic, something heroic is released from the event. And Francis appears precisely to be an ancient hero ». (Pietro Scarpellini)

(XX) **The Death of St. Francis**

Upon the departure of Blessed Francis a friar saw his soul ascend to heaven in the form of a brilliant star.

(XXI) **The Apparition of St. Francis to Brother Agostino and the Bishop of Assisi**

The Superior of the Friars, who was near death and for some time had been unable to speak, shouted, « Wait for me, father, for I am coming with you ». And, upon dying, he followed his holy father. The Bishop of Assisi, standing on the Monte di San Michele

Upper Basilica, nave, Francis preaching before Honorius III, detail (1292–96)

the Archangel, saw Blessed Francis who said to him, « I am going to heaven now ». And in that hour Blessed Francis died.

(XXII) **The Confirmation of the Stigmata**

At the Porziuncola, as Blessed Francis lay dead, Master Girolamo, a famous doctor and learned man, moved the nails, and with his hands touched the wounds in the hands, feet and side of the Saint.

The episode, which occurred in the open, is set by the painter inside a church. The lacunar apse is barely distinguishable in the background, and in the foreground there is a beam supporting three paintings. It is probably located in the Upper Basilica, which had a similar iconostasis supported by two corbels which are still present at the entrance to the presbitery.

(XXIII) **The Mourning of the Poor Clares**

The crowd which had gathered, carrying branches and many torches, escorted the holy body, adorned with celestial jewels, to the city of Assisi where it was seen by Blessed Clare and the holy virgins.

(XXIV) **Canonization of St. Francis**

His Holiness the Pope, arriving in person at the city of Assisi, diligently examined the miracles which were supported by the testimony of the friars. He then canonized Blessed Francis and added his name to the list of saints.

The feast of the canonization of St. Francis was celebrated on July 16, 1228 by Gregory IX in the Piazza del Comune of Assisi. In the painting are represented both the platform from which the Pope made the announcement and, in the foreground, the casket containing the body of the Saint, which at the time was kept in the Chiesa di San Giorgio.

(XXV) **The Apparition to Gregory IX**

As Pope Gregory had some doubts regarding the wound in the side, Blessed Francis said to him in his sleep, « Give me an empty vial ». And when he had given it to him, it was seen to fill with blood from his side.

(XXVI) **The Immediate Healing of a Devoted Follower**

Blessed Francis removed the bandages and gently touched the wounds of John of Lerida, who had devotedly summoned him upon being wounded. At that moment he was completely healed, although he had been mortally wounded and was considered by the doctors to be dying.

(XXVII) **The Confession of a Woman Brought Back to Life**

Blessed Francis brought a dead woman back to life. In full view of clergymen and others present, she confessed a sin that she had not yet confessed and then died to sleep in the Lord; and the devil fled confused.

(XXVIII) **The Liberation of the Penitent Heretic**

Blessed Francis freed a prisoner who was accused of heresy and had been placed in the custody of the Bishop of Tivoli by order of the Pope. The prisoner was freed on the feast of Blessed Francis, following the eve on which he had fasted according to the customs of the Church.

Stained glass windows

The Upper Basilica preserves an extraordinary collection of medieval stained glass windows, which is the most complete in Italy in spite of extensive remaking. The

Upper Basilica, nave, Giotto, The Miracle of the Spring (1292–96)

oldest are those of the apse, which perhaps precede the consecration of the Basilica in 1253 and are attributed to German workmanship. Soon afterwards, French masters influenced by Gothic culture did the four–light window in the left transept as well as part of the nave. The four–light window of the right transept, and various windows in the nave, are attributed to the Maestro di San Francesco and are dated after 1263 due to their themes, which were taken from the *Legenda Maior* of St. Bonaventure.

Apse Vault (German masters). In the left two–light window, in the first light, from below are: *The Tree of Jesse; Gideon Squeezes Water From the Fleece; The Burning Bush; Aaron's Rod; The Offering of Little Samuel; Salomon and the Queen of Sheba; Saul Having the Priests Killed; Moses Fleeing From the Pharaoh; The Arch of the Temple of Dagon*. The second light was redone, with the exclusion of the cusp, by the Moretti firm of Perugia in 1928. From below are: *Joachim and Anne Meet at the Golden Gate; Annunciation; Nativity Scene; Announcement to the Shepherds; Presentation at the Temple; Adoration of the Magi; Slaughter of the Innocents; Flight to Egypt; The Idols Collapse on the Arrival of the Holy Family in Egypt*.

In the first light of the central two–light window are: *Solomon Enthroned (?); The Bath of Naaman (?); Moses and the Eternal Father; Manasseh Purifying the Temple; Entrance of Elisha in Damascus; Abraham and the Three Angels; Institution of Passover; The Prayer of Elijah; Abner Betrayed by Joab (?)*. In the second light are: *The Dispute in the Temple; Baptism in the Jordan River; The Transfiguration; The Merchants Driven From the Temple; Entrance of Christ into Jerusalem; The Washing of the Feet; The Last Supper; Sermon in the Garden; The Capture of Christ*. In the lunette is the *Coat of Arms of Sixtus IV*.

In the first light of the right two–light window are: *Sacrifice of Abraham; The Brazen Serpent; Moses Causing Water to Spring From the Rock; Jonah being Thrown Back by the Fish; Hagar and the Angel; The Shunemite and Elisha; Joseph Reveals Himself to His Brothers; Elijah is Taken to Heaven; The Spirit of Moses Descending Upon the Jews (?)*. In the second light are: *Ascent to Calvary; Crucifixion* (modern); *Burial of Christ* (modern); *Resurrection; Christ in Limbo; Noli Me Tangere; Disbelief of Thomas; Ascension; Pentecost.*

Four–light window in the left transept (French masters). From the lower left, in the first light are: *Creation of Sky and Earth; Creation of the Firmament; Separation of Land and Sea; Creation of Moon and Stars; Creation of the Animals; Creation of Man and Woman; The Seventh Day*. In the second light are: *Original Sin; Expulsion from the Garden of Eden; Labor of the Progenitors; The Offerings of Cain and Abel; Cain Murdering Abel; The Eternal Questioning Cain; The Mourning of Cain over Abel's Death*. In the third light are: *St. Agatha; St. Lucia; St. Clare; St. Catherine; Angel with Thurible*. In the fourth light are: *St. Barbara; St. Margaret; St. Cecilia; St. Agnes; Angel with Thurible*. In the quadrilobate decorations of the lunette are represented: *Christ Conferring His Blessing Between St. Francis and St. Anthony; Virgin with Child Between Two Prophets*. In two roundels are shown *Jeremiah* and *Abraham* (modern).

Four–light window in the right transept (Maestro di San Francesco). The two lights on the left have geometric designs. In the third light, from above, are: *Angel's Announcement to Sarah; Angel's Announcement to Zachary (?); Apparition of the Angel*

Upper Basilica, nave, Giotto, The Sermon to the Birds (1292–96)

to Gideon; Tobias Leaving His Father (?); The Three Children in the Burning Furnace; Daniel in the Lion's Den. In the fourth light are: *Apparition of Christ to the Marys; Christ Appearing to Peter; Christ Appearing to Two Disciples on the Road to Emmaus; The Voyage of the Pilgrims to Emmaus; The Supper in Emmaus; Jesus Appearing to the Apostles*. In the rose in the lunette is the *Ascension*. In two roundels are *David* and *A Prophet*.

Nave. The first window on the right wall is by the Maestro di San Francesco. In the left light, from below, are: *St. Francis; The Cross in the Chiesa di San Damiano Speaking to St. Francis; The Saint Healing a Cripple; The Dream of Innocent III; The Sermon to the Birds; The Stigmata*. In the right light are: *St. Anthony of Padua; St. Ludwig of Toulouse* (taken from a stained glass window in the Cappella di Santo Stefano); *St. Anthony Facing Ezzelino da Romano; St. Anthony Liberating Prisoners; St. Anthony Saving a Ship from a Storm; St. Anthony Preaching at the Arles Chapter when St. Francis Appears*.

The second window on the right wall is also by the Maestro di San Francesco. In the left light, from below are: *St. Bartholomew; St. Bartholomew Freeing a Possessed Man; The King's Messengers Inviting Him to the King's Palace; St. Bartholomew Healing the Daughter of Polemius; King Polemius Offering Him Gifts; Martyrdom of the Saint*. In the right light are: *St. Matthew; St. Matthew Receiving Homage From the Queen's Eunuch; St. Matthew Putting to Sleep the Dragons of the Magicians Zaroes and Arphascal; St. Matthew Returning to Life the Daughter of King Aegyppus; St. Matthew Venerated by the People with a Golden Crown; St. Matthew Killed in the Temple*.

The third window on the right wall is by French masters. In the left light from below are: *St. John the Evangelist; St. John Coming Out of the Caldron of Boiling Oil; St. John Returning Drusiana to Life; St. John Drinking Poison and Returning Two Dead People to Life; Jesus Appears to St. John to Announce His Death; Death of the Saint*. In the right light are: *St. Thomas; St. Thomas Blessing Pelagia and Dionysius; St. Thomas Distributing Goods to the Poor; St. Thomas Is Released from Prison; St. Thomas Is again Imprisoned; Martyrdom of the Saint*.

The fourth window of the right wall is also by French masters. In the left light is *St. James*; in the right light is *St. Andrew*. The first window of the left wall is by the Maestro di San Francesco. In the right light, from below, are: *Christ Introducing St. Francis; Three Angels*. In the left light are: *Madonna with Child; Three Angels*.

The second window of the left wall is by the Maestro di San Francesco. In the right light, from below are: *Isaiah and Jeremiah; Micah and Amos; Hosea and Joel; Ezekiel and Daniel; Two Prophets; The Redeemer*. In the left light are: *Two Sainted Bishops; St. Sylvester and St. Gregory; St. Nicholas and St. Martin; St. Rufino and St. Vittorino; St. Ambrose and St. Augustine; The Redeemer Conferring His Blessing*.

The third window of the left wall is also by the Maestro di San Francesco. In the right light is *St. Philip*; in the left light is *St. James the Lesser* (modern).

The fourth window of the left wall, by the Maestro di San Francesco, has *St. Simon* in the right light and *St. Judas Thaddeus* (modern) in the left light.

In front of the porch of the Lower Basilica is the façade of the former **Oratorio di San Bernardino,** built by Lombard workers between 1459 and 1472 for the Franciscan Third Order. The small, smooth façade has an elegant Rennaisance portal

Upper Basilica, right transept, Stained Glass Window (second half of the 13th century)

with two arches supported by three pillars decorated with candelabra. In the lunette is a relief of *St. Bernardino Showing the Monogram Between Two Angels*, done by local sculptors Franceschino Zampa and Girolamo di Bartolomeo, who left their names in the inscription in the frieze: *HUIUS PORTE AD APICE USQUE FRANCISCUS PATRONUS PRO ANIMA SAUXIT. OPUS FRANCISCHINO ZAMPA IHERONIMO QUONDAM BARTHOLOMEI AUCTORIBUS ASSISIENSIBUS. MCCCCLXXXVIII.*

Through a portal is the entrance to the **Sacro Convento** (not open to visitors). In the outer wall is the tomb of Guglielmo di Pietro di Buonguglielmi of Perugia († 1363). Beyond the portineria (the doorman's office) on the right is a polygonal fountain with a marble basin, brought from the upper square where its presence was documented in 1310. Passing through an internal courtyard one enters a large hall. On the walls are eight bas reliefs with events from the death, burial, and discovery of the body of St. Francis which were done by Franceso Gianfredi of Rome (1851) for the crypt of the Basilica. By the same artist are the two large marble statues of Pius VII and Pius IX (1855), removed from the crypt and placed in the cloister of Sixtus IV in 1936.

The Convento hosts the Istituto Teologico of Assisi, a Center for Franciscan Documentation, and an important **Library**, opened to the public in 1979. In 1981 the Fondo Antico della Biblioteca Comunale (Ancient Section of the City Library), which contains manuscripts dated from before 1800, was transferred here. The library contains 709 codices from the 12th to the 16th century, many of which are decorated with splendid miniatures; 356 incunabula; 3256 « cinquecentine » (valuable books printed in the 16th century); over 92,000 volumes; and a few thousand booklets. The music section is particulary extensive, containing about 2,500 manuscripts. In addition, the Biblioteca and the Archivio Vescovile (Episcopal Library and Archives), as well as various private collections, were added to the library between 1984 and 1987. In the rooms of the Istituto Teologico are kept several paintings from the 17th century which were removed from the baroque altars of the church. In a large room, once used as a refectory, is a fresco portraying *The Last Supper*, by Dono Doni (1573). In the refectory is a large painting of *The Last Supper* by the Neapolitan painter Francesco Solimena (1717).

Second Itinerary

FROM THE UPPER PIAZZA DI SAN FRANCESCO TO THE PIAZZA DEL COMUNE

Biblioteca Comunale, Oratorio dei Pellegrini, Monte Frumentario, Foro Romano and Museo Civico

Following the contruction of the Basilica of San Francesco at the lower end of the hill at about 300 meters from the old Roman wall, a wide street was designed to go directly from the church to Portella di Panzo (Panzo's Gate). In fact, Colle del Paradiso (Paradise Hill) is in an odd position with respect to the route beginning at the monumental gate beneath Palazzo Fiumi–Roncalli that was connected with the Via Francesca, going across Ponte San Vittorino (Bridge of San Vittorino). Ever since medieval times, this street has been called Via Superba, in order to distinguish this new monumental entrance into the city from the dark narrow streets of the urban center. In 1265, Pope Clement IV banned the construction of any churches or monasteries within a distance of 300 « canne » (an ancient measurement equivalent to 2 to 3 meters) of the Sacro Convento. This was to protect it from being surrounded by the Benedictine convents that had closed in the countryside and were being established in the city. Hospices were built at the bottom of the hill to provide shelter for pilgrims and aid to the sick. Homes for ordinary citizens were built on the other side of the street. These buildings were transformed into aristocratic homes during the 16th and 17th centuries.

In front of the main supporting wall of the upper square of San Francesco (no. 16) is the **Sala del Pellegrino** (Pilgrim's Hall). In 1918, Father Emilio Norsa transformed this 1774 building into a concert hall and called it Scuola Davidico Serafica. Norsa commissioned the painters Zanetti, Aldi and Ciocci to decorate the hall with eight scenes from the *Life of David* and the balcony with the *Glory of St. Francis.*

To the left is the beginning of Via Cardinale Merry Del Val, which follows the steep slope to Porta San Giacomo. At the beginning of Via San Francesco is the staircase to **the Oratorio dell'Immacolata Concezione**, which is served by the Capuchin Friars, who came here in 1881 from the monastery of Sant'Antonio near Porta Cappuccini. The painting above the entrance is the *Apparition of the Virgin Mary to St. Francis.* The oratory, a simple room with a cross vault, was decorated by Augusto Malatesta and features friezes and Franciscan coats of arms. On the main altar is the *Immaculate Conception* (19th c.) and to the left is the *Vision of St. Clare* (20th c.). The adjoining **Museo degli Indios dell'Amazzonia** (Museum of the Amazon Indians), was opened in 1972 and features materials coming from the Capuchin missions in Latin America. This collection, which is exhibited on three floors, includes three sections dedicated to the Indian civilization, to the flora and fauna of the Amazon region and to the works of the missionaries.

At No. 12/A is the monumental **Palazzo Bernabei**, formerly known as Sperelli. It

Loggia dei Maestri Comacini (Masters of Como, 15th century)

was designed by Giacomo Giorgetti after 1646 for the heirs of Francesco Sperelli, Bishop of Sanseverino Marche. The Roman prince Alessandro Torlonia gave the building to the Capuchins in 1881. In 1928, it became the Franciscan Museum, an important collection of paintings, drawings and prints depicting Franciscan subjects. The collection was moved to Rome in 1955.
At No. 19 was the old hospital of the Confraternita di San Gregorio, which was documented as far back as the 14th century. In the vestibule there is a lunette depicting the *Madonna with Child, St. Gregory and St. Francis* (17th c.).
Located at No. 14 is the **Loggia dei Maestri Comacini**, so named for the symbols of the master bricklayers (a compass, a rose, a mallet and a T–square). These images can be seen in the architrave of a door dated to 1485, as well as in the keystones of the windows. The house was built in the 13th century but it was enlarged in 1477, as indicated in the coat of arms to the right. The addition to the tower dates to this century. It is traditionally thought that this was the headquarters of the skilled Lombard masons who worked in Assisi to construct the Basilica and Convent of San Francesco.
Behind the house, the steep steps of Vicolo Sant'Andrea lead to the monastery of the same name and to one of the city's characteristic medieval quarters.

This part of the street is dominated by the long façade, of **Palazzo Giacobetti** (no. 12/F), which houses the Biblioteca Comunale (City Library), the Accademia Properziana del Subasio and the Istituto Magistrale, which is a a high school. The building was constructed by the Breccia–Vigilanti family of Assisi, whose coat of arms appears in the frescoes of the *piano nobile* (first floor). It was later owned by the Giacobetti family, who had their coat of arms placed on the façade. In the entrance portico, there are two ancient granite columns with a small overhanging balcony. A second balcony, supported by four spiral modillions, is in the center of the building near the ballroom. The motto *IN DOMINO CONFIDO* is inscribed on the architraves of all the windows. The 17th century artistic decorations in the rooms on the first floor are very well preserved, but the access to these rooms is granted only to scholars, with the permission of the Library Director.
The *Salone delle Feste* (ballroom) has a vault with an architectonic perspective scheme representing a loggia, on which allegorical figures and portraits of the patrons appear. The portraits thus depict Paolo Giacobetti and his wife Settimia della Genga. The painting in the center of the vault portrays the *Triumph of Virtue over Vice*. This work has been attributed to the Sienese painter Ventura Salimbeni who, in 1603, worked on the Chapel of the Deposition in Santa Maria degli Angeli, which was founded by the Breccia–Vigilanti family.
The *Sala di San Francesco* was named after the figure of the saint in ecstasy depicted on the vault, which was painted by Antonio Circignani, known as Pomarancio. The grotesque landscapes were done by the Perugine painter, Matteuccio Salvucci. The *Sala di Giuseppe Ebreo* was done, again, by Pomarancio, who copied the cycle of frescoes found in Palazzo Mattei di Giove in Rome. The *Sala di Salomone*, the *Sala di Davide* and the *Sala di Mosè* were frescoed by an anonymous painter at the beginning of the 17th century. In another wing of the palazzo, there is a room with

Palazzo Giacobetti, Matteuccio Salvucci, Grotesque (beginning of the 17th century)

neo-classical frescoes depicting *Moral Allegories*. Several paintings hang in the Biblioteca, two of which bear mentioning: the *Glory of St. Dominic* (1673) by Francesco Providoni, and the *Ecstasy of St. Philip Neri* (18th c.) by Giuseppe Laudati.
The **Biblioteca Comunale** or City Library has a wealth of books – 46,000 volumes – about 4,000 of which belong to the Accademia Properziana del Subasio. The city's historical archives are very important sources regarding local history. The main archives consist of 509 parchments dating to the 13th century, and the notary archives contain over two thousand registers dated from 1372 to 1820. The Archives of St. Francis, consisting of a collection of ancient documents, that also includes a very rich collection of manuscripts with miniatures, was transferred to the Library of the Sacro Convento. In addition, there is a collection of 1,117 drawings done by seventeenth and eighteenth–century Assisi painters (Sermei, Giorgetti, Martelli, Marinelli, etc.) that were given to the city by the painter Augusto Malatesta.

On the right–hand side of the street is the imposing building of the **Ospedale della Misericordia.** This hospital was opened in 1814 in the Benedictine monastery of Santa Maria degli Episcopi, which had formerly been located outside Porta San Giacomo and was then relocated inside the city walls in 1401. The building was restructured in 1883 by Alfonso Brizi. It was transformed into private homes in 1989–90. From the portico on the left, one can enter into the little chapel of the monastery. Cesare Sermei frescoed the vault with figures of the saints. The *Mystical Wedding of St. Catherine* (1586), on the right wall, has been attributed to Arcangelo Aquilini.

At No. 13/A is the Istituto Suore Francescane Missionarie del Giglio. This institute is housed in a small palazzo built in the neo–Renaissance style (1880–83), based on plans drawn up by Attilio Cangi. It was built on the site of a pilgrims' hospital run by the Confraternita dei Santi Giacomo ed Antonio for pilgrims who were visiting the city's sanctuaries. In 1417, a group of citizens from Assisi went on a pilgrimage to the tomb of St. James the Apostle in Santiago di Compostella in Galicia, Spain. When they returned, they united to found a hospital for the poor, which they named after this saint. In 1424, another hospital was added on to it and it was dedicated to St. Anthony of Vienne. The façade of this building, completed in 1422, was decorated by Ottaviano Nelli of Gubbio. His frescoes depicting the *Virgin between St. James and St. Anthony Abbot* and the *Annunciation* were removed and are now kept in the Pinacoteca Comunale.

Next to it is the **Oratorio dei Pellegrini,** which was built in 1457 as a small chapel to be used by the hospital bearing the same name. The very simple façade has a round arch portal and an overhanging roof supported by large corbels. It is decorated with what now remains of a fresco painted by Matteo da Gualdo depicting the *Redeemer in Glory between St. Anthony and St. James, and the Angel Musicians.* The interior of the Oratory presents one of the most important fifteenth–century pictorial complexes in Assisi. It was commissioned to exalt the images of the patron saints and the charitable activity of the Confraternity.

The wall near the altar is framed by *trompe–l'oeil* architecture featuring a false architraved portico, above which naked *putti* are playing and making garlands. In the upper part, which is divided into two sections by the window, is the *Annunciation,* whereas in the lower part are scenes of the *Enthroned Madonna and Child with Angels Playing Musical Instruments.* On the sides are *St. James and St. Anthony with Two Angels Bearing Candles.* The name of the artist and the date 1468 are written on a small tablet to the left, which read: *HOC OPUS FACTUM FUIT SUB ANNO DOMINI MILLESIMO QUATROGENTESIMO SESSAGESIMO OCTAVO. DIE PRIMA JUNII. MACTEUS DE GUALDO PINSIT.*

The vault and the walls were decorated by Pierantonio Mezzastris, an artist from Foligno, who stipulated his contract with the confraternity in May of 1477. Depicted in the webs of the cross vault are the *Doctors of the Church.* Depicted on the right wall are two miracles of St. James, inspired by a well–known legend of the late Middles Ages that recounted the story of a young pilgrim who had been unjustly accused of stealing and was thus condemned to death. These are the *Miracle of the Resurrected Cockerels that Proclaim the Young Man's Innocence*, signed *PETRUS ANTONIUS DE FOLIGNO PINXIT*, in the tablecloth and the *Miracle of the Hanged Man Miraculously Held up by the Saint and Found still Alive by His Parents.* St. Anthony the Abbot is the subject of the two paintings on the left wall: *The Saint Receives the Unguided Camels Bringing Provisions to the Monks and The Saint Distributes Alms to the Poor.* The counterfaçade is divided into two parts by a false architectural cornice. In the upper part is the *Benedictory Christ Inside a Mandorla*

Decoration of Cherubs and Adoring Angels. Saints James, Anthony and Ansano are depicted in the lower section. When he painted the latter figures, once thought to have been done by Pietro Perugino, Mezzastris was assisted by the Assisi painter Andrea Aloigi, known as l'Ingegno, who studied under Perugino.
At N. 8 is the sixteenth–century **Palazzo Bartocci–Fontana** (originally called Filippucci and then Bindangoli), which is made up of various medieval houses. It has a lovely portal embellished with diamond–shaped ashlars. The building's design has been attributed to Giulio Danti.
At No. 5/A is the **Portico del Monte Frumentario,** formed by seven segmental arches supported by small columns with carved capitals. These are crowned with trilobate arches. The rear wall was completely frescoed by one of Giotto's followers known as the Maestro del Farneto, who worked between the end of the 13th century and the beginning of the 14th century. The fresco presents three scenes, which are now very fragmentary. On the left is the *Apparition of Christ to a Saint*; behind the Barberini coat of arms is the *Madonna with Child and a Saint*, and the final scene is the *Last Judgement*.
The interior consists of a long, narrow room whose ceiling is supported by arches. There is a large window to the rear that looks out onto the valley.

This was the ancient hospital of the community, one of Italy's first public hospitals. It was built in 1267 by the Council of the Traders and Rectors of the Arts, which had obtained permission from the Provincial Minister of the Franciscans, Brother Illuminato da Rieti. This was done in spite of Clement V's papal bull prohibiting the construction of any churches within a distance of 300 « canne » from the Basilica. The brothers of the Sacro Convento brought a lawsuit to court, so that in 1270, all religious ceremonies in the adjoining oratory were banned. The hospital was managed by the Ospedale della Misericordia in Perugia. In 1746, Bishop Ottavio Ringhieri transferred the headquarters of the Monte Frumentario to this site. According to the declaration on the stone that is walled over the portal, the Monte Frumentario had been founded in 1633 by Cardinal Antonio Barberini, brother of Pope Urban VIII, to help the poor of Assisi. In 1877, the place was transformed into a small theater and more recently, it has been reserved for other secular use.

Attached to the portico is the **Fonte Oliviera,** traditionallly attributed to the Perugian architect Galeazzo Alessi. It is a narrow rectangular basin in travertine that rests against a wall decorated with coats of arms. It was constructed by Oliviero Lodovici in 1570. A plaque above the fountain offers a warning: *PENA UNO SCUDO E PERDITA DEI PANNI PR CHI LAVA IN QUESTO FONTE (PENALTY OF ONE SCUDO AND LOSS OF LAUNDRY FOR ANYONE WHO WASHES IN THIS FOUNTAIN)*. Next to the fountain is the house in which the scholar Francesco Antonio Frondini (1759–1841) resided. Going down Vicolo Frondini on the right, one will reach Vicolo degli Esposti, whose name is derived from the orphanage connected to the community hospital. A 13th century loggia with round arches supported by sturdy pillars are all that remains of the orphanage. Above the entrance is a mediocre fresco depicting the *Madonna of Mercy*, dating to the 17th century. This building is now the temporary headquarters of the State Archives Department.

Oratorio dei Pellegrini, Pierantonio Mezzastris, Miracle of the Roosters (about 1477)

At the end of the street is the **Arco del Seminario**, known as *Portella di Panzo* during the Middle Ages. The arch is located along the ancient Roman wall. To the left of the arch is an inscription marking the house of Giuseppe degli Aromatari, a doctor and scholar from Assisi who lived during the 17th century. Past the archway on the right is a pink–and–white–striped stone wall. This is all that remains of the women's convent of Sant'Angelo di Panzo, which had been founded in 1270 by a Benedictine community that came from the monastery of Panzo on Mount Subasio. In the niche, there is a fresco by Girolamo Marinelli depicting the *Apparition of the Virgin to St. Francis* (1628). When Marcello Crescenzi was bishop, the monastery was the site of the **Seminario diocesano** (Diocesan Seminary). This was enlarged by Bishop Niccolo Sermattei in 1778. The monastery's church, which was

Monte Frumentario (1267) and Fonte Oliviera (1570)

dedicated to St. Charles Borromeo when the seminary was founded, is at No. 7. Some 14th century frescoes that were removed from the church are now kept in Villa Santa Tecla near Assisi.

On the other side of the street is the large building of the former **Collegio Missionario Teologico** (Theological Missionary Institute) of the Conventual Friars, which was designed by Attilio Cangi in 1911.

Next, at No. 5, is **Palazzo Rossi,** with its elegant Renaissance façade, which is traditionally attributed to Galeazzo Alessi. Across from this is Vicolo Aloigi, a characteristic alley that winds its way up to the church of Santo Stefano. In the small square nearby, Piazzetta Verdi, is the **Teatro Comunale Metastasio** (city theater), which was designed by Lorenzo Carpinelli in 1836. At one time, the interior was comprised of a horseshoe–shaped floor plan with three tiers of boxes and a gallery, originally decorated by Raffaele Fogliardi. The theater was inaugurated in the fall of 1840 with a performance of Giuseppe Mercadante's opera, « Emma of Antioch ». In 1956, following a rather questionable decision, it was transformed into a movie theater.

At this point, the street enters into the ancient Roman layout leading to Piazza del Comune. In the Middle Ages, it was called **Via Portica,** perhaps to commemorate the porticos that surrounded the Roman square. Others say that it was named after the fountain protected by an arch, located at the bottom of the hill, whose existence was first documented in 1204. On the rear wall is the coat of arms of the

Mammoni family. The motto that had been inscribed there, *QUI BIBERIT EX HAC AQUA SITIET ITERUM*, has since disappeared. The house above this has a coat of arms (1461), whose identity is uncertain: perhaps it was the coat of arms of a textiles guild. At No. 16 is Palazzo Brizi. There is a bust of Eugenio Brizi, an Assisi patriot, on its façade. At No. 9 is the « spetiaria » degli Aromatari, (apothecary of the Aromatari family), also known as the « bottega del moro » (shop of the moor) on account of the head sculpted on the coat of arms. The portal is decorated with relief work attributed to Franceschino Zampa (around 1479), which features candelabras and « putti » on the jambs, and festoons and heads on the architrave.
According to the historian Fortini, the store of Pietro di Bernardone was located in the narrow alley to the left.
The entrance to the **Cripta di San Niccolò** (crypt of St. Nicholas) and to the **Museo Civico** (Civic Museum) is located at No. 2. The underground portion is all that remains of the Church of San Niccolò *de pede platee*, the existence of which was documented as early as 1097 and which was a parish in 1227.
The crypt, which was converted into a store in the 15th century, was rediscovered in 1924. One of the well–known episodes regarding the conversion of St. Francis took place in San Niccolò in 1209. Here, together with his first followers, Pietro and Bernardo da Quintavalle, Francis questioned the Gospel three times in order to glean a way of life from it.

Having finished their prayers, blessed Francis took the closed book and, kneeling before the altar, he opened it. The first time he opened it, he found this advice from God: « If you want to be perfect, go, sell everything you have, give everything to the poor and follow me, and you will find treasure in heaven ». Blessed Francis rejoiced at this and he gave thanks to God. But because he was a true lover of the Trinity, he wanted to confirm his commitment with another testimony and so he opened the book a second time and a then third time. The second time he opened it, he found the admonition, « You will take nothing with you ... » and in the third opening, he found « ... whoever wants to come with me must deny himself ... ». Each time he opened the book, Blessed Francis thanked God for confirming his intention and wish and after the third time, he said to his chosen men, Bernard and Peter, « Oh brothers, this is our life and our rule for all those who want to join

"Spetiaria" of the Aromatari (about 1470), detail

us. Go therefore and, as you have heard, fulfill it ».
(*Legend of the Three Companions*, 28–29)

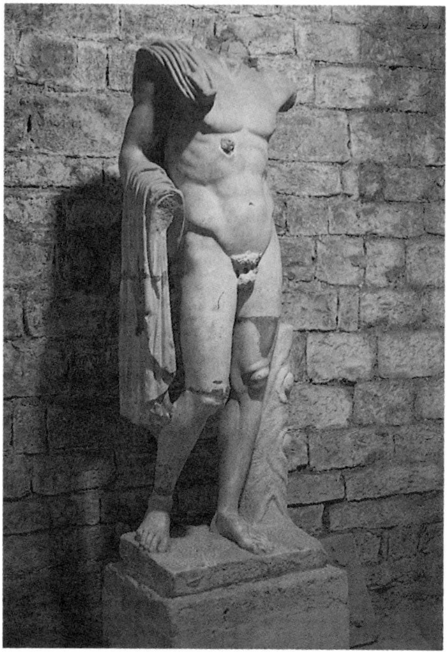
Museo Civico, Nude (1st century A.D.)

Museo Civico. The interior is rectangular and is divided into naves by two sturdy pillars supporting a cross vault. The floor level of the museum corresponds to the old Roman square. The remaining wall on the right may have been part of the terracing that defined the boundaries of the square in ancient times.
The museum was founded in 1793 by the Accademia Properziana del Subasio, which had collected many stelae exhibited in the pronaos of the Temple of Minerva. The collection, which has grown thanks to donations and to new discoveries, was set up in its current headquarters in 1933. Its material, composed of Umbro–Roman pieces, still requires a more systematic arrangement. The most important pieces are as follows: to the left, beyond the entrance, is a 3rd century A.D. *strigiled sarcophagus* with a bacchanal scene depicted in the center; between the two pillars is a sarcophagus with a double–sloped lid; against the pillar is a fragment of a *draped female statue* that dates to the Augustan age. On the upper right wall is a pre–Roman inscription casting, written in Latin characters, concerning the boundaries between Assisi and Perugia (the original is in the Museo Archeologico in Perugia). Located along the rear wall to the right are a *cippus* referring to the Municipium of Assisi; a headless statue of a man in a toga (1st century A.D.); a *stela of Ottiedius Attianus*, a soldier from the IX Praetorial Court; and a *headless statue of an heroic figure* dating to the Julian–Claudian age. In the left nave is the *fragmentary statue of a seated divinity*, which is believed to be the goddess Minerva to whom the temple was dedicated. On the walls and the display cases are some terra–cotta and glass objects, some stucco fragments, decorative frescos, and coins coming from the « domus » (Roman house) excavated under Palazzo Rocchi in 1864; from the same place comes the figure of *Mercury* bearing the caduceus and petasus. From the casa romana called Casa di Properzio (House of Propertius) are varius marble fragments, one of which with the figure of a dancing satyr and a large fresco of geometric wall decorations featuring marine motifs. There are also various Egyptian objects, bronzes and a small coin collection.
There is a passage along the right–hand wall that leads to the original square. The excavations under the actual Piazza del Comune were begun by the French archi-

tect August–Pierre Famin in 1836 and were continued by Lorenzo Carpinelli. The original stone–slab flooring is still visible and a small water run–off channel runs along its entire length. Lined up along the ground and on the walls are various types of inscriptions and funerary stelae, some of which refer to the *gens Propertia.* Against the temple wall there are column fragments, a Doric capital, and the remains of a peristyle that may have encircled the area. There is an opening in the wall for the staircases that led to the temple. The holes for the braces that once held the bronze decorations are visible. In the area in front of the stairs is a low two–level podium that may have been used as an altar or as a base for statues. Next to this is the travertine base of the shrine that held the statues of Castor and Pollux, to whom the still–existing inscription dating to the late Republican age refers. Ahead on the left are the well–preserved remains of a cistern near the stairs leading to the terrace on the upper floor. At the end of the corridor one can see the remains of the columns of the portico that closed the square off on the north side, as well as some walls that may be the remains of *tabernae*. The passage at the end on the right–hand side leads to the underground areas of Palazzo dei Priori, known as the Sala delle Volte, which preserves part of the original square floor. Within a portico located outside the museum is the *Fonte di San Niccolò*, which rests on the original level of the old Roman square. The pulpit above it comes from the façade of the Palazzo del Governatore. It has five restored panels that are supported by a tuft–shaped corbel carved by Niccolò da Bettona in 1354. The street ends in Piazza del Comune.

Third Itinerary

FROM THE LOWER PIAZZA DI SAN FRANCESCO TO THE PIAZZA DEL COMUNE GOING THROUGH VIA FONTEBELLA

Fonte Marcella, Confraternita di San Francesco, House of St. Bernardo da Quintavalle

The lower piazza of San Francesco leads to the valley via Porta San Francesco and Porta San Pietro.
By proceeding along Via Fontebella, one can reach the Piazza del Comune, taking a route that is less common but whose urban views and landscapes are equally impressive. The first part of this route, Via Frate Elia, coincides with the road leading to the sanctuary, a route used by visitors who today, as in the past, come up to Assisi from the valley. A 1618 guide for pilgrims arriving at this point at the end of a tiring day of visits suggested the following: *Let's go toward Porta San Francesco to find a hotel. The Osteria dell'Angelo is where M. Santi Santucci, known as the « king of the innkeepers », will treat you wonderfully.*
Its privileged location has helped the hotel and commercial development of this part of Assisi, which attracts growing crowds of visitors. The oldest inn is the Minerva, which is thought to have been a depot for mail couriers. Other distinguished hotels are the Subasio (1868), Giotto (1900) and the Windsor–Savoia (1911). With the great increase in mass tourism during the past few decades, souvenir shops have proliferated.

At the southern end of the square, at the small gate named Portella di San Francesco, which had already been mentioned in 1246, is the beginning of Via Frate Elia. At No. 1 is the entrance to the Istituto Lodovico da Casoria, an institute for the blind and handicapped founded in 1871 in the house that once belonged to the Tini family. The historic Hotel Subasio is opposite it, at No. 2. It was built in 1868 over the site of the old spinning mill owned by Andrea Rossi, who established the hotel to cater to the growing demands of tourists in search of quality lodging. Many famous visitors have passed through the rooms of this hotel, including the french historian Paul Sabatier, whose writings contributed to spreading a mystical vision of the city and of its saint throughout the world.
Also along Via Frate Elia, at No. 8, is the Ospedale per sacerdoti poveri (hospital for poor priests) attending the Assisi Pardon, founded in 1624 by two brothers, Dioleto and Deodato Matrigiani. Attached to it was the small Church of Nome di Gesù, frescoed in 1631 by Vincenzo Giorgetti and Cesare Sermei. Outside there is a small shrine dedicated to the *Immaculate Conception.*
In front of the shrine is the steep stairway of Vicolo Venanzi, an alley that runs along the site of the houses once belonging to the Confraternita di San Pietro. In the shrine on the first flight, there is a fragment of a 14th century fresco. The entrance to the oratory, known to have existed prior to 1329, was at No. 25/A of Via Domenico Stella. By continuing on the right, going through Via Giorgetti, one can return to Via Fontebella. Piazzetta Ruggero Bonghi is formed by the crossroads of several streets. In the middle of the crossroads is a fifteenth century house and on

12.

13.

14.

15.

16.

17.

18.

19.

20.

21.

22.

23.

Via Fontebella, Fonte Marcella (1556–57), etching by Laurenzio Laurenzi

its façade is a shrine containing a majolica (1930) by Amerigo Lunghi, inspired by Lorenzetti's « Madonna of the Sunsets ». To the right is the 14th century **Porta di San Francesco,** a tower crowned by Guelph merlons. Inside the arch is the coat of arms of the city and of Pope Urban V, which were painted by Pace di Bartolo in 1367. The road leads through the gate to Piazza Unità d'Italia, now the site of a parking lot and bus stop. In earlier times, the street continued on toward Perugia, passing alongside the Sacro Convento.

Proceeding directly toward Piazza San Pietro, one reaches the Church of San Pietro. At No. 18/A there is a fresco of the *Madonna with Child and San Rocco*, which could be an early 16th century work done by Francesco Tartaglia.

The Hotel Giotto, which opened in 1900, is at No. 41 of Via Fontebella. The 17th century Palazzo Illuminati, formerly Palazzo Benigni–Graziani, is at No. 25. The Ospedale della confraternita di San Pietro (hospital of the Confraternity of San Pietro), known to have been established by the year 1354, was at No. 23. On its façade is a niche frescoed with a *Madonna with Child between St. Peter and St. John the Baptist*, whereas *St. Vittorino and St. Francis* are depicted in the intrados (late 14th century). The house located at the corner of Via Giorgetti (No. 1) has a niche with a fresco dating to the early 17th century: it depicts *St. Francis Receiving the Stigmata.* Another fresco with the image of the *Madonna with Child*, attributed to Cecco di Bernardino, can be seen on the façade of the house at No. 14: the year 1548 is inscribed on the architrave.

At this point, the street offers a beautiful view of the Umbrian valley, while its left–hand side is dominated by the Monte Frumentario, at the base of which is **Fonte Marcella.** Commonly known as Fontebella, this travertine fountain was built in 1556–57 by the Sienese governor Marcello Tuto. The front of the fountain is composed of a rectangular basin divided into three panels with roses, the municipal insignia and the emblem of Marcello Tuto. Water spouts from three carved lions' heads placed in the methops of a doric frieze. The fountain is crowned with the coat of arms of Pope Paul IV flanked by volutes.

Vicolo degli Esposti begins behind the fountain. Opposite the alley is a typical medieval home with sculpture fragments imbedded into its wall and a 14th century mullioned window. On the ground floor of this house, whose entrance is located on the little steps of Via Giuseppe Aromatari, there is an 18th century public washbasin. The plaque at No. 3 indicates that it was the house of the scholar Francesco Pennacchi (1860–1932).

In ancient times, the Roman walls crossed the road at Vicolo Frondini. It is possible that at the end of the 13th century, there was a small gate that connected the new street leading to San Francesco, parallel to via Superba. All that remains of this supposed gate is the corbel imbedded in the corner of Palazzo Fiumi–Roncalli. Via Pennacchi leads to the Pro Civitate Christiana.

Palazzo Fiumi–Roncalli looks out onto Piazzetta Garibaldi (No. 1). The palazzo belonged to the most powerful family in Assisi, a family that, in its fight with the Nepis family, dominated the city's history in the late Middle Ages. The palazzo was built above the ancient Roman city gate that was the starting–point of the road

leading to Perugia, passing by way of the modern–day Via del Fosso Cupo. The gate, which is not open to the public, had a double arch made of travertine blocks, with a square attic. The façade was decorated with a cornice similar to the cistern of San Rufino. On the 17th century façade of the palazzo is a plaque commemorating Giuseppe Garibaldi's stay in Assisi in the fall of 1848.
Adjoining the palazzo is the **Confraternita di San Francesco**, also known as Confraternita di San Leonardo or delle Stimmate. The existence of this group of disciples has been documented to before the year 1329. At that time, the brothers met in the Church of San Leonardo in the Porta San Giacomo district of the city. In 1428, Gentile di Bernardo Fiumi donated his buildings to the fraternity with the proviso that they build new headquarters, which they did the following year.
The oratory is situated parallel to the street. Above the entrance is a frescoed niche depicting the *Stories of the Pardon*, whereas *God, St. Francis and St. Leonard* are portrayed in the intrados. On the outside is the *Annunciation* (circa 1439), which has been attributed to Pietro di Giovanni Mazzaforte. It was extensively repainted during the 17th century.
Fragments of the *Seven Works of Mercy*, painted in monochrome on the adjoining wall, date to this same period and may have been done by the same artist. The fragments illustrate the evangelical commitment that inspired the life of the confraternity and, as viewed from the left, they are: *To Offer Refuge to Pilgrims, To Quench the Thirsty, To Feed the Hungry, To Visit Prisoners, To Visit the Sick, To Clothe the Naked and To Bury the Dead.*
The interior is composed of a two–bay hall covered by a cross vault (permission to visit the hall can be obtained from the Pro Civitate Christiana). A large fresco of the *Crucixion with St. Leonard, St. Francis and the Chastised*, on the wall by the altar, was painted by Giovanni di Corraduccio of Foligno at the time the oratory was built. The figures of *St. Ives* (?) and *St. Bartholomew* were also done by the same artist. The painted friezes were done in 1875 by Augusto Malatesta. On the right wall is the altar of the Virgin Mary, with a *Madonna with Child* done by Gaetano Alessandrini (about 1875), inspired by Sebastiano Conca. Hanging on the walls are prints of the *Via Crucis*, etched by Bartolomeo Bartoccini and Giuseppe Ferretti based on drawings by Friedrich Overbeck. The *Concession of the Pardon* (1598), a work signed by Giuseppe Gisleri, is frescoed on the vault of the meeting hall; the *Crucifixion* (1583) on the far wall and the *Stories of St. Francis* that are alternated with images of *Saints* (1597–98) in the lunettes, are the work of various artists. These paintings were commissioned by members of the confraternity, who are portrayed in devotional postures in the medallions.
Going down Via Cristofani, the homes of the Confraternita di San Francesco are located at No. 15. They were restored in a neo–Gothic style in 1926. A plaque at No. 8 marks the home of Assisi historian Antonio Cristofani (1828–1883). The street ends at Piazza del Vescovado.
The path of the ancient Roman road that connected the Temple of Minerva with the city gate is now Via Brizi. The Leonelli house, restored in a neo–Gothic style in 1926, is located at No. 1. Via Giotto leads into Via Portica, which continues on to Piazza del Comune. At No. 10 of Via Bernardo da Quintavalle is the house of Ber-

Confraternita di San Francesco

nardo da Quintavalle, St. Francis' first companion. It is part of a Romanesque structure that was incorporated into the 17th century Palazzo Sbaraglini. There is a plaque on the wall that evokes a famous episode in the life of St. Francis, an event that took place in Bernard's room, which has now been converted into a chapel (not open to the public).

And then Bernard wished to contemplate his saintliness and he made up a bed in his own room in which a light always burned through the night. And St. Francis, who wanted to conceal his saintliness, immediately threw himself on the bed as soon as he entered the room and pretended to sleep. After some time, Bernard likewise lay down to sleep and began to snore as if he too were sleeping. St. Francis, believing that Ber-

Chiesa di S. Gregorio

nard was asleep, rose from his bed, raised his eyes and his hands to heaven, and cried out with great fervor and devotion, 'Oh my God, my God!'and he continued to cry out and to weep in this manner until morning. As Bernard could see St. Francis' great devotion in the lamplight, he devoutly considered his words and was touched and inspired by the Holy Spirit to change his way of life.

(*The Little Flowers of St. Francis, II*)

Opposite the house is the **Church of San Gregorio** (go to the parish of Santa Maria Maggiore for permission to visit the church). This was the headquarter of the Confraternita dei the Disciplinati di San Gregorio, the oldest confraternity in Assisi. According to seventeenth–century tradition, it dates to 1179, although it is considered more likely to have started in the second half of the 13th century. It would appear that the confraternity was originally located in Via Portica near the Teatro Metastasio and that Bishop Teobaldo Pontano had it moved to its new headquarters in 1325, which is where it remained until it was abolished in 1772.

The building's exterior is composed of a curtain made of small rows of pink and white Subasio stone done in a typical thirteenth–century style. The entrance on Via San Gregorio was restored during the 17th century. The niche has a fresco in very poor condition that depicts the *Madonna with Child and the Angels, St. Francis and St. Gregory*, which was painted in 1633 over an older image, possibly by Puccio Capanna. Inside the building is a large Baroque altar bearing the coat of arms of Bishop Tegrimio Tegrimi (1630–1641). In the gable there are stucco statues representing *Faith and Hope*. In the center, there is a copy of Caravaggio's *Deposition*, the original of which is in the Vatican Gallery. To the left is the *Visitation*, dating to the early 18th century, and on the right is *St. Anthony the Abbot*, done by Giacomo Giorgetti. On the left wall, there are fragments of frescoes dating to the second half of the 14th century. These frescoes depict the *Annunciation, Madonna with Child, St. Christopher and St. Helen.*

Next to the church, at Via San Gregorio No. 12, is the headquarters of the Centro internazionale per la pace fra i popoli (International Center for Peace Among Nations), which is housed in a medieval building. The lovely round–arch doorway has a keystone marked with an emblem, a circle with four points crowned by a cross. According to Ludovico da Pietralunga (circa 1570) this was Pietro di Bernardone's store.

Going along this road (Via Portica)*, near the piazza there is a fountain, whereas a bit behind it on the right is a house with stores, that was the storeroom of the father of St. Francis. That he was a merchant is indicated by the sign sculpted in stone on the façade.*

At No. 16 of Via Bernardo da Quintavalle is the former Palazzo Rocchi, now the convent of the Franciscan Sisters of Alcantara, who came here in 1947. There is a modern private chapel, designed by Angelo Polissella, on the ground floor (not open to the public). The keystone over the portal at No. 10 bears the emblem of St. Anthony the Abbot. This may have been an ancient hospital. Piazza del Comune can be reached by proceeding along Via Sant'Antonio and then continuing on Via dell'Arco dei Priori.

Fourth Itinerary

LA PIAZZA DEL COMUNE (Town Hall Square).
Temple of Minerva, Palazzo del Capitano del Popolo and Torre del Popolo (City Hall Tower), Palazzi Comunali (City Government Buildings), Pinacoteca Comunale (Municipal Art Gallery), Chiesa Nuova

The Piazza del Comune is a large, rectangular–shaped area at the medieval city's Topographic center. Its major axis is parallel to the mountain, and it is located at the intersection of the main roads leading to the city gates. Along its perimeter stand the city government buildings, the encounter of ancient and medieval civilizations expressed by the remarkable pairing of the noble structure of the Temple of Minerva with the tall Torre del Popolo. Most of the city's life, particularly intense during the tourist season, takes place within the square.

It is still uncertain, due to the lack of an adequate excavation program, whether the space below the present Piazza del Comune hosted the ancient Forum of the Roman Municipality or a holy place of worship similar to the Temple of the Fortuna Primigenia in Palestrina. Because of the steep slope of the site, the wide terrace was supported on the lower side by a wall located in the present Via dei Macelli Vecchi. The upper side was bordered by a thick support wall about eight meters high located behind the temple and made of rectangular stones. This was topped by a narrow terrace which dominated the square below and was connected to it by stairways. The square was closed on three sides by a Doric columned arcade which hosted a few taverns. At each end were two huge fountains, perhaps connected with an early cult of Castor and Pollux, to whom a four–columned shrine placed in the middle of the square was dedicated.
Following the crisis of the Roman municipality, the area was ransacked during the devastating sieges of Totila (545) and Charlemagne (773) mentioned in the 14th century chronical by Brother Elemosina. Having been abandoned, the Piazza became filled with débris which caused the street level, uncovered in 1836 at more than three meters below the present one, to be raised substantially. It was crowded with buildings belonging to the nobility and the religious which overlooked a square named in the medieval chronicles *platea mercati* (market place). The Piazza recovered its prominence with the birth of the free Commune following the uprising of 1198, during which the palaces of the *boni homines* (the nobility) occupying it were torn down. When it was made the seat of the city government in 1212, the Piazza was renamed *platea comunis*, or *platea populi.* In 1228 it was widened on the side toward the mountain by the elimination of the dwellings crowding it for the canonization of St. Francis, which took place in the new Piazza del Comune in the presence of Pope Gregorius IX.
The city government buildings on the lower side were the last major constructions to influence the appearance of the Piazza. In 1881 several buildings on the eastern side were torn down to create an additional throughway to ease traffic along what is now Via San Gabriele dell'Addolorata.

In 1988, strips of travertine were inserted in the present pavement to mark the outlines of the wall which supported the temple, the adjacent base, and the four–columned shrine. The Piazza del Comune is unique due to the presence of the Temple of Minerva, one of the best preserved examples of Roman religious architecture. For centuries it has attracted the admiration of travelers for the classic beauty of its form, especially that of its façade. Giotto portrayed it in the first episode of his Franciscan cycle. Palladio included it among the most outstanding examples of ancient architecture in his famous treatise *The Four Books of Architecture*. Giovanni Antonio Antolini was the first in the modern age to dedicate an historical and philological study to it. Among the many reports by celebrities that visited it, the page from *Italian Journey* by Wolfgang Goethe stands as one of the most lively and passionate due to the profound impression the building made on the German poet, who visited Assisi on October 26, 1786:

I asked a handsome youth the way to Santa Maria della Minerva. He accompanied me up to the town, which is built on the side of a mountain. Finally we arrived at the ancient part of the town, and there, in front of my very eyes, stood that celebrated monument, the first complete monument from antiquity I had ever seen. It is not a grandiose temple, as would be expected for such a small town, and yet it is so perfect, so well–conceived, that it would fit anywhere. And now, first of all, I will describe its position. Since the time I read in Vitruvius and Palladio how temples and public buildings should be laid out, I have had great respect for these monuments. In these matters as well as in others, the ancients possessed great instinct. The temple is placed halfway along the slope on a wide surface where two hills meet which is still called « La Piazza ». This slopes slightly and four roads converge on it, forming a typical St. Andrew's cross. Two roads climb up from below and two descend from above. Presumably, the buildings standing opposite to the temple and blocking its view did not exist in ancient times. Were they not there, one's eye could wander toward the south overlooking a wealthy region, and the Tempio della Minerva could also be seen from all sides. The layout of the roads must be ancient, since they follow the shape and the slope of the mountain. The temple does not stand in the middle of the square, but is placed in such a way as to appear foreshortened and very impressive to travelers arriving from Rome. One should draw not only the building, but also its well–chosen position.

I was so amazed by the mastery of its author that I could not take my eyes off the façade. The style of the columns is Corinthian, and the distance between them is slightly more than twice their diameter. It seems that the columns and their bases rest on pedestals, but this is so only in appearance as the stylobate is cut five times between the columns and in each gap five steps lead up between the columns to the floor, which is level with the temple entrance and on which the columns actually rest. The bold idea of cutting the stylobate was very appropriate for otherwise, the temple being on a slope, the stairway leading to it would have extended farther, thus reducing the area of the square.

It is difficult to say how many steps are covered. Except for a few, most of them are buried or extend under the pavement. Reluctantly I had to leave this sight and decided to call the attention of all architects to this monument so that an accurate plan of it may be made available. I say this because on this occasion I realized how unreliable tradition can be. Palladio, whom I trusted completely, produced a drawing of this temple; but he cannot have seen it with his own eyes, for he represents pedestals resting on the ground. Thus, the columns rise out of proportion and this balanced, harmonious monument, which so satisfies the eye and the intellect, is replaced by a deformed structure reminescent of the ruins of Palmyra. I find no words to express what the contemplation of this monument stirred in me. It will bear fruit forever.

According to tradition, the **Temple** was dedicated to Minerva but there are those who favor a dedication to Castor and Pollux due to the alleged existence of an early cult connected with curative waters.

The monument dates from between the beginning of the 1st century B.C. and the time of Augustus. On the frieze was a dedication written in bronze letters, reconstructed by Eugen Bormann based on the position of the support holes: *CN. T. CAESII CN. F. TIRO ET PRISCUS IIII-VIR. QUINQ. SUA PECUN. FECER.* (Gneus Caesius Tiro and Titus Caesius Priscus, sons of Gneus, and belonging to a four–member magistrate court for a five–year term, built this monument at their own expense). During the Middle Ages, the building was assigned to the monks of the Abbey of San Benedetto al Monte Subasio, who made it into a church dedicated to San Donato. In 1212, Abbot Maccabeo conceded it to the City, which used it as residential quarters for the magistrates and as a prison. From 1456 the temple resumed its ancient religious function, and in 1539 it was dedicated to **Santa Maria della Minerva** by order of Pope Paul III Farnese. The church passed to the Fathers of St. Filippo Neri in 1758 and is now officiated by the Terz'Ordine Regolare di San Francesco.

Temple of Minerva (1st century B.C.), a capital

The six–columned façade has Corinthian columns with an attic base and high plinths. The pediment was marked with bronze decorations, perhaps a clypeus or a crown. The pronaos, onto which the cell doors extend, originally had a coffered ceiling.

The interior of the church occupies the cell of the temple, lengthened in 1634 following the project by Giacomo Giorgetti, and is covered by a barrel vault. Giorgetti also designed the baroque altar frame with the figure of *The Eternal* painted in the fastigium. Along the sides are the statues of *Purity* and *Charity*. Above the altar is a niche for the statue of the Madonna of Lourdes. Previously the wall had been occupied by a painting representing *The Ecstasy of St. Filippo Neri* by Baldassarre Orsini which is now kept in the sacristy of the Cathedral. Along the two sides are the 18th century statues of *St. Peter* and *St. Paul.* The lateral altars were designed by Pietro Carattoli in 1758. On the right side is a painting representing the *Death of St. Andrea Avellino* by Anton Maria Garbi. On the left side is the *Death of St. Joseph* (1764), by Martin Knoeller. On the vault are the *Glory of St. Filippo Neri* and the *Cardinal Virtues*, by Francesco Appiani; behind the altar are the *Theolog-*

ical Virtues. On the counterfaçade are choir stalls from the mid 18th century with an organ restored in 1956. Several paintings are kept in the sacristy which was designed by Pietro Carattoli. Among these are *The Virgin* and *The Angel of Annunciation*, by Girolamo Martelli; and *Crucifixion*, by Francesco Appiani.

On the left of the temple stands the very tall **Torre del Popolo**. It was the first residence of the Capitano del Popolo (a magistrate) and dates from the mid 13th century. One of the bells is dated 1274 and bears the name of Capitano Rustichello del Poggio engraved upon it. Perhaps at that time the first floor and the belfry already existed, since they were represented in the first episode of Giotto's Franciscan cycle. Its construction was completed in 1305, while Capitano Cabrino da Parma was in office, as is inscribed in the memorial tablet on the left of the portal: (*HEC TURRIS EXPLETA FUIT TEMPORE NOBILIS MILITIS DOMINI CABRINI DE BURGO PARME HONORABILIS CAPITANEI POPULI ASISII ANNO MCCCV INDICTIONE III*). From the beginning of the 16th century to 1707 it was the seat of the Notaries' Guild. During the celebrations for the 7th Franciscan centennial, the *Campana delle Laudi* (Bell of Praises) was put in the belfry in the presence of King Vittorio Emanuele III. Along its border is engraved the following inscription written by the Podestà Arnaldo Fortini: *TO THE CITY OF ASSISI IN THE SEVENTH CENTENNIAL OF THE DEATH OF ST. FRANCIS THE CITIES OF ITALY DONATED THIS BELL SO THAT IN THE MORNING AND IN THE EVENING IN SUMMER AND WINTER IT MAY RING RESOUNDING THE PRAISE TO GOD AND ALL HIS CREATION. XII SEPTEMBER MCMXXVI.*

The tower is a building with a quadrangular floor plan, 47 m high, divided into three registers by stringcourse cornices, and crowned by swallowtailed battlements uncovered in 1896. In both upper registers are pairs of large one–light windows. In the lower register are the clock and narrow, one–light windows arranged irregularly. The portal was reconstructed in 1524 by the Guild of Notaries following the design by Cecco di Bernardino. On the frieze is the motto *UNICA MUNDI FIDES*. On the arch's keystone are the insignia of the Guild with its emblems: books, inkpot, and pen.

A tablet on the base of the tower illustrates the measures used in Assisi in the

Measures of Assisi (1348)

Palazzi Comunali (City Government Buildings) (13th–15th century)

14th century with roof tiles, floor tiles, and bricks; the measures for wool, linen, and silk fabric; the « piede » (foot) and the « formone » for wood. It was placed there in 1349 by Capitano Angelo di Latero da Perugia (*A. D. MCCCXLVIIII FACTUM FUIT HOC OPUS TEMPORE ANGELI LATERI DE PERUSIO CAPITANEI ASISII*). Passing through a room on the ground floor (which is not open to the public) one would enter a small court located at the left side of the temple. On the curtain–wall there is what remains of a pilaster with a Corinthian capital. This marked the original position of the cell's rear wall before it was extended.

Connected to the Tower is the **Palazzo del Capitano del Popolo**. It was completed in 1282, when Guidone de' Rossi da Firenze was Capitano del Popolo. He posted a memorial tablet on the curtain–wall, which reads: *A. D. MCCLXXXIII TPR. DNI. GUIDI DE FLORENTIA CAPITANEI POPULI ASISII.* Almost completely destroyed when Assisi was sacked by Niccolò Piccinino (1442), it was restored in the 16th century, when it became a public school.
The building is made of white stone from Mt. Subasio. It has three storeys and four large portals with semicircular arches. At one time it hosted salt shops and warehouses. On the façade are attached the insignia of Podestas and the tablet of the Terziere (town district) of Santa Maria. The flat–topped battlements, added in 1926, replace the original gable roof. The rooms on the ground floor were decorated by Adalberto Migliorati with tempera paintings inspired by the local art of embroidery (Assisi Stitch) and pottery, and with the insignia of the city (1924). On the first floor are both the seat and the library of the International Society of Franciscan Studies. Fragments of the decorations found in the halls were saved and are now kept in the Pinacoteca Comunale (Municipal Art Gallery) and in several museums abroad.
The western side of the square was bounded by the Romanesque Chiesa di San Niccolò, next to which stood the shrine of the Madonna del Popolo, where public masses were held. The church was torn down in 1925, after being used first as carabinieri barracks (1848) and then as the seat of the Società Operaia di Mutuo Soccorso. In 1927 the **Palazzo delle Poste** (Post Office Building) was built in its place, in neo–Gothic style, by Silvio Gabrielli and Ruggero Antonelli. The fresco of the *Madonna del Popolo*, painted before 1318 by a local follower of Simone Martini, has been placed in a shrine. Originally, it contained a St. Francis (now in the Pinacoteca) and a St. Clare, both kneeling before the Madonna and interceding for Assisi. The altar stone comes from the Sasso (Mountain) della Verna. The entrance hall was decorated in neo–Gothic style by Adalberto Migliorati, with *St. Francis Consulting the Gospel, St. Bernardino, and Insignia of the City* (1927).

The southern side of the square is entirely occupied by the **Palazzo Comunale** and by **Palazzo Bonacquisti** (No.6). The latter was built in the 16th century by Galeazzo Filippo Pomponio Bonacquisti, Count of Panzo and one of the founders of the Accademia del Monte. His name appears in the portal. In the architraves of the windows on the second floor is inscribed a motto which, concealing the family name, alludes to the vanity of worldly matters: *BONA ACQUISITA. MUNDANA*

Volta Pinta (1556), detail

TRANSITORIA. MOMENTANEA VANA. The building hosts the Cassa di Risparmio di Perugia (Perugia Savings Bank), The Circolo Cittadino (Citizens' Club) « Subasio », and the Commissariato di Pubblica Sicurezza (Police Station).

The Palazzi Comunali (City Government Buildings) consist of four units joined together in different periods between the 13th and 15th century. They are connected by the two archways, the Arco dei Priori (Priors' Arch) and the so–called Volta Pinta (Painted Vault). The external appearance of the buildings is typical of the local building style of the late Middle Ages, emphasized by a « purist » restoration done in 1926 which is responsible for the fake battlements of the Palazzo dei Priori. The upper floors house the seat of the Municipio (City Government). The Pinacoteca Comunale and the Azienda di Promozione Turistica (Tourism Promotion Agency) are on the ground floor.

The earliest part of the complex includes, on the left side, the *Palazzo dei Priori*, which was built on what was left of the buildings owned by Ser Vagnozzo and purchased by the Commune in 1275. It was completed by 1295, when papers from the city archives refer to it as *Palatium Novum Comunis Assisii.* On the upper floor was the Ufficio dei Magnifici Priori, office of five sages who governed the city together with the Podestà and the Capitano del Popolo. On the ground floor were shops which were rented out to grocers, barbers, taylors, and butchers. This custom was maintained until 1926. In a convenient location, cereals were weighed and a standard, 12½ lb weight sample was kept along with two precise scales.

The second structure was sold to the Commune in 1337 by the Florentine banker Bono di Nello and by the Compagnia dei Bardi for the purpose of extending the Palazzo dei Priori on the right side, as is inscribed on a tablet on the front. The building was severely damaged when it was sacked by Piccinino in 1442, and was restored after 1456 by Cardinals Savelli and Orsini and by Pope Sixtus IV, whose arms appear on the façade. High above, a large tablet commemorates the action taken in 1542 by Governor Giovanni Andrea Cruciani on behalf of Pope Paul III Farnese. The ancient subdivision of the city into five gates was replaced with a subdivision based on three districts (terzieri): San Francesco, San Rufino, and Santa Maria Maggiore. This was done in order to stop the internal struggles between the *Parte de Sopra* (Upper Side) and the *Parte de Sotto* (Lower Side). In 1493 the Mon-

te di Pietà (City Pawnshop), instituted in 1468 by Brother Barnaba Manassei da Terni, as well as the Archivio Comunale (City Archives) were placed on the ground floor.
In 1450 a new wing of the building was under construction in the area occupied by the garden of the Palazzo dei Priori which was destined for use by the Apostolic Governor or his lieutenant.
The vault in the lower part of the building is commonly called **Volta Pinta**. It gave access to the city brothel, for which records exist dating from the 14th century. In 1453 it was decided, for the sake of decency, to close the back wall. Afterwards the area was utilized as an exchange floor for grains. The vault is decorated with figures done in the grotesque manner painted in 1556 by one *Raphael Pictor* on commission by Governor Marcello Tuto, whose insignia, a club with shoots, is represented in all the stories illustrated. In the center is the insignia of Pope Paul IV Carafa. On a clypeus are represented the scenes of a muse inspiring a poet and a contest between Apollo and Marsyas. On another clypeus was the portrait of the Assisan poet Sextus Propertius, now replaced by an inscription in memory of the restoration done in 1900 by the Accademia Properziana del Subasio (Propertian Academy of Mt. Subasio). The complex decoration, separated by festoons, includes intricate series of allegories, erotic aphorisms, fables, and myths.

Pinacoteca Comunale (Municipal Art Gallery), Puccio Capanna, Maestà (1341), detail

The interiors of the buildings were radically restructured in the first half of the 20th century. The Sala della Conciliazione (Lateran Pacts Hall), which formerly hosted the Teatro del Leone (Lion's Theater) which was dismantled due to the damage suffered during the 1832 earthquake, was decorated with tempera frescoes by Enzo Morelli (1926–31). On the back wall is represented *St. Francis in Glory;* on the left is *St. Rufino and Three Friars,* one of them Elia with a model of the Basilica; on the right is *St. Clare and Three Poor Clares;* on a band is written the Canticle of the Creatures. Above the stalls is the *Portrait of Cardinal Merry del Val* (1933), Pontifical Legate to the 7th Franciscan Centennial, by F. Zonghi Lotti. On the side walls are emblems of the city. On panels above the entrance are pairs of allegoric figures, alluding to Peace and Work. On the back wall was recently placed a large oil painting by Lorenzo Fonda, entitled *Fragments for Peace.*
The entrance wall of the Council Hall is decorated with *Views of Assisi Castles* and

coats of arms of the local noble families, painted in 1870 by Alessandro Venanzi. On the walls are portraits of famous Assisans (18th and 19th centuries). The vault of the Sala del Consiglio (Council Hall) was painted by Carlo Gino Venanzi (1910) with *Allegories of School, Charity, Work, and Hygiene, Praising Harmony in Times of Justice and Freedom*. In the lunette are monochromes with portraits of famous Assisans.

The ground floor of the Palazzo dei Priori hosts the **Pinacoteca Comunale.** The collection, assembled due to the efforts of the Accademia Properziana del Subasio and inaugurated in 1912, consists largely of frescoes removed from road–side shrines and from the seats of Assisan brotherhoods following the suppression of religious institutions ordered by the Pepoli Edict in 1860. Along the walls are displayed capitals, decorative fragments, inscriptions, and emblems of various origins and epochs with walnut chairs and stools placed between them.

First Room. No.1, *Knightly Procession;* No.2, *Month of November;* No.3, *Month of October;* fragments of a cycle dedicated to the Months of the Year, formerly in the Palazzo del Capitano del Popolo, painted around 1282 by a Master inspired by the Anjou tradition of chivalry; No.8, *Crucifix Venerated by a Sainted Woman and Two Groups of Devout People,* fresco removed from the Confraternita (Brotherhood) di San Biagio, by a local painter from the early 14th c.; No.15, *St. Francis*, fragment from the Maestà di Piazza placed on the outside of the Palazzetto delle Poste; No.9, *Crucifix*, by the Maestro Espressionista di Santa Chiara, brought from the Monastero di Sant'Apollinare; No.23, *Prayer in the Garden*, fresco by Pace di Bartolo removed from the Confraternita di San Biagio; No.22, *Madonna with Child and Angels*, as for No.23; No.19, *Madonna with Child and St. Francis*, fragment of a Maestà detached from the dismanteled city gate next to the Cathedral, commissioned to Puccio Capanna and Cecce di Saraceno in 1341; No.16, *St. Stephen's Martyrdom*; No.17, *Figure of Man at Arms*; No.18, *Benedictory Hand*, fragments from a story of St. Stephen, removed from the Monastero di Santa Caterina, by the same author as the Nativity painted on the left transept in the Chiesa di Santa Chiara; No.20, *Christ Conferring His Blessing*, fragment from a decorative band removed from the Confraternita di San Biagio, mid 14th century; No.30, *Annunciation and St. James*, fresco removed from the façade of the Ospedale dei Pellegrini, attributed to Ottaviano Nelli (1422); No.10–11, *St. Onofrio Hermit with the Figure of the Donor at His Feet and St. Biagio with the Instrument of Martyrdom*, votive frescoes detached from the Confraternita di San Biagio, by a follower of the Maestro Espressionista di Santa Chiara; No.13, *Three Figures of Men at Arms*, fragment removed from the Monastero di Santa Caterina, attributed to the Maestro Espressionista di Santa Chiara; No.24, *St. Catherine of Alexandria*, fresco removed from the Monastero di Santa Caterina, by a follower of Pace di Bartolo active until the end of the 14th century; No.25, *Figure of Saint*, as for No.24; No.7, *Madonna in Maestà*, large scene brought from a room of the Palazzo del Podestà, Giotto's school (prior to 1305); No.27, *Head of Saint*, from the Confraternita di Santa Caterina, by the Maestro dello Stendardo di San Leonardo; No.31, *St. Lucia*, brought from the façade of the Ospedale dei Pellegrini and attributed to Ottaviano Nelli (1422).

Second Room. No.29, *The Virgin with Child between St. James and St. Anthony*, fresco removed from the façade of the Ospedale dei Pellegrini, by Ottaviano Nelli (1422); No.32, *St. Benedict the Abbot*; No.33, *St. Scolastica*; No.34, *St. Catherine of Alexandria*; No.35, *St. Rufino*; No.36, *Madonna with Child*; No.37, *God the Father*, removed from a shrine outside the Ospedale dei Pellegrini, done by an imitator of Ottaviano Nelli; No.44, *Processional Banner*: side A, *Madonna of Mercy*; side B, *St. Biagio Enthroned between St. Rufino and St. Francis*; below, two *Stories of St. Biagio*, brought from the Confraternita di San Biagio and painted shortly after 1462 by Niccolò di Liberatore, known as l'Alunno; No.46, *Crucifixion*, cyma of No.44; No.62, *Madonna with Child and Seraphim*, fragment of a Maestà removed from a small chapel near the Fonti di Moiano, by Tiberio d'Assisi; No.61, *St. Rufino*, as for No.62; No.47, *Madonna with Child Surrounded by Seraphim*, large lunette removed from the Porta San Giacomo (St. James Gate), attributed to Andrea of Assisi, known as l'Ingegno; No.28, *Mural Triptych with Crucifixion and St. Agnes and St. Catherine on Both Sides*, removed from a shrine, by a mediocre painter of the end of the 14th century; No.48, *St. Julian Killing His Parents*; No.49, full–figure of *St. Lucia* (1494); No.50, *St. Anthony of Padua*; No.51, *Head of a Bishop*; No.52, *St. Christopher with the Infant Jesus*, fragment; Nos. 53 and 54, *St. Lucia*, fragments; No.57, *Sainted Bishop*, remains of a decoration intended for devotional purposes, removed from the parish church of Castello di Mora, by a mediocre local painter active at the end of the 15th century; No.63, *Virgin with Child between St. Francis and St. Anthony*, fresco removed from an arch of Vicolo Sant'Antonio, by Tiberio d'Assisi. Inside a reliquary is a valuable oriental carpet from the 16th century.
Third Room. No.64, *Annunciation*; No.65, *Madonna of Mercy between St. Rufino and St. Francis*; No.66, *SS. Rocco and Anthony the Abbot*; No.67, *St. Rocco*; No.68, *St. Catherine of Alexandria*; No.69, *Madonna with Child*; No.70, *St. Rocco*; No.71, *St. Sebastian*, votive frescoes removed from a chapel near the Castle of St. Gregory, by a follower of Tiberio d'Assisi, perhaps his brother Diofebo.
Fourth Room. No.79, *Head of a Sainted Woman*, of unknown origin, 16th century; No.82, *Madonna with Child and a Nun*, fragmentary fresco removed from the Sala del Consiglio del Palazzo Comunale, beginning of the 17th century; No.80, *Virgin with Child Surrounded by St. Jerome, St. Francis, and St. Clare*, painting by Durante Alberti brought from the Chiesa di Sant'Antonio dei Minori Cappuccini; No.83, *The Blessing of St. Francis to the City of Assisi*, from the Sala del Consiglio del Palazzo Comunale, painting by Cesare Sermei (1626); No.75, *Stigmata of St. Francis*, from the Cappella del Palazzo Comunale, painting by Dono Doni (1566); No.87, *St. Rufino and St. Vittorino Receiving the Crown of Martyrdom*, from the Palazzo Comunale, painting by Giacomo Giorgetti; No.88, *St. Elisabeth of Hungary Visiting Dying St. Clare*, as for No.87; No.89, *Mystic Wedding of St. Catherine*, of unknown origin, 17th century. In a room of the **Azienda di Promozione Turistica** (No.27) are two paintings by Dono Doni, portraying the *Crucifixion* and the *Annunciation* (1565), and brought from the Cappella del Palazzo Comunale.

At the eastern side of the square is the **Fonte di Piazza**. The fountain already existed in 1303. It was reconstructed in 1467 by Polimante di Maestro Gentile and as-

Chiesa Nuova (1615–21)

sumed its present configuration in 1762, after work done on it by Giovanni Martinucci who followed a design by architect Valeri. The pool is supported by a base surrounded by small columns holding a wrought iron transenna and has nine smooth panels. The water gushes from the jaws of three lions. At the center of the fountain a baluster rises, holding another pool which is circular in shape.
On the side of the square opposite the Palazzo dei Priori stands a 16th century building on the front of which is a loggia (18th century) with five arcades supported by Tuscan Order columns and crowned by a balustrade. Vicolo della Fortezza (Fortress Alley) ascends on the right side of the building. At No.3 stands a small, three–storey building which has a stone front marked in the entrance by a cross and by the *Agnus Dei* and which perhaps was once the seat of a hospital. During the 19th century it belonged to the Compagnia del Sacramento. From the left side begins Vicolo Sant'Agata, named after the Romanesque church torn down in 1577. Continuing along the Vicolo della Fortezza, one arrives first at Via Santa Maria delle Rose and, further ahead, at the Rocca.

Having passed through the Arco dei Priori, one arrives at No.2 which is the entrance to the underground vault of the Palazzo, called *Sala delle Volte*. This area is level with the ancient square and contains ruins of the original Roman pavement. On the left side is **Piazza della Chiesa Nuova**, called the *Platea Macelli* in medieval records since it hosted several butchers' shops. A bronze sculpture by Roberto Joppolo, representing the parents of St. Francis, *Madonna Pica and Pietro di Bernardone*, was placed against the back wall in 1984. In a niche is a *Madonna with Child* (1927), a majolica by Amerigo Lunghi.
The **Chiesa Nuova** was built above the house of Giovan Battista Bini, where supposedly St. Francis was born. It was purchased in 1615 by Brother Alessandro di Trejo, Vicar General of the Minori dell'Osservanza, with money granted by the King of Spain Philip III. The first stone was laid by Bishop Marcello Crescenzi on August 30, 1615, as is stated on a tablet attached to the façade. It was already in use in 1621, although it was not consecrated until 1691.
The design of the building, based on that of Sant'Eligio degli Orefici in Rome, is an interesting example of Renaissance revival architecture. From the records it appears that the work was done by Brother Rufino da Cerchiara.
The brick façade is marked by four pilasters supporting a Doric trabeation with an attic and tympanum above which rises a hemispheric dome. The architrave portal has a divided tympanum on corbels which bears the coat of arms of Philip III bordered by the emblems of the Franciscan Order and of Alessandro di Trejo. The floor plan is that of a Greek cross with an octagonal center (A). The extensions as well as the center are covered by domes.
The surface the interior is entirely covered with frescoes dated around 1621 and largely restored in 1925. The stucco decoration was done in 1769. Beyond the entrance, on the left, is the *Cappella del Crocifisso* (1) frescoed with monochromes attributed to Cesare Sermei. Above the altar, where the relics are now displayed, was a painting representing the *Blessed Salvador da Horta Healing the Sick*, now inside the Convento. On the vault, in a roundel, is *SS. Francis and Clare*; in the panels is

Appearance of the Virgin to St. Clare and *Miracle of St. Clare*; on the walls, on the left is *Miracle of the Breads Marked by a Cross*; on the right is *St. Clare Putting the Saracens to Flight*. Opposite is the Cappella di San Bernardino (2). Above the altar is a painting attributed to Vincenzo Giorgetti, portraying *St. Bernardino Surrounded by SS. Bonaventure, Ludwig of Toulouse and Two Franciscan Saints Showing the Monogram*. On the vault and on the walls are monochrome frescoes attributed to Cesare Sermei, portraying *Episodes from the Life of St. Bernardino.*
On the piers supporting the central dome are *Eight Episodes from the Life of St. Francis*, attributed to Vincenzo Giorgetti. The *Four Evangelists* (1925) on the webs are by Giovan Battista Conti and replace the original decoration by Brother

CHIESA NUOVA AND ORATORIO DI SAN FRANCESCO

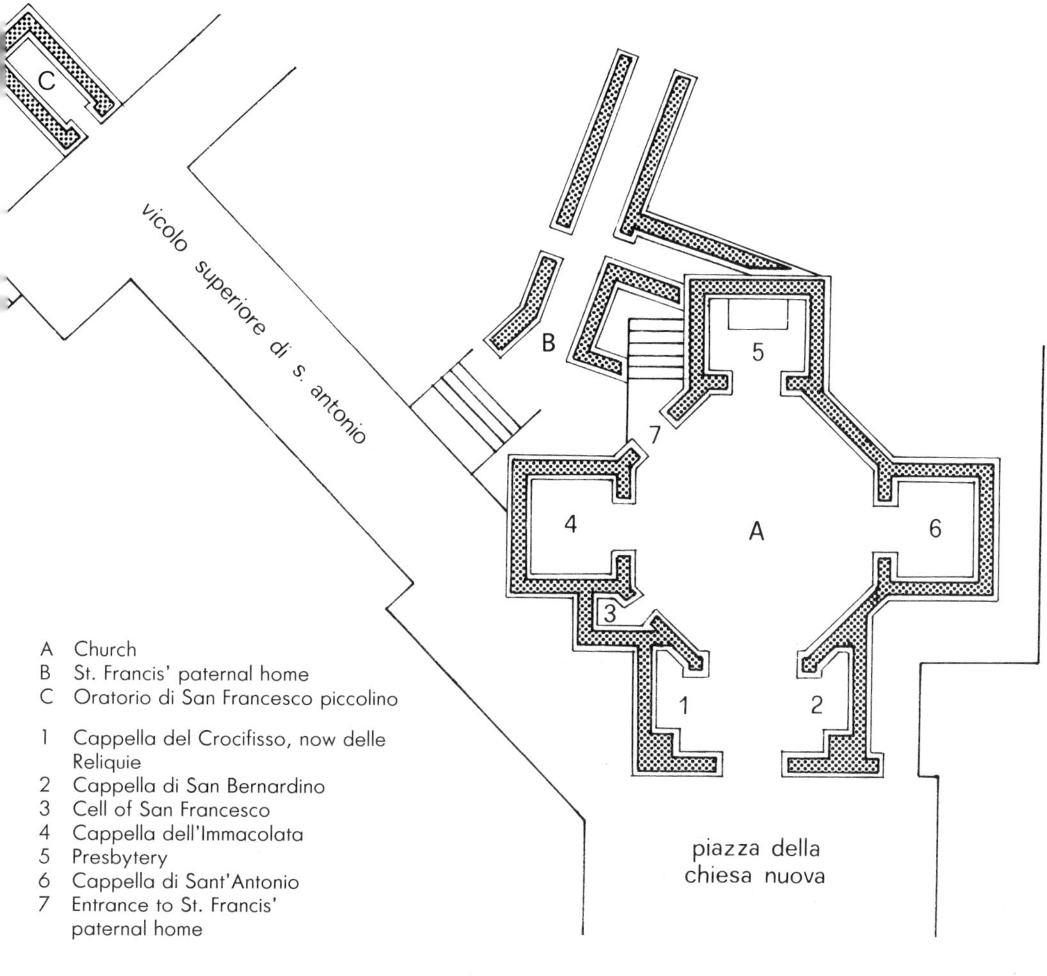

Emanuele da Como. On the first pillar on the left is represented the cell (3) where Pietro di Bernardone confined young Francis in chains to divert him from his life of penitence and from his love for the poor. The interior hosts a wooden statue representing the Saint in prayer (17th century).
The news of what was happening spread through the squares and streets of the town until it reached his father's ears. As soon as he had heard how people were mistreating his son, he went out immediately to fetch him, not to free him, but to put an end to the matter. Furious, he jumped on him like a wolf on a sheep and, staring at him threateningly, his face contorted with anger, grabbed him and dragged him home. There he locked him up in a dark storeroom for several days, and tried everything from words to blows to bring him back to worldly vanity.
Francis let himself be influenced neither by words nor by chains nor by blows. He withstood all with patience, becoming even stronger and more adept in following his ideal. But his father had to leave on urgent business, and so the prisoner was left alone with his mother. Not approving of her husband's behavior, she talked to her son in a loving way but could not, however, dissuade him from his plan. Overcome by motherly love, one day she broke his chains and allowed him to go free.
(*Legend of the Three Companions*, 17–18).

In the left wing is the *Cappella dell'Immacolata* (4). Above the altar is a painting by Andrea Polinori with the *Madonna of the Cordon* which was brought from the Santuario di Pantanelli, near Todi, and replaced an *Immaculate Conception* by Francesco Providoni. The frescoes are by Giacomo Giorgetti. On the left wall is *Birth of the Virgin*; on the right wall is *Original Sin*. In the lunettes are *Angels with the Marys* and *Virtues*. In the presbytery (5), above the altar, is a painting by Cesare Sermei with the *Dream of St. Francis*. Also by Sermei are the frescoes: on the left wall is *Martyrdom of the Franciscans in the Flanders*; on the right wall is *Martyrdom of the Franciscans in Morocco*; in the lunettes are *Puttos Holding Curtains*. According to tradition, the altar was constructed where there was once the room in which St. Francis had the vision of a palace full of arms.

The following night, while he slept, the goodness of God allowed him to see a large and beautiful palace. It was filled with arms marked with the Cross of Christ to demonstrate how the Compassion he had shown the poor knight, for love of the Supreme King, would be reciprocated with an incomparable reward.
He asked to whom these arms belonged and a voice from heaven reassured him that they were all for him and his knights.
When he woke up in the morning, he interpreted the vision as a premonition of glory. Indeed, he could not yet perceive through appearences what was the invisible truth of invisible matters. Therefore, still ignoring the Divine plan, he decided to go to Apulia in the service of a noble count. He hoped in this way to acquire the title of Knight, as the vision had shown him. Shortly thereafter, he began his journey; however, as soon as he had arrived at the nearest town, during the night he heard the Lord who, in a loving tone, said to him, « Francis, who can help you most – the lord or the servant, the rich or the poor? ». « The lord and the rich », replied Francis. And at once the Voice in-

Chiesa Nuova, Giacomo Giorgetti, Original Sin (17th century), detail

sisted, « Then why are you leaving the Lord for the servant? Why are you leaving God who is so rich, for man who is so poor? ».
And Francis asked, « Oh Lord, What Shall I do? ». « Return to your land », replied the Lord, « because the vision that you had portrays a spiritual mission which must be realized within yourself, not by human will, but by Divine order ».
(Bonaventura da Bagnoregio, *Legenda Maior*, I, 3).

On the right wing of the transept is the Cappella di Sant'Antonio (6). Above the altar is a painting by Tommaso da Ascoli with *SS. Anthony, Emidio and Pasquale Baylon* (18th century). On the walls are frescoes attributed to Vincenzo Giorgetti. On the left wall is *Martyrdom of the Franciscans in Ceuta*; on the right wall is *Martyrdom of the Franciscans in Japan*. In the lunettes, from the left, are: *SS. Giacomo della Marca and Bernardino; SS. Bonaventure and Lugwig of Toulouse;* and *SS. Giovanni da Capestrano and Alberto da Sarteano*.
Through a door located under a pillar (7) one enters a small court opening onto a medieval wall in which there are the doors of what supposedly was St. Francis' paternal home (B). On the wall is a modern ceramic panel portraying *St. Francis Taking Leave from His Mother*. An alley leads to the store, now an oratory, where Francis did his trading.
In the antechamber of the Convento are several plaster casts by Vincenzo Rosignoli. In an area which was originally part of the small church of the abolished Confraternita dello Spirito Santo is an important library specialized in Franciscan studies (access allowed only to scholars). Its archives host a rich collection of manuscripts, many of which are miniated. A new section of the library which includes a hall for congresses was inaugurated in 1990.

On the left side of the church, along the Vicolo Superiore di Sant'Antonio, is the **Oratorio di San Francesco Piccolino** (C) (Oratory of Infant St. Francis). According to a holy legend, the mother of St. Francis found shelter in this stable when he was born. On the ogival portal is written: *HOC ORATORIUM FUIT BOVIS ET ASINI STABULUM. IN QUO NATUS EST SANCTUS FRANCISCUS MUNDI SPECULUM* (This oratory was the stable of an ox and a donkey. In it was born St. Francis, mirror of the world). The narrow room is covered by a rustic vault with an ogival section. On it are frescoes from the 14th century which were brought to light during the 1926 restoration.

Fifth Itinerary

FROM THE PIAZZA DEL COMUNE TO PORTA SAN GIACOMO (St. James Gate)
Churches of San Paolo, Santo Stefano, San Giacomo de Murorupto

At one time, the town district of San Giacomo hosted the residential towers of feudal nobility which were torn down during the popular uprisings of 1198. Although it lacks any noteworthy monuments, it offers visitors unexpectedly scenic views within the context of the original public housing which, to a large extent, is still well–preserved.
Between the Palazzetto delle Poste and the Palazzo del Capitano, begins Via San Paolo (St. Paul Street). At No.2, in a room on the ground floor of the Convento di Sant'Antonio del Terz'Ordine Regolare, open for temporary exhibitions, are the ruins of both the walls and the terrace pavement flanking the Temple of Minerva.

At No.5 is The **Chiesa di San Paolo.** Benedictine Priorate subordinate to the Monastero of San Benedetto al Monte Subasio, it was founded in 1071 by Abbot Eginaldo. Before 1481, the building was given to the Canon Regulars of San Salvatore in Lauro of Rome, subordinate to the Congregation of San Giorgio in Alga in Venice, who kept it until the abolition of the Congregation in 1652. Shortly afterwards it became part of the Chapter of the Cathedral. In 1581 it became the seat of the Shoemakers' Guild. At present it belongs to the Confraternita di San Rufino.
The entrance is on the right side of the church. Above the portal is a fresco from the end of the 16th century with *SS. Paul, Benedict and Lorenzo Giustiniani*, and the emblems of the monks of San Giorgio in Alga. The interior maintains the original Romanesque structure with a nave and a cross vault, and is divided into seven bays with arches supported by columns taken from other buildings. In the third bay are two small chapels. On the terra–cotta floor are represented two swords, the symbols of St. Paul, and the symbols of the Shoemakers's Guild: sole, awl, and shoemaker's knife. On the bottom wall is the *Madonna with Child Surrounded by SS. Lucia, Ansano, and Donor* (1475), a fresco by Matteo da Gualdo. Under the plaster it is possible to see, indistinctly, several votive figures.On the right, in the Cappella del Crocifisso, is a banner decorated on one side with the *Deposition of the Cross*, and on the other with *SS. Rufino, Francis, and Clare Invoking Protection for Assisi*, attributed to Antonio Maria Garbi (18th century) and originally kept at the Confraternita di San Rufino. The wall is frescoed with emblems of the Passion. In the underside of the arch are *St. Anthony the Abbot* (end of the 16th century) and *St. Francis*, attributed to Cesare Sermei (about 1630). In the Cappella della Madonna are *Madonna with Child and SS. Crispino and Crispiniano; Annunciation;* and *SS. Lucia and Catherine* (1581). Behind the altar is an oval with *St. Paul* (18th

century). Against a wall is a processional banner with the *Matyrdom of St. Rufino and the Miracle of the Cart Pulled by Oxen* (1783). In an empty room is a fresco with *Madonna with Child and SS. Crispino and Crispiniano* (1606).
Next to the church was the ancient Benedictine Priorate (No.7), of which remain the equilateral arch portal with a relief cross and the ruins of the monastic cloister (privately owned). Farther ahead, on the right, is part of an imposing substructure wall from Roman times with a beautiful curtain–wall of pink stone from Mt. Subasio. At the center of the wall, in a private building, is a 12 m high, quadrangular cistern. At No.19 was the hospital of the Confraternita di Santo Stefano, indicated by a tablet attached to the wall with a column, whip, and the cross, emblems of the Confraternita, and the inscription: *HOSPITALIS FRATERNITATIS S. STEFANI.*
Next, at No.21, is the seat of the **Confraternita di Santo Stefano**. The Confraternita dei Disciplinati (Brotherhood of the Flagellants), already in existence in 1316, built its oratory in 1325 with the permission of Bishop Teobaldo Pontano. In 1327 it wrote a statute which served as a model for many of the religious associations of Assisi. Very important in the life of the Flagellants was the chant of the laudes which accompanied flagellation within the oratory or in public processions. In the archives of the Cathedral is an important laude book which was written in 14th century Italian vernacular and is one of the oldest in Italy. Some of the laudes it contains were written for dramatization.
The building has a very simple appearance and a papal insignia dated 1664, and is divided into two storeys. The lower storey hosts the church (not open to visitors), which is still served by the brotherhood. Its present appearence dates from 1845, when it was remodeled by Angelo Brizi. On the walls are several paintings and a processional banner with the *Martyrdom of St. Stephen*.

On the upper floor there was once a conference hall which is now occupied by municipal offices; a tablet recalls its restoration in 1788. At the sides are two wooden panels on which the list of charitable donations is painted. On the back wall is a fresco from the 18th century with *The Appearance of the Trinity to St. Stephen*.
Next to the oratory begins the Vicolo di Stefano along which is found a tabernacle with very poorly preserved frescoes. In the intrados are the busts of the *Redeemer between Two Prophets, St. John the Baptist* and *St. Catherine of Alexandria*. On the front is an *Annunciation*. There is a record of one Brother Pace di Bartolo being paid for the frescoes in 1363. In the niche a *Crucifixion* (1650) was placed on behalf of the Accademia Properziana del Monte Subasio.

Farther along, the alley becomes wider and leads to a small garden with a beautiful view of the Umbrian Valley. Amidst the green of the valley appears the apse of the **Chiesa di Santo Stefano**, already a parish church in 1166.
It is a modest building of pink stone from Mt. Subasio and has a gable façade through which a simple portal opens. Above this was a window that was closed in ancient times to host a fresco which has been completely lost. According to a holy tradition, the bells of the small, rib vaulted bell tower rang spontaneously upon the death of St. Francis at the Porziuncola. The interior, very striking for its bare sim-

Chiesa di Santo Stefano, bell tower

plicity, has one nave covered by wooden beams and by four brick arches. The presbytery is still covered by the original stone vault. On the left wall is an *Enthroned Madonna with Child between St. Francis and St. Stephen Who Introduce the Donors*, fresco from the early 14th century, painted in a style similar to that of the Maestro delle Vele. All of the heads, except for the donors', were restored in the 17th century. Farther along the wall is a fragmentary *Crucifixion* attributed to Dono Doni. The modern interior was designed by architect Giuseppina Ciampani (1963). The *Madonna with Child* in terra–cotta beside the altar is by Francesco Prosperi.

Returning to Via San Paolo, at Nos. 21/A–23 is the former Orfanotrofio Femminile (girls' orphanage) di Sant'Ildebrando, founded in 1752 with a legacy by musician Pietro Benedetti and already functioning in 1763; it is now a private residence. Above the main altar in the oratory is a painting with *The Immaculate Conception between St. Francis and St. Clare*, attributed to Georg Adler. At No.32 is the Renaissance Palazzo Locatelli, now Opera Casa Papa Giovanni (visits upon request). A modern chapel designed by Franco Moroni was built utilizing a room on the ground floor. The 16th century tabernacle was brought from the castle of Palazzo, near Assisi. The wooden *Crucifix*, done in the style of the Tuscan school of the 15th century, was donated by Mary Berkley. On the right wall is a *Madonna with Child*, a terra–cotta by Francesco Prosperi. On the second floor, several rooms are decorated with *Allegories of Virtues, Arts, and the Locatelli Family* (1619).
At No.36 is the 16th century Palazzo Aloigi which belongs to the family that gave

birth to Andrea of Assisi, known as l'Ingegno, the disciple of Pietro Perugino praised by Vasari. On the Piazza stands the ugly Palazzo Spagnoli, built for Sigismondo Spagnoli in 1925; *The crazy unaccomplished dream.....hanging over the city like a nightmare* (Giovanni Astengo). In the building's garden is the small church of Sant'Antonino, already in existence at the end of the 12th century and seat of the brotherhood bearing the same name. Of the original Romanesque structure, only the apse survives.
Leaving Via San Paolo and continuing along Via Metastasio, on the left one can admire the scenic Umbrian Valley. At No.5 is the Casa di Riposo (retirement home) Andrea Rossi. This occupies the buildings of the former Monastero del Giglio, founded in 1689 by Sister Angela Maria de Lilio, Franciscan Tertiary, for whom it was named. After 1860, the community moved to Via San Francesco.
At No.14/D is the home of Felice Trapassi, father of Pietro Metastasio, renowned author of dramas and poet at the court of Vienna.

Leaving Via Metastasio and climbing up the steps of Via Santa Croce, one reaches the **Monastero (convent) di Santa Croce delle Suore Tedesche (German Nuns)** (No.4). This once belonged to the Benedictine nuns of Santa Croce dei Galli, who moved here shortly before 1382 from their Monastero in the Tescio River Valley and remained here until their abolition by Napoleon in 1810. In 1878 the building was passed on to a community of German Capucine Poor Clares, founded by four sisters from Steinkirchen, Bavaria, who had settled in Assisi in 1720. The entire complex was reconstructed in 1901 based on a design by Attilio Cangi. The exterior lunette with the *Stigmata of St. Francis* is by Luigi Balducci. The chapel is built in neo–Gothic style and above the altar is a wooden *Crucifix* by Giuseppe Frenguelli.
Via di Santa Croce continues between the high walls of cloisters, and soon reaches the **Oratorio della Confraternita di San Rufinuccio** (for visits, one must call at the Monastero di Santa Croce).
The Brotherhood of Flagellants already existed in 1329, at which time their statute was written and perhaps the small oratory on the Colle della Rocca also existed. The oratory definitely existed by 1348, when it was mentioned in a will. The building has a curtain–wall with bands of white and pink Mt. Subasio stone and a full-arch portal above which there is a brick shrine, frescoed by Cola Petruccioli (end of 14th century). The interior consists of a large, barren room and a presbytery covered by a cross vault. An arch and a Gothic gate separate the room from the presbytery. At one time the walls of the presbytery hosted an important decoration with stories of the Passion painted by Puccio Capanna (about 1334), now displayed in the Museo della Cattedrale. With the removal, the preparatory sinopites portraying the *Flagellation, Crucifixion, and Deposition in the Sepulcher*, were uncovered. Another sinopite with a *Madonna with Child between Two Angels*, damaged by vandalism, was done for a fresco by Pace di Bartolo, also moved to the Museo della Cattedrale. On the underside of the arch is a beautiful fresco by Puccio Capanna representing *St. Anthony the Abbot*. On the vault is *God*, by F. Savonanzi (18th century).

From Vicolo di Santa Croce one descends to Via Metastasio. The vicolo also leads to Via Capobove, which continues to the center of town. From the same vicolo, ascending a small stairway on the left, one reaches Via del Colle. A small street amidst olive and cypress trees and bordered by stone walls, it ascends toward the top of Colle Asio (Asio Hill) to the Rocca. Returning to Via Metastasio one finds, at No.18, the **Monastero di San Giacomo de Murorupto**.
The Chiesa di San Giacomo was built in 1088 thanks to a donation by Ubertino di Guittone of Assisi to the Monastero (convent) of Farfa to satisfy the penance of 300 years imposed upon him by Bishop Giuliano of Gubbio. The church was given the name *de Murorupto* (broken wall) because it is located near the ruins of the city walls. In 1256 Abbot Giacomo of Farfa donated the Monastero to Abbess Benedetta of the Damianite nuns. She in turn gave it to the canons of the Cattedrale, receiving in exchange the Chiesa di San Giorgio where St. Clare was buried. In 1323 the nuns of San Donato de Flebulle on the Colcaprile acquired it but transferred to it only in 1458, when the Parish was suppressed, and remained there until 1897. Since 1902 it has hosted the Laboratorio di San Francesco, founded by Harold Goad for the poor young women of Assisi and supervised by the Suore Francescane Angeline. The laboratory hall is now used as a theater dedicated to Catherine Goad.

The entrance to the Convento (visitors must ring the bell) leads to a small, trapezoidal cloister closed at the far end by part of a Romanesque portico. Still preserved are its arches, which are supported by a pillar and two stocky columns with crutch–shaped capitals decorated with plant motifs, animal protomes, and volutes. Above the door is an oil painting of *St. James* from the 19th century. The interior of the Romanesque church, reopened for worship in 1927, consists of a nave, divided into three bays with cross vault and supporting arches, and a transept. The apse, which has a one–light window in the center, has two small chapels on the sides. On the left wall are two frescoes: *St. Catherine of Alexandria* (end of the 14th century) by the Maestro dello Stendardo di San Leonardo; and *Madonna with Child* (mid 15th century) by the Maestro di San Quirico. On the apse arch is a *Crucifix* from the 17th century. Through a door in the left transept one exits to the city walls. In the garden below, a part of the original Roman walls is exposed. From the terrace one can enjoy a view of the Tescio Valley and the surrounding hills which extends from Porta San Giacomo to the polygonal tower of the Rocca Maggiore. In the sacristy is a votive fresco with a *Nursing Madonna and SS. Francis, Rocco, Benedict, Rufino, Clare, and Sebastian* (1536), painted by Cecco di Bernardino for Sister Giovanna di Giovanni da Perugia.

Descending along Via San Giacomo, one finds at Nos.20–22 the home of the Tini family, largely restored in 1926 and decorated with archeological finds embedded in the walls. Under a large arch on the left, in one of the best–preserved locations of the medieval city, begins Vicolo Sant'Andrea. Following a winding path one arrives at Piazzetta Santa Margherita, from which it is possible to enjoy a most impressive view of the Upper Church of San Francesco.

Monastero (Convent) di San Giacomo de Murorupto, cloister (11th century)

The existence of the small parish church of **Santa Margherita** is documented since 1246. In its interior is a wooden altar dating from the 17th century with a polychrome statue of *St. Margaret*. To the left of the entrance is a baptismal font with a sculpture of *Musician Angels* (1970) by Luigi Balducci. On the wall to the right of the façade is a statue of *St. Francis* (1965) by Giuseppe Capitanucci.

Farther along Vicolo Sant'Andrea, at No.5, is the **Monastero di Sant'Andrea** (Convent of St. Andrew). The church was already in existence in 1231, first subordinate to the Monastero (convent) of San Giacomo *de Murorupto* and after 1316 subordinate to the Abbazia (Abbey) of San Pietro. At the end of the 15th century it was purchased by the nuns of San Giovanni Battista (delle Lucrezie) di Todi who established in it their own community of Franciscan Tertiaries. At present it is the seat of the Suore Francescane di Gesù Bambino.
Above the portal is a shrine with a poorly preserved fresco of a *Madonna with Child* from the 16th century. Inside (visits are possible on request) is a chapel decorated with frescoes by Giacomo Giorgetti. In the lunettes are *Busts of Apostles, Allegoric Figures,* and *Vocation of SS. Peter and Andrew*. Above the altar are reliquaries and a polychrome wooden statue of *St. Andrew* (17th century). In an area of the convent marked by the presence of a well is a fresco of the early 15th century portraying a *Nursing Madonna*. On the walls are several paintings of the 17th century, among which are a *Madonna with Child between St. Andrew and St. Christopher*, by Pietro Rancanelli, and a *Trinity and SS. Luigi Gonzaga and Theresa*, by

Anton Maria Garbi. In the modern chapel designed by architect Giovanni Muzio (1970) is a *Crucifix* and a painting with *The Immaculate Conception*, both from the 17th century. On the walls is a *Via Crucis*, engraved by Bartolomeo Bartoccini and Giuseppe Ferretti following a design by Friedrich Overbeck.

The steep stairway of Vicolo Sant'Andrea ends at Via San Francesco. Returning to Via San Giacomo, one soon arrives at the gate bearing the same name which opens through a section of the 14th century wall which coincides with the Roman wall. The keep has a rectangular floor plan, two storeys, and no battlement. A cypress that started growing spontaneously in earth accumulated by the wind has been on top of the tower for over 150 years. On the façade are the insignia of the Patrimony of St. Peter, the City, and Cardinal Albornoz, who had the city gates restored between 1354 and 1367.
Via San Giacomo continues along the internal side of the city walls toward the Piazza Superiore di San Francesco. Outside the gate, however, the street descends steeply toward the Tescio River Valley, which it crosses near the Ponte dei Galli beside which are the ruins of the **Monastero di Santa Croce dei Galli**. In 1276 the building was used as a hospital. There is no record of this Benedictine community before 1316, but before 1382 the nuns founded another Monastero inside Assisi. The small church in pink stone has a gable façade with a full–arch portal and what was once a window, now closed, with a ceramic of the *Stories of the Passion* (1983), by Gianni and Lella Berti of Assisi. In the interior is a *Crucifixion with St. Helen and St. Catherine* (1643), most likely done by Girolamo Marinelli.
According to a 14th century chronical, the bridge was crossed by the troups of Charlemagne who was on his way to Rome to be crowned emperor by Pope Leo III. It is referred to in a 1166 document as *Pons Gallorum*. The present two–barrel–vault configuration dates from 1356 and utilizes travertine ashlars of probable Roman origin. Over the bridge, on the right, is a construction which was used as a mill until the last century and which dates from the 12th century. Following the road along the stream, about 500 m farther, there is a medieval bridge. The valley is dominated by the imposing, white structure of the Basilica di San Francesco and the Sacro Convento, which contrast sharply with the blue sky and the green of the surrounding vegetation. Near the San Vittorino bridge the road joins Route 147 to Perugia.

From Porta San Giacomo, a shady lane with cypress trees leads to the cemetery, built on a rocky buttress. In ancient times the site was occupied by a Roman villa, of which there remained a now lost mosaic floor decorated with little fish. Most likely it was part of a small pool connected with the Sanguinone aqueduct. Ruins of the aqueduct were still visible on the hill of the Rocca until twenty years ago. Within the cemetery perimeter is the church of **Santa Maria degli Episcopi**, referred to in medieval records as *de Piscolis*, (of the fish), perhaps in connection with the original use of the site. The Monastero already existed in 1291, when it belonged to a Benedictine community of nuns which moved to a new Monastero on Via Superba before 1434.

The church has a simple stone façade with a portal decorated by a pink stone equilateral–arched lintel and a one–light window. The interior has one nave covered by an ogival vault divided into two bays by a supporting arch. On the apse vault is a fresco representing the *Death of the Virgin and St. Joseph with Infant Jesus* (1650), by Girolamo Marinelli, and a *Nursing Madonna*, from the 14th century, which has been to a large extent repainted. On the walls are two 17th century paintings with *St. Francis Interceding for the Souls in Purgatory*, and *The Immaculate Conception and Saints*, a wooden *Crucifix*, and a votive tablet painted by Giustino Cristofani with *St. Clare and St. Francis Invoking Protection for the Cemetery* (1941).
The lane continues along the northern side of the Colle della Rocca past several pink stone quarries and, near Porta Perlici, ends at Route 444 in the direction of Gualdo Tadino.

Vicolo Superiore di Sant'Andrea

Sixth Itinerary

FROM THE PIAZZA DEL COMUNE TO THE CATTEDRALE AND TO THE ROCCA MAGGIORE.
Cattedrale, Museo della Cattedrale, Rocca, Anfiteatro, Rocchicciola

From the upper side of the Piazza del Comune ascends Via San Rufino. This is the continuation of the ancient road which, by leading from Porta San Francesco through Via Fontebella to Porta Perlici, connected the numerous terraces of the Roman city. Despite several restorations, the steep road preserves its typical medieval appearance. At No.2 is a façade with a stone curtain–wall. By walking under a large arch on the right, one arrives at the Piazzetta delle Erbe, a widening of Via San Gabriele dell'Addolorata shaded by linden trees. Here produce from the countryside is sold on market days. At No.10 is a portal with the heraldic « bees » of the Barberini family which is the entrance to what was formerly the seat of the Monte Frumentario (Grain Pawnshop), founded in 1633 by Cardinal Antonio Barberini for the town's poor. To the right begins Via del Pozzo della Mensa, a narrow alley lined with medieval houses which in ancient times belonged to the Canons' refectory. At the end of the alley is a large tower constructed with square stones from Roman times and holding a cistern for which the street is named. At No. 41 is Palazzo Falcinelli which has a 16th century portal decorated with a mascaron. On the façade of the opposite building is a wooden shrine with a *Cruicifix, St. Francis and St. Clare* (1926). The street ends in **Piazza San Rufino**, which is dominated by the Romanesque façade of the Cathedral.

The medieval square is located on a Roman terrace bordered on the upper side by a long substructure wall still visible under the pavement and inside the church. According to a recent hypothesis this was the Forum, of which so far no ruins have been identified. According to an unconfirmed tradition, a small basilica was built on the site around 412 A.D. to host the body of St. Rufino, the first bishop of Assisi who was martyred in 238 A.D. at the Chiascio River near Costano. St. Pier Damiani writes in one of his sermons of the controversy originating between Bishop Ugone and the people of Assisi over the destination of the sarcophagus containing the body of the Saint. Opposed to the wishes of the bishop, who wanted it moved to the Cattedrale di Santa Maria Maggiore, the people demanded a contest. This resulted in the prodigious victory of the seven champions of the people who pulled the heavy marble coffin in a tug–of–war against the sixty pulling it for the bishop. Ugone then allowed the church to be rebuilt shortly before 1029 when a rectory was already functioning next to it and, before 1036, invested it with the title of Cathedral. Of the Basilica built by Ugone, which occupied a large portion of the church square, there remain the crypt below the present façade and the Romanesque bell tower. In 1134 the Canons' Chapter, presided over by Prior Rainerio, decided to tear down the building and to build a new temple behind the old one. The church was begun in 1140 by architect Giovanni da Gubbio, as is inscribed on a tablet enclosed in the outside wall of the apse: *AN-*

NO DOMINI MILLENO – CENTENOQUE QUADRAGENO – AC IN SOLIS CARDO – SUUM EXPLET ILLO ANNO – DOMUS HAEC EST INCHOATA – EX SUMPTIBUS APTATA – A RAINERIO PRIORE – RUFINI SANCTI HONORE – EUGUBINUS ET IOANNES – HUIUS DOMUS QUI MAGISTER – PRIUS IPSE DESIGNAVIT – DUM VIXITQUE AEDIFICAVIT. The work proceeded slowly and was not finished in 1210, when a reconciliation pact between the Maiores and Minores of the town, which is still kept in the Municipal Archives, ordered the continuation of the work *(opus nove ecclesie Sancti Rufini vadat in antea)*. By that time the presbytery was completed and St. Rufino's body was taken there in 1212. The altar was consecrated by Gregorius IX in 1228, but it was only in 1253 that Innocent IV consecrated the completely built church.

The **Cattedrale di San Rufino** represents one of the masterpieces of Umbrian Romanesque architecture, both for its harmonious form and the variety of its decorations. The façade, reminescent of that of the Duomo and the Church of San Pietro in Spoleto, was completed during the 13th century. In the original project it should have been much lower, terminating with a gable, or perhaps with salients in order to emphasize the differing heights of the aisles. Later, however, the cusp was elevated, as is evidenced by an overlap on the wall, to obtain a more slender structure.
The magnificent **façade** is divided by pilasters into three sections, reflecting the internal structure of a nave and two aisles. It consists of three registers separated by cornices supported by small hanging arches. The lower register consists of panels, following the design of the Cappella di San Giovenale in the Duomo di Narni. The moldings enclosing the three portals are of unequal width and increasing height to create an ascending sequence. The largest portal is illustrated with a series of allegorical figures referring to the Apocalypse. The entrance is guarded by two crouching lions meant to admonish the faithful. The one on the left is devouring a man with his head thrown back and a sickle at his belt; the other is holding a ram with its claws. The jambs and the architrave are decorated with geometric motifs and hollows for mosaics, and with vines and leaves. The arch is decorated with vines enveloping allegorical figures which allude to the authority of the Church and the Order of Creation. In the lunette, inside a roundel, is *God Between the Moon and a Star*. To the left is an *Enthroned Madonna Nursing the Infant Jesus* and to the right is a *Saint Holding a Book in His Hand*, perhaps John the Evangelist. On the lower edge are three human heads, the meaning of which is not clear. Around the lunette is a curb formed by small intertwined columns from which hang harpies and pairs of monstrous animals, half reptile and half bird, which are engaged in fierce battles. The archivolt is decorated with eight groups of unidentified figures which suggest Cosmic Harmony. On the outside edge is another band with vines inside which human and animal figures are entwined, which is enclosed by a molded, dentated cornice. The lateral portals are simpler in design. The one on the left is interpreted as an allegory of the Eucharist and has two mutilated *dragons* holding the jambs which are divided by pateras decorated with flowers, deer, dragons, and fish. The same motif is repeated in the architrave where the *Mystical Lamb* is represented between two eagles, and on the archivolt where the Cross is surrounded by flowers and leaves. In the lunette two *lions* drink from a vase. The portal on

Cattedrale di San Rufino, façade (13th century), detail

the right, which is perhaps inspired by the grace obtained through Baptism, has a similar pattern. At the base are two *winged lions*; in the architrave are the *Symbols of the Evangelists* shown next to the *Mystical Lamb* and in the lunette are two *peacocks* drinking from a vase.

The median register of the façade has three rose windows and is divided by a stringcourse cornice supported by corbels with monstrous forms above which there is a blind gallery. The gallery is decorated by two wolves (one on each end) and by two taurine protomes (one on top of each of the central pilasters). The central rose window has three concentric circles made of small arches and ribbons and is supported by three telamones standing on fantastic animals in a niche. On the four sides are the *Symbols of the Evangelists*. The figure between the angel and the lion fell in 1880 and was replaced by a copy. The figure originally on a corbel between the eagle and the ox has been lost. The rose window on the left has two concentric circles of small arches with *St. Michael the Archangel Stepping on the Dragon* in the middle. On the sides are two *Saints* in *relief*, perhaps St. Peter and St. Paul. Virtually identical is the rose window on the right, at one time surrounded by four animal figures, one of which remains. The tympanum has an ogival arch resting on a cornice, perhaps meant for a mosaic decoration. On the cusp is a lamb and along the slopes are several pateras.

On the left flank is the **Bell Tower** of the old Ugonian Basilica, built by Giovanni da Gubbio. It has a rectangular floor plan and five registers separated by stringcourse cornices and scanned by pilasters and small hanging arches. On the first

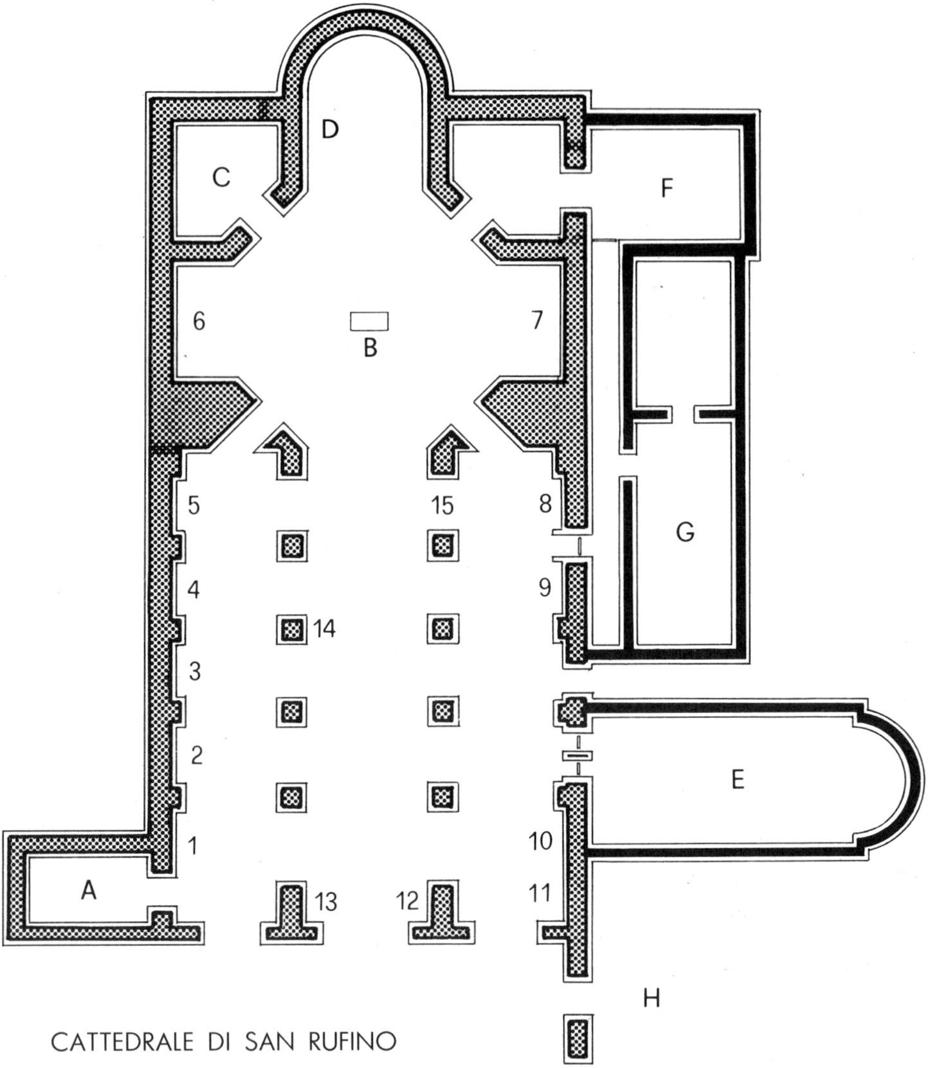

CATTEDRALE DI SAN RUFINO

A Roman cistern
B Main altar
C Cappella della Madonna del Pianto
D Wooden choir
E Cappella del Santissimo Sacramento
F Sacristy
G Museum
H Cloister and entrance to the Crypt

1 Altare di Santa Maria della Consolazione
2 Altare di Sant'Emidio
3 Altare della Immacolata Concezione
4 Altare del Crocifisso
5 Altare di San Gaetano di Thiene
6 Altare di San Rufino d'Arce
7 Altare di San Vitale
8 Altare di San Francesco
9 Altare della Madonna Addolorata
10 Altare di San Giuseppe
11 Fonte battesimale
12 Statue di San Francesco
13 Statue di Santa Chiara
14 Pulpit
15 Statue of St. Rufino

register is a clock with one hand. The belfry is opened on each side by two pairs of large two–light windows. The oldest bell was brought from the Abbazia di San Benedetto al Monte Subasio, and bears the date 1278 and the name of Bono da Pisa.
The **interior** of the church has lost its original Romanesque appearance which featured a nave flanked by stocky pillars dividing it from the two aisles, a raised presbytery and a crypt, due to radical changes by Galeazzo Alessi which were carried out between 1571 and 1585. Above the vaults (not open to visitors) one can still see the pillar capitals, the upper part of the outer walls, and the webs of a dome. The restoration by Alessi, made necessary by the instability of the original structure, gave the interior a typical late Rennaissance structure due to the superimposition of a body with an elongated floor plan onto one with an octagonal floor plan. The effect must have been more striking before 1848, when entrance doors were opened at the far end of the aisles and the altars below the cupola were eliminated. The nave is divided into five bays marked by square–section pillars with archivolts, topped with a Doric–style frieze with metopes and triglyphs. The center bay has a barrel vault with large reinforcement arches, while the lateral bays have simple cross vaults. The presbytery is dominated by a polygonal dome and has a tall choir at the back wall. The nave vault, the choir, and the dome were once decorated by temperas by Alessandro Venanzi (1881) and were whitewashed in 1982. The left wall is built on a Roman wall which was partially uncovered when the altar tops were eliminated. Through a door at the entrance of the nave one reaches the base of the bell tower, part of which consists of a monumental, square–shaped **Roman cistern** (A) covered by a barrel vault. The water entered through a vertical opening in the back wall. Above the entrance is an inscription, the cast of which is kept in the Museo Civico, where the names of six persons qualified as *Marones* are mentioned. They are indicated as each being responsible for an important construction assigned to them by the senate: an arch, the cistern, and the wall itself which extended from the arch to the circus.
In the aisles and corresponding with the bays, are ten altars which are alternated with statues of prophets in stucco by the Ticinese Agostino Silva (1672). Beginning with the left aisle are: (1) altare di Santa Maria della Consolazione (1681), built by the Corporazione dei Calzolai (Shoemakers' Guild), with a painting by an unknown author portraying a *Madonna with Child Surrounded by SS. Crispino, Crispiniano, Monica, and Augustine* (about 1745); (2) altare di Sant'Emidio designed by Giacomo Giorgetti (1664), with a painting by Francesco Appiani representing *The Trinity, the Madonna, and SS. Anthony of Padua, Emidio, and Francis Interceding for Assisi* (1752), commissioned as a vow after the 1751 earthquake; (3) altare della Immacolata Concezione with stuccos by the Ticinese Agostino Silva (1672); (4) altare del Santissimo Crocifisso with stuccos by Silva (1672) and a *Wooden Crucifix* by an unknown author (1561) carried through the city streets on Good Friday processions; (5) altare di San Gaetano di Thiene founded by Canon Lattanzio Sermattei, with a wooden band by Fabrizio Lorenzi (1660), a painting by Francesco Refini portraying a *Madonna with Child between St. Peter the Martyr and St. Gaetano di Thiene* and, in the cyma, the *Trinity* (about 1674).

The presbytery was modified in 1848 based on the design by Angelo Brizi. Under the table of the main altar (B) are kept the remains of St. Rufino. From the left are: (6) altare di San Rufino d'Arce with a *Crucifixion* by Dono Doni (1563); Cappella della Madonna del Pianto (C) (1894), named after a polychrome terra–cotta *Pietà* from the 15th century which was miraculously seen to be crying in 1494, stolen in 1982 and replaced by a *Pietà* by Francesco Passeri (1985). On the left wall is a bronze relief in memory of Bishop Placido Nicolini, by Enrico Manfrini (1973). In the apse is a valuable wooden choir (D) with 22 stalls inlaid by Giovanni da Piergiacomo da Sanseverino (1518–1521). The choir conceals the apse of the Romanesque church where, on the sides of a one-light window, there are two frescoes with *St. Peter and St. Paul* from the 14th century. On the right is the altare di San Vitale (7), with altarpiece by Dono Doni portraying a *Deposition* from the Cross (1563).

Returning to the right aisle one sees the altare di San Francesco (8) founded by Bishop Lodovico Giustiniani, with stuccos by Agostino Silva with the four *Cardinal Virtues* (1672). The altar piece, by Dono Doni, portrays *Christ in Glory between St. James and St. John the Evangelist*; below are *SS. Rufino, Vitale, Anthony the Abbot, Clare, and Francis* (1550). Below the statue of Prophet *Moses* is the entrance to the Museo Capitolare (Chapter's Museum). Further along the aisle is the altare della Madonna Addolorata(9), reconstructed by the Confraternita di San Lorenzo (1650); in a niche is a polychrome statue of the *Madonna of Sorrows* (about 1672), carried in procession on the evening of Good Friday. Through a Romanesque portal one exits from the right side of the church, reaching Via Dono Doni by means of a stairway.

Farther along one finds the **Cappella del Santissimo Sacramento** (E), the most perfect example of the Baroque style in Assisi, built in 1663 with a legacy by Girolamo di Ortorio Paci to the Compagnia del Sacramento, a group composed of the Canons of the Cathedral and the local nobility. The architectural design by Giacomo Giorgetti was realized by Angelo Sbraca. Above the entrance door the Genoan Andrea Carloni frescoed the *Sacrifice of Elijah* (1673). By the same author are the paintings on the walls of the oratory. On the left are *St. Tobias and the Angel; David Receiving from Achimelech the Loaves of the Proposition; Sacrifice of Isaac*. On the right are *Hagar in the Desert; David Praying to Stop the Plague; Elijah and the Angel*. In the apse are *The Nativity; Supper at Emmaus*; and *Resurrection*. In the apse vault is *Victory of Gideon over the Madianites* and *Allegories of the Theological Virtues*, by Carloni. In an oval in the vault are *Allegory of the Eucharist*, by Giacomo Giorgetti (about 1663); *Collection of the Manna* and *Moses and the Brazen Serpent*, by Giovanni Antonio Grecolini (18th century). In the counterfaçade, above the choir made of gilded, carved wood, is the *Last Supper* (1696) by Brother Emanuele da Como. The altar, made of polychrome marble, dates from 1764 and on its sides are two Baroque angels in gilded wood.

Returning to the nave one finds the altare di San Giuseppe (10), reconstructed in 1628. The banner with *St. Joseph Showing the Wedding Ring to the Members of the Company of St. Joseph* is by Berto di Giovanni. Below the altar is a predella with *Stories of St. Anthony, of the Virgin, and of St. Bernardino.* At the back of the nave

Cattedrale di San Rufino, Dono Doni, Deposition (1563)

is the ancient font (11) where St. Francis, St. Clare, St. Agnes and, according to a legend, Emperor Frederick II were baptized. The terra–cotta band was done by Raffaele Angeletti and Francesco Biscarini (1882); the painting with the *Baptism of St. Francis* (1882) was done by the Viennese Franz Von Rohden. In the pillar of the façade, below a grate, is a stone with a foot print left by a mysterious pilgrim who stood as godfather at the baptism of St. Francis. On the sides of the portal of the nave are the statues of *St. Francis* (1882) by Giovanni Duprè (12), and *St. Clare* (1888) by Amalia Duprè (13). On a pillar of the nave, on the left, is a pulpit (1882) carved by Vincenzo Rosignoli (14); on the opposite side is a statue of *St. Rufino* (1823) by Paul Lemoyne (15).

Through a door in the wall of the right aisle which is located below the statue of Moses, one enters a corridor running along the external flank of the church, the curtain–wall of which is exposed. In the middle of the wall is a one–light window with a fresco by the Maestro Espressionista di Santa Chiara which portrays a *Madonna with Child*. In the corridor are kept numerous stone fragments among which are capitals once belonging to the Basilica Ugoniana and which were found inside the crypt below the façade, and various paintings from the 17th century brought from the Cathedral and other churches in the Diocese. Among these are: *Jesus Surrounded by Doctors*, from the Palazzo Vescovile (Bishop's Palace), by an anonimous painter from the early 17th century; *Appearance of the Virgin to St. John in Patmos*, from the Palazzo Vescovile, by Giacomo Giorgetti; *St. Francis Consulting the Gospel in the Church of St. Niccolò*, from the Chiesa di San Niccolò, beginning of the 17th century: *Madonna with Child and St. Francis* (1636), from the Cathedral, by Cesare Sermei; *St. Nicola di Bari*, from the Chiesa di of San Niccolò, by Cesare Sermei.
At the end of the corridor is the entrance to the **Sacristy** (F) (visits on request), decorated by Carlo Gino Venanzi in 1907. On the walls are several paintings: *St. Anthony of Padua Receiving the Christ Child from the Madonna* (1664), from the Cathedral, by Giacomo Giorgetti; *Dying St. Francis Blessing the Town of Assisi* (1640) from the Palazzo Vescovile, by Cesare Sermei; *SS. Rufino, Cesidio, and Rufino D'Arce*, from the Cathedral, by Cesare Sermei; *Ecstasy of St. Filippo Neri* (1764), from the church of Santa Maria della Minerva, by Martin Knoller; *Ecstasy of St. Filippo Neri* (1781), from the church of Santa Maria della Minerva, by Baldassarre Orsini; *St. Rufino in Glory* (1676), from the Cathedral, by Girolamo Marinelli.
From the Sacristy it is possible to reach a small underground chapel, called the Oratorio di San Francesco, in which the Saint used to pray before going to preach in the Cathedral. In the biographies of St. Francis it is narrated how, while he was praying in this cell, the friars in Rivotorto saw him go through the sky in a fiery chariot, an episode represented in a bas–relief by Francesco Prosperi.

It was about midnight, and while some of the friars were asleep and others were fervently praying in silence, a brilliant fiery chariot entered through the door of the building and moved around the room two or three times. It was carrying a large globe

Cattedrale di San Rufino, Cappella del Santissimo Sacramento, Giacomo Giorgetti, Allegory of the Eucharist (about 1663)

which, like the sun, lightened the darkness of night ..... In the end they understood that it was the Soul of their holy father which glowed so extraordinarily, and that it was mostly because of his purity and the affectionate care with which he looked after his children that he had deserved the blessing of that singular gift from the Lord.

(Tommaso da Celano, *Vita* I, 47)

In the same corridor is the entrance to the **Museo della Cattedrale** and to the **Archivio Capitolare** (G). The collection was inaugurated in 1941 in rooms built in the area previously occupied by the cemetery of the canons and consists of paintings brought from the Cathedral and from churches in the Diocese. Very important to the history of local art are the frescoes removed from the Confraternita di San Rufinuccio. It is suggested that one begin the visit with **Room No.2,** which contains: fragment with *Head of the Virgin*, fresco removed from the crypt of the Basilica Ugoniana, beginning of the 12th century; *Head of the Madonna of Sorrows; Nativity and Annunciation to the Shepherds*; *Benedictory Hand*, frescoes removed from the left apse of the Cathedral, by the Maestro della Santa Chiara; *Flagellation; Crucifixion; Deposition in the Sepulcher*, frescoes removed from the Confraternita di San Rufinuccio, by Puccio Capanna and Cecce di Saraceno; *Madonna with Child, Angels and Donors; Prayer in the Garden*; frescoes removed from the Confraternita di San Rufinuccio, by Pace di Bartolo; *Processional Banner* with, on one side, *St. Francis Enthroned Surrounded by Angels Playing Music* and *St. Francis Being Adored by Flagellants, with Corpse in the Middle* and, on the other side, *Crucifixion, Stigmata of St. Francis and St. Leonard* (1378), from the Confraternita di San Francesco, by an anonymous follower of Pace di Bartolo from the end of the 14th century, named for this banner the Maestro di San Leonardo. Also contained in the room are: Polyptych by Niccolò Liberatore known as l'Alunno (1462), brought from the main altar of the Cathedral, with *Enthroned Madonna with Child and Angels* in the central panel, *Sainted Deacon and St. Rufino* on the left panel, *St. John the Evangelist and a Sainted Deacon* on the right panel, and *Martyrdom of St. Rufino in the Burning Oven, Discovery of the Saint's Body in the Chiascio River, Removal of the Saint to Assisi* on the predella; *Madonna with Child, St. Anthony the Abbot and St. Francis*, from a shrine removed from the rectory of the Cathedral, by Matteo da Gualdo; tryptich with *Madonna with Child between St. Sebastian and St. Francis* (about 1475), from the Chiesa di Santa Maria delle Grazie in the castle of Palazzo near Assisi, by Matteo da Gualdo; *St. Bernardino of Siena, St. Anthony of Padua*, from the left apse of the Cathedral, by the Maestro di San Quirico; *Processional Cross* from the 13th century; *Reliquary with Wood from the Holy Cross*, gilded silver (mid 15th century), shaped like a small temple supported by a stand containing a small *Cross* from the 12th century.

Room No.1: St. Rufino (1520), inlay from the choir of the Cathedral, by Giovanni di Piergiacomo da San Severino; *St. Gregory the Great and Flagellants* (1563), altarpiece predella with *Deposition* of cross situated in Cathedral, by Dono Doni; *St. Lawrence and Flagellants* (1563), predella of an altarpiece with *Crucifixion* now in the Cathedral, by Dono Doni; *Madonna with Child and Saints, God Conferring His Blessing and 15 Stories of the Rosary* (1581), brought from the Chiesa di Santa Ma-

Museo della Cattedrale, Niccolò di Liberatore, Enthroned Madonna and Saints (1462)

ria delle Rose, by Lorenzo Doni; *Baptism of Christ in the Jordan River* (1556), doors of the baptismal font of the Cathedral, by « Master Raphael »; *St. Rufino d'Arce* (1573), from the Cathedral, by Giovanni Maria Pelogallo; *Crucifixion*, of unknown origin, end of 16th century; *Pietà between St. Francis and a Holy Bishop*, of unknown origin, 16th century; *Crucifixion*, of unknown origin, 16th century; *Mourning over Christ's Death* (1620), of unknown origin; *St. Vitale Restoring the Power of Speech to a Youth* (about 1613), from the Cathedral, by Cesare Sermei; *St. Jerome and St. Rufino d'Arce* (1637), from the Cathedral, by Cesare Sermei; *St. Francis, St. Anthony of Padua*, from the Cathedral, by Cesare Sermei and collaborator; *Madonna of the Rosary, St. Dominic and St.Catherine of Siena, 15 Mysteries of the Rosary and Saints* (1618), from the church of San Cristoforo di Mora.
Room No.3: Processional banner (1627) with *Martyrdom of St. Catherine* on one side and *SS. James and Anthony the Abbot* on the other side, by Orazio Riminaldi, from the Confraternita di Santa Caterina; *Slaughter of the Innocents*, based on a theme by Rubens, by Curzio Savonanzi. In a showcase are displayed valuable liturgical vestments from the 17th and 18th centuries.
In an adjacent room is the Archivio Capitolare, which preserves an important collection of parchments, the most ancient dating from 963 A.D., and several miniated liturgical codices of the 13th–15th centuries. The archives of the city brother-

Cattedrale di San Rufino, crypt, sarcophagus (3rd century A.D.)

hoods, with the 14th century statutes and a famous laud book belonging to the Confraternita di Santo Stefano, were brought to this center.
On the right side of the church square of the Cathedral is the Palazzo della Canonica (17th century) with its simple travertine portal. A few tombstone fragments are attached to the external wall. At the corner with the façade is a noteworthy metope with a *Knight Holding a Horse* and at the opposite corner is a slab with *Knight between Two Small Columns* of Roman republican times.
A door on the right leads to rooms where the rectory of the Cathedral of Bishop Ugone was once located and where there can still be seen a well and the remains of the 11th century cloister, with twin arches supported by crutch–shaped capitals alternated with pillars. Beyond an arcade, on the left, is the entrance to the **Cripta della Basilica Ugoniana** (H), rediscovered in 1895. Shaped like an oratory, it is divided into seven small aisles and an apse. The cross vaults are supported by columns connected by arches, topped partly with capitals taken from elsewhere. On the left of the entrance is the door that once lead to the nave. Behind the left jamb is attached a tablet with braided motifs and a cross. The apse wall was painted with a sequence of saints, of whom only *St. Costanzo* remains. On the vault are the *Symbols of the Evangelists* (11th century). In the center of the apse is a Roman sarcophagus from the 3rd century A.D., in which the body of St. Rufino was buried. It is decorated on the front with the *Myth of Diana and Endymion*, on the sides with *Diana on the Charriot and Endymion Leaning on a Shepherd Stick*, and on the back with the portrait of the Saint, painted by « Master Raphael » in 1556. Hanging from a wall is the front part of a clypeate sarcophagus with *Images of a Funeral Sacrifice*. On the wall opposite the entrance is visible an extended portion of the Roman wall that used to support the terrace above. Below it is a small water channel for drainage.

Until 1925 a bronze statue of St. Francis, now inside the Vescovado (Bishop's Palace), stood in the middle of the church square. On the left side of the church square is the house that belonged to Favarone di Offreduccio and Ortolana, parents of SS. Clare and Agnes. At No.6 is Palazzo Sermattei (18th century), named after a noble Assisan family related to the Della Genga family, the family into which Pope Leo XII (1823–1829) was born. Against the façade of the building, at a corner of the square, is a rectangular pool with seven panels and a band decorated by six lion heads. It is utilized as a fountain and drinking trough. Perhaps it was to this fountain, or to another one in the middle of the square, that the metope to the right of the fountain belonged. On the metope are the Lion of Assisi, inscriptions dated 1278, and the name of the Capitano del Popolo Bonifacio dei Samaritani. The present arrangement dates from 1532, as indicated on a tablet with both the emblem of the Commune of Assisi and that of Governor Virgilio de Bernardi.

On the side of the square facing the church is Palazzo Agostini (17th century), now called Minciotti, with a balcony on the corner tower. Next to it, on Via Santa Maria delle Rose, is a building with a beautiful stone curtain–wall and two Romanesque two–light windows in the attic which was the first seat of the Consular

Court of Law. It was probably here that Pietro di Bernardone spoke to the town Consuls to request that his goods be returned to him by his son Francis, who had used them to restore the Chiesa di San Damiano. The building next to it rests on limestone blocks from Roman times. At No.4, is the former Monastero della Santissima Concezione, formerly belonging to the Franciscan Tertiary nuns, also known as « Della Benedetta », after the name of the founder, Benedetta Fiumi. The existence of the community is on record since 1453 but it probably began at an earlier date. In the chapel (not open to visitors) is a Baroque altar with a painting attributed to Giuliano Presutti (about 1530), portraying a *Madonna with Child between St. Jerome and St. Anthony of Padua* and *God* in the lunette.
The street is crossed by Vicolo della Fortezza, which on the left descends steeply to the Piazza del Comune, enclosed by low garden walls and with the municipal tower in the background. In the opposite direction one ascends to the Rocca.
The street terminates in a small square shaded by linden trees and bound by a low wall beyond which one can enjoy a scenic view of the valley. Overlooking the square is the former Parish church of **Santa Maria delle Rose**, called Santa Maria Minore in ancient times to distinguish it from Santa Maria Maggiore near the Vescovado, and also called Santa Maria del Sopramuro (above the wall). It is built above the mighty wall behind the Temple of Minerva. At the beginning of the 19th century architect Antolini discovered in it the ruins of a pagan temple. The church is first mentioned in 1198 as one of those administered by the Bishop, but its construction occurred at a much earlier date, as the rough carvings on a lateral entrance indicate. On the simple, white Mt. Subasio stone façade is attached a tablet, surrounded by early medieval decorations, in remembrance of the reconsecration of the church by Bishop Marco Palmerini in 1726. The interior (not open to visitors) has been turned into a cinema; behind its screen are several frescoes (1618). Attached to the church is an arch with a double barrel vault, built with blocks taken from the Roman temple and roughly carved in the early Middle Ages (10th century). From the same period is the lateral entrance of the church with an architrave decorated with stylized flower motifs and supported by carved corbels. In a niche is a fresco with *Madonna with Child* (end of the 12th century). On the opposite wall are fragments from the 15th century. Beyond the arch is the beginning of Via Joergensen. At No.8 is the house in which the Danish poet Johannes Joergensen, biographer of St. Francis, once lived.
Descending along Via Santa Maria delle Rose, which crosses one of the most fascinating and least crowded districts of town, one can see, at an intersection, a shrine decorated with a poorly preserved *Madonna with Child between St. Sebastian and St. Francis* (beginning of the 16th century). On a portal is a slab with a hospital monogram indicating the original function of the construction. By taking Via Alfonso Brizi, an alley on the Rocca hillside, one arrives at Via San Giacomo. Continuing along Via Capobove (Oxhead), perhaps so named because of the presence in ancient times of a decoration with a bucranium, one reaches Via San Paolo. After the steps of Vicolo Tiberio d'Assisi, from which the characteristic Vicolo del Cipresso begins, one arrives at the Piazza del Comune. From Piazza San Rufino begins Via Perlici. This passes through one of the best preserved districts of the

Via Santa Maria delle Rose, cast iron fountain (1887)

Vicolo di San Lorenzo, etching by Laurenzio Laurenzi

medieval town, both for the integrity of its architectural layout and its traditional atmosphere. The urban area is centered on the original nucleus of Roman Assisi, which was built on a flat area enclosed by the hillside, the saddle of Piazza Nova, and the wall below the Cathedral.

The Roman town, which is square in design, was protected by a mighty wall which is still partly visible in the basements of buildings found within the area delineated by Via del Torrione, Vicolo Bovi, and Via del Comune Vecchio. A gate, called Porta della Bonamater during the Middle Ages, stood on Via del Torrione near the ruins of an ancient Roman mausoleum. Another gate was located at the intersection of Vicolo Bovi and Via del Comune Vecchio, and was protected by a tower. Ruins of the walls and the Tower of Perlici, along with ashlars of the archivolt, were brought to light in 1923 in the foundations of the Assunti house. Next to the tower, the bases of four columns of a large portico of the 1st century A.D. were found. A fragment of a column was taken and placed on the wall which surrounds the Assunti house on Piazza Nova.

At No.9 on Via Perlici was the Hospital of the **Confraternita di San Lorenzo,** which had an oratory (not open to visitors) dedicated to St. Lawrence, located at the top of the steps of the alley bearing the same name and positioned against the Rocca. From here one can enjoy a splendid view of the upper part of the façade of the Cattedrale di San Rufino and the bell tower rising above the rooftops. The Confraternita dei Disciplinati (Flagellants) already existed in 1329, when it was given a statute. It was abolished in 1772 by Bishop Niccolò Sermattei in order to provide the Diocese Seminary with all of its needs. The church continued to function through the efforts of the Confraternita di Sant'Antonino. With the abolition of ecclesiastic property in 1860, the complex passed into private hands. In 1933 it was purchased by the English noblewoman Mary Lowell Berkley, under whose ownership it assumed its present appearance and who used it as an exclusive salon frequented for about forty years by distinguished members of the international cultural community. Looking behind a gate through the green cypress trees, one sees the side of a church with a 16th century portal decorated by the emblem of the Saint. In the old wall enclosing the Brotherhood is a shrine with a *Madonna with Child Surrounded by St. Francis, St. Lawrence, and the Flagellants*. On the underside of the arch is *St. Rufino and St. Vittorino* (about 1394), signed by the Orvietan painter Cola Petruccioli. Continuing the ascent, one soon reaches the Rocca.

At No.17 of Via Perlici are the medieval houses of the Mammoni family, recognized by the coats of arms on the façade, two felines sustaining a tower, chosen by the *Parte de Sopra* as its insignia. In an alley on the left is the seat of the **Confraternita di San Vitale** (not open to visitors).
The Company of Flagellants was founded on the flanks of Mt. Subasio before 1362 by the Blessed Hermit Vitale, and was moved to the town at the end of the century. After its abolition, in 1773 the building was assigned to the Confraternita del Terz'Ordine Secolare di San Francesco which is still in existence. One enters through a portal on which the emblem of the Third Order is painted. On the external wall is a shrine with an 18th century fresco of the *Crucifix and Four Saints*.

On the internal side of the wall is a poorly preserved *Madonna of Mercy.*
The church has a single nave divided into four bays. On the counterfaçade is a choir with an organ from the 18th century. On the walls are several paintings from the 17th and 18th century: *St. Francis Conferring the Cordon to the Prior of the Brotherhood* (end of 18th century); *Crucifixion between St. Vitale and St. Benedict and Donor* (1601); above the altar, *Madonna with Child and SS. Rufino, Vitale, and Francis* (1647), by Girolamo Marinelli; *St. Vitale Invoked by the Sick* (1655), by Francesco Providoni; *Holy Family* (17th century); *St. Francis* (18th century).

On the right begins Via del Comune Vecchio, a straight narrow alley which leads to Piazza Nova and is flanked by attractive medieval houses positioned against the Roman city wall. At No.14 is a two story house with archivolt keystones in the shape of stars, similar to those found in the house of The Masters of Como on Via San Francesco.
Farther on, the alley passes through a gate which was opened in a portion of the Roman wall in 1199 by Consul Tancredi to facilitate travel in the direction of the Marca. A tablet attached to the external side is inscribed with the words: *HOC OPUS FACTUM EST ANNO DOMINICE INCARNATIONIS MCLX/XXXVIIII INDICTIONE II VI KALENDAS. IUNII STU/DIO CUNTADINI BARTOLI LONBARDI-/BRUNELLI. HAEC EST PORTA Q/UA ITUR IN MARCHIAM DOMINO/TANCREDO CONSULE.*
Having crossed through a court familiarly called « gli Archicciol i», a part of a medieval section of town built on the Cathedral premises, one passes under another arch which was opened in a wall constructed before 1237 to protect this section of town.

Deviating to the right along Via Perlici, one sees part of the Roman Aqueduct of the Sanguinone which once carried water from Monte San Rufino to the amphitheater. During the Middle Ages, the aqueduct was reutilized by Brother Elia to carry water over the northern flank of the Hill of the Rocca to the Basilica di San Francesco. The street terminates at the medieval **Porta Perlici,** built on a rocky ridge early in the 14th century. From it departs Route 444 to Gualdo Tadino. Deviating to the left along the northern side of the Colle della Rocca, one reaches Porta San Giacomo. On the left, the street ascends toward the **Rocca** to the top of the Colle Asio (Asio Hill). From there, on a clear day, one can enjoy a panoramic view of the Umbrian Valley and the surrounding hills. To the east is Mt. San Rufino, with the Rocchicciola, the Perlici town district, the Cathedral, the Basilica di Santa Chiara, and the Piazza del Comune at its base. To the south is an overview of the city and the valley, with the dome of the Santuario di Santa Maria degli Angeli in the middle and, at the far end, Bettona and the Monti Martani. To the west are the gentle hills of Perugia, with the complex of the Basilica di San Francesco in the foreground. To the north are the deep gorge of the Tescio River and the Colcaprile hill. It appears that the Assisi of the ancient Umbrians was located at the top of the hill above the Perlici area, where the Roman city developed. Learned opinion is in conflict as to whether the hill was occupied by an Etruscan fortress, an Umbrian holy place, or a necropolis. When the walls of the Roman city were extended the Asio Hill was included within their perimeter and was probably chosen as the site for the Acropolis. This hypothesis, however, lacks archeological evidence. In 545, at the time of the Gothic Byzantine war, the for-

24.

25.

26.

27.

28.

29.

30.

31.

32.

33.

tification was devastated by Totila and was probably reconstructed when Assisi became part of the Duchy of Spoleto. Following the conquest of the town by Archbishop Christian of Mainz (1174), the Rocca was taken over by Emperor Frederick Barbarossa who lived in it in 1177 issuing a number of diplomas. It became a residence of Duke of Spoleto Conrad of Urslingen, to whom Emperor Henry VI had entrusted the custody of young Frederick II. However, due to pressure by Pope Innocent III, the Duke was forced to abandon it in the spring of 1198, and it was torn down by the people of Assisi, who opposed German rule. With the return of the Holy See from exile in Avignon, the Rocca was rebuilt in 1365 on its original location by Cardinal Egidio Albornoz, who installed a garrison in it for control over the city. For over a century–and–a–half, the fortress played a dominant role in the dramatic political events during which Assisi was under domination of Biordo Michelotti (1394–1398), Giangaleazzo Visconti (1401), Guidantonio da Montefeltro (1409–1419), Braccio Fortebraccio da Montone (1419–1424), Francesco Sforza (1438–1442), and Niccolò Piccinino (1442). Its possession was indeed vital to the control of the city. Considerable work was done on it at the time of Biordo Michelotti, who elevated the keep, and placed his coat of arms on its southern side and on a washbasin in the landlord's chamber. In 1458 Giacomo Piccinino began construction of the polygonal tower on the west side which was completed under Pius II in 1460. In 1478, during the reign of Pope Sixtus IV Della Rovere, the castle lord Urbano Vegerio had the keep and the vaults of the living quarters restored. Pope Paul III added the circular bastion between 1535 and 1538, as if to place the seal of papal dominion over the city. No longer used for any mil-

The Rocca

itary purposes after the second half of the 16th century, the Rocca was then used as a prison. After 1860, when it became property of the Italian state, the Rocca was heavily damaged by vandalism on the part of the population which looked for mythical, hidden treasures, or more simply for construction material. In 1883 it was purchased by the City Government, which began its restoration.

Located on the summit of the hill, The Rocca is protected by a mighty barbican of trapezoidal floor plan equipped with loopholes and machicolations and reinforced with towers at the corners. Within is a small castle dominated by an imposing keep. The entrenched field, used in ancient times for military exercises and terminating with two bartizans, extends toward the mountain. Here the complex joins the city walls which descend along the hill and ascend again toward Porta Perlici and the Rocchicciola. To the west is an isolated tower with a dodecagonal floor plan and two registers, connected to the castle by a grandiose wall. The tower bears the insignia of Pius II (1460) and the Masters of Como who built it. From the tower, the city walls continue along the crest of the hill to reach Porta San Giacomo.
A door next to the circular bastion opens onto the entrenched field. The entrance to the fortress is located in the lower part of a tower, at one time equipped with a drawbridge and double portcullis and which is supported by an escarpment and crowned by corbels and machicolations. On the curtain–wall are attached the coats of arms of Urban V, the Papal States, Cardinal Albanese, Cardinal Albornoz, and finally that of the Boncompagni family damaged during the anticlerical uprising of 1848. Through a covered passageway one enters the court which extends around a two story construction with a square floor plan from which rises the keep. The entrance is located on the southern side, through a portcullis portal which leads into a narrow court. To the left were service rooms, the pantry, the kitchen, and a dining room. The living quarters for the soldiers were on the upper floor and could be reached by an external stairway. By passing over a wooden bridge, formerly a drawbridge, one enters the keep, divided into five superimposed rooms connected by a spiral staircase. The upper room, now without a ceiling, served as living quarters for the castle lord. From its three wide windows can be enjoyed the most impressive view in the Assisan area.
In 1565, the supervisor for the papal fortresses, Cipriano Piccolpasso, noted: *These living quarters are in good condition and well ventilated; however, during my service, the quarters had begun to fall into disrepair, for no help was provided for financing the cost of their maintenance*.
The polygonal tower can be reached by means of a long passageway provided with loopholes, and by a dark, spiral staircase. From the summit one has a splendid view of the Basilica di San Francesco.

Once again in Piazza San Rufino, one continues along Via del Torrione which passes under the **Arco del Vento** (Arch of the Wind), so named for the blustering gusts of northern wind which often batter it forcing passersby to hang onto the railings on the wall. On the right is the belltower. On the left, inside a marble–cutting shop, are the ruins of three arcades with two registers which have been considered, without sufficient evidence, part of a theater, but which are most likely

part of a 1st century A.D. building connected with the amphitheater. Beside the ruins is the ancient mill of St. Rufino, still used today for making olive oil.
Beyond an enclosing wall one can see the apse of the Cathedral, semicircular in floor plan and divided by a cornice which used to mark the level of the presbytery. It is partitioned by pilasters and crowned by small hanging arches which are decorated by animal protomes and an eagle sculpted by Giovanni da Gubbio and are similar to those in the Chiesa di Santa Maria Maggiore.
At the end of the street, at the corner of Piazza Matteotti, are the ruins of an imposing, two story **burial monument**, with a funeral chamber vaulted with blocks of travertine (access from the St. Rufino garden; for visits contact the Cathedral parish priest). The upper portion, in concrete, is without its original covering. The tomb, from the 1st century A.D., stood just outside the city walls, nearby the Porta della Bonamater.
Piazza Matteotti is a large rectangle area which is used as a parking lot and a bus terminal. In ancient times the plain was occupied by a necropolis. Numerous cinerary urns from the 1st century B.C. were found during the construction of the Convitto Nazionale school. During the Middle Ages it was called *Prato* (lawn) or *Platea Novi Mercati* (the new market place) because until recent times it hosted a market. The etymon still survives in familiar use as *Piazza Nova*. The urban development plan drawn up in 1316 contemplated the construction in the middle of the square of a chapel dedicated to the Virgin Mary and a fountain supplied with water from Perlici. On the left side of the square stand Palazzo Bovi (1614), formerly Mazzichi, the modern Carabinieri station and, on the corner, Casa Assunti (No.5), designed in neo–medieval style by Giuseppe Paccoi (1918–26) and with a statue of *St. Francis* by Prospero Prosperi (1926) on its façade. The foundations of the building rest on the Roman walls of a place called Montarone in ancient times. From these also came the travertine utilized for its construction. The column shaft with base found on the right side of the fence comes from the underground vaults near Via del Comune Vecchio.

By taking Via Villamena from Piazza Matteotti one reaches the 14th century **Porta Perlici.** At the bottom of the square a row of buildings conceals the ruins of an **Anfiteatro Romano** which was built in a depression in the ground and dates from the 1st century A.D. The best view of the amphitheater is from a natural terrace on the opposite side, accessible from Via dell'Anfiteatro. The area which was once occupied by the stands measures 80 x 110 m. Its elliptical form can still be distinguished between the garden wall which bounds the ancient arena and the surrounding buildings. It had two orders of concrete tiers with an *opus reticolatum* lining which is partially preserved. The entrance faced the piazza, where there is still a portal with pillow–shaped ashlars from the 16th century. It has been hypothesized that the arena was designed to host naumachias using water from the Sanguinone, which flowed in a large channel under Piazza Nova and out into the garden of the Cattedrale di San Rufino. On Via dell'Anfiteatro is the **Fonte di Perlici,** known colloquially as *Gorga (fountain) di Perlascio*. It was constructed in 1294 by order of Capitano del Popolo Guido di Giacomo da Cortona, who was also responsible for

Fonte di Perlici, washing trough (1736)

the restoration of the Fonti di Moiano and whose coat of arms appears on the bottom curtain–wall. On a corbel is carved the figure of a bear. Next to the fountains is a roofed washhouse built in 1736 and restored in 1826. In the amphitheater area were located the homes of the wool dyers, who were assigned the job of cleaning the fountains twice a year.

Against the amphitheater, at No.9 of Piazza Matteotti, stands the complex of **Santa Caterina** (visits upon request). The Monastero (convent) was founded shortly before 1278 by a community of Benedictine nuns who had moved to Assisi from the original seat near Viole. In 1521 their religious community was banned due to their scandalous behavior, and a few years later the Monastero was assigned to a community of Cistercians from the Church of Santa Giuliana of Perugia. In 1595 the building was given to the Confraternita di San Giacomo e Sant'Antonio, which still occupies it, in exchange for the Oratorio di Sant'Antonio given by the Capucine Minors. The entrance on the right flank of the oratory was opened after the church was given to the brotherhood. The room was formerly divided into two floors. The monastic church was on the upper floor, as is demonstrated by several 14th century frescoes removed from the garret and now kept at the Pinacoteca Comunale.
The interior consists of a single room with a trussed roof and walls which are bare, with the exception of the back wall which has a fresco with a *Madonna in Glory and SS. James, Francis, Anthony the Abbot, Vitale, and John the Evangelist* (end of 16th century). Around this are a few 17th century paintings: *Martyrdom of St. Catherine* (1608) by Cesare Sermei; banner with *Martyrdom of St. Catherine* (17th century); *Crucifixion* and *Immaculate Conception and St. James and St. Anthony the Abbot* by Francesco Appiani. A banner attributed to Prospero Mallerini bears on one side the *Martyrdom of St. Catherine* and on the other *St. Anthony the Abbot and St. James*. In a room of the Convento, entrance at No.8 at the Circolo Arci (visits upon request), is a fresco with *St. Anthony the Abbot and St. Paul the Hermit* (1612).
On the upper side of the square is a series of well–preserved houses, what is left of a medieval town district destroyed to provide space for the Convitto Nazionale Principe di Napoli, a large construction built in 1925 according to a project by Osvaldo Armanni for the children of the teachers. It was described as *the enormous mass of stones, with arches and two–light windows; gigantic parody of the modest, gracious, and authentic medieval houses* [which it replaced] (G. Astengo). In addition to a boarding school, the Convitto hosts a day school with a complete program for compulsory education, a hotel management school, and a scientific high school.

Behind the Convitto, on Via Paul Sabatier, is the **Parco Regina Margherita,** commonly called *Pincio* like the famous park in Rome. Realized by Alfonso Brizi in 1882, it consists of a number of terraces connected by pleasant back streets lined with shrubs of viburnum and laurel which lead to an open air theater and a pond surrounded by willows. It has many holm oaks, wych elms, lindens, and cedars, in addition to a large black poplar.
In front of the Pincio is the Monumento ai Caduti (First World War Memorial)

designed by Giovanni Giovannetti in 1930 and built with Roman travertine found in the foundations of the Assunti home. At the sides of the memorial are two Lebanon cedars; around it are holm oaks and lindens.
On the left side of the Convitto, one ascends along Via delle Carceri up to **Porta dei Cappuccini**, or Porta di Sant'Antonio, a partially destroyed 14th century tower with double barrel vault. The underside of the arch still preserves traces of Gothic frescoes with the emblem of the city. The gate is named after the neighboring Chiesa di Sant'Antonio Abate, on record since 1198 as the seat of the Ospedalieri and passed on to the Confraternita di San Giacomo e Sant'Antonio in the 14th century. In 1595 the Convento was given to the Capucine Minors who used it until the abolition of ecclesiastical property in 1867. At present the premises are used by the Convitto Nazionale.

Turning to the left along an unpaved road flanking the internal side of the walls, one arrives at the *Cassero di Sant'Antonio* (St. Anthony's Donjon, not open to visitors), familiarly called **Rocchicciola**, built by Cardinal Albornoz in 1367 on the northeastern end of the walls as protection for the city in the direction of the mountain. The fortress consists of a barbican, partially destroyed, and a high donjon with a trapezoidal floor plan which includes an internal court dominated by a majestic tower and a chapel decorated by a *Crucifixion* by Matteo da Gualdo.
Outside the Porta Sant'Antonio is the beginning of the road leading to the Eremo delle Carceri (The Hermitage, 3.8 Km).

Seventh Itinerary

FROM PIAZZA DEL COMUNE TO THE ABBAZIA DI SAN PIETRO, PASSING THROUGH THE BASILICA DI SANTA CHIARA.
Basilica di Santa Chiara, Borgo Aretino, Chiesa di Santa Maria Maggiore, Monastero delle Clarisse (Poor Clares) di San Quirico, Monastero delle Benedettine di San Giuseppe, Pro Civitate Christiana, Abbazia (Abbey) di San Pietro

Following the construction of the Basilica di Santa Chiara beside the ancient walls, a new center of development became active toward the east, opposite the Basilica di San Francesco, at the other side of the hill. After the widening of the city walls at the end of the 13th century the design of the city attained a characteristic spindle shape, later enhanced by the urban development plan of 1316. This led to the establishment of the new town districts of Borgo Aretino and San Pietro, and diminished the importance of the area around the Bishop's palace. Many convents and lay brotherhoods were established within the new urban layout. In recent times, the modern complex of the Cittadella Cristiana was built within it.

On the eastern side of the Piazza del Comune begins **Corso Mazzini**, the main street, formerly called Via del Ceppo della Catena (Chain Shackles Street) due to the presence, in the Middle Ages, of chains bounding the square. At the beginning of the street, on the left side, a tablet attached in 1542 marks what used to be the threshold of the Santa Maria district of town. In Roman times the pavement was considerably lower than the present one, as indicated by the walls uncovered recently in several private basements. (No.25b, 31).
The street is dominated by the façades of palazzi built by the aristocracy. At Nos.13–17 is the Palazzo Cilleni Nepis from the late Renaissance (1598). Now Albergo dei Priori, it was built on the site once occupied by the homes of the noble de Nepis family, antagonist of the Fiumi family during the cruel urban struggles of the 15th century. At Nos.12–14 is the 18th century Palazzo Bini–Silvestri, at the base of which is an arch, decorated by a modern ceramic with a *Nativity* under which pass the steps leading to the Oratorio di San Francesco Piccolino. At No.20a is a house with a beautiful medieval curtain–wall with two seashells, the coat of arms of the Taccoli family, on its portal.
At the end of the street is the **Portella di San Giorgio** (Portella di Santa Chiara), redone during the Middle Ages to replace the ancient Roman gate, of which several travertine ashlars, largely buried due to the elevation of the pavement, remain at the level of the foundations. On the imposts of the arch are sculpted a head and the coat of arms of the City of Assisi. Beyond the gate is the wide and irregular **Piazza di Santa Chiara,** dominated by the imposing structure of the church bearing the same name.
The square is located on an artificial terrace built in the second half of the 19th century. From the railing on the southern side it is possible to admire a panoramic view of the Umbrian Valley with the apse of the Chiesa di Santa Maria Maggiore in the foreground to the right. In the opposite direction, one has a striking view of

Basilica di Santa Chiara (St. Clare) (1257–65)

the hill of the Rocca. The northern side of the square is bound by a series of medieval buildings, mostly redone in the 19th century.
In the middle of the square is a polygonal fountain constructed in 1872 according to a design by Attilio Cangi.

At the time of St. Francis, the area was still outside the city walls and hosted a small church dedicated to St. George (on record since 1111) to which were connected a hospital and a school belonging to the canons of the Cattedrale di San Rufino. St. Bonaventure reports that it was here that young St. Francis learned how to read and later gave his first sermon. Upon his death, which occurred at the Porziuncola on October 3, 1226, the Saint's body was first carried to the Chiesa di San Damiano to allow St. Clare to bid him farewell, and then to the church of San Giorgio, where it remained in the crypt for four years. The canonization ceremony on July 16, 1228 was also held in this church. Upon St. Clare's death, which occurred on August 11, 1253 in the Convento of San Damiano, her body also was temporarily placed in the Chiesa di San Giorgio. Immediately thereafter, the Damianite sisters made an attempt to transfer to the site of the tomb of their holy founder, proposing to the Cathedral's canons the trading of the Convento of San Damiano for the Chiesa di San Giorgio. However, it was only in 1257 that, after countless difficulties and due to the firm intervention of Pope Alexander IV, they obtained the ownership of the small church and began the construction of a basilica in honor of the Saint, canonized in 1255. The work proceeded rapidly and on October 3, 1260, her body was entombed under the main altar of the new choir. Five years later, on September 6, 1265, Cardinal Rodulphus de Chevrières consecrated the church while Pope Clement IV solemnly consecrated the main altar.

The **Basilica di Santa Chiara** has a nave divided into four bays and covered with a cross vault, a protruding transept, and a polygonal apse. It has the same T–shaped floor plan as the Upper Church of San Francesco, but with more slender proportions. The very simple exterior is covered by a curtain–wall consisting of rows of white and pink stone. The simplicity of the structure is emphasized by two horizontal cornices in the front and two polygonal buttresses on the sides. The gable façade with a triangular tympanum has a single, semicircular portal with two superb bas–relief lions on the sides of the impost. In the lunette is a very poorly preserved fresco by Giacomo Giorgetti showing the *Appearance of the Virgin Mary to St. Clare*. Above the portal is a large rose window with four concentric circles formerly decorated by mosaic, and in the tympanum is a circular eye. On the sides are three large flying buttresses (1351) to support the vault. Those on the right side are hidden inside the Monastero (convent); the others are projected onto the square, giving it its characteristic appearance. The space enclosed by the flying buttresses used to be occupied by a washhouse, on record since 1283 and torn down in 1872, the foundations of which were uncovered during repaving work on the square in 1988. To the right of the apse rises the **Campanile** (bell tower), the tallest in Assisi. It is divided into four registers, the third of which has two two–light windows on each side. The belfry has wide, one–light windows. The cone–shaped spire was rebuilt in 1926.
The simplicity of the exterior of the church is further stressed by the plain **interior,** the bareness of which is interrupted only by the light entering through modern

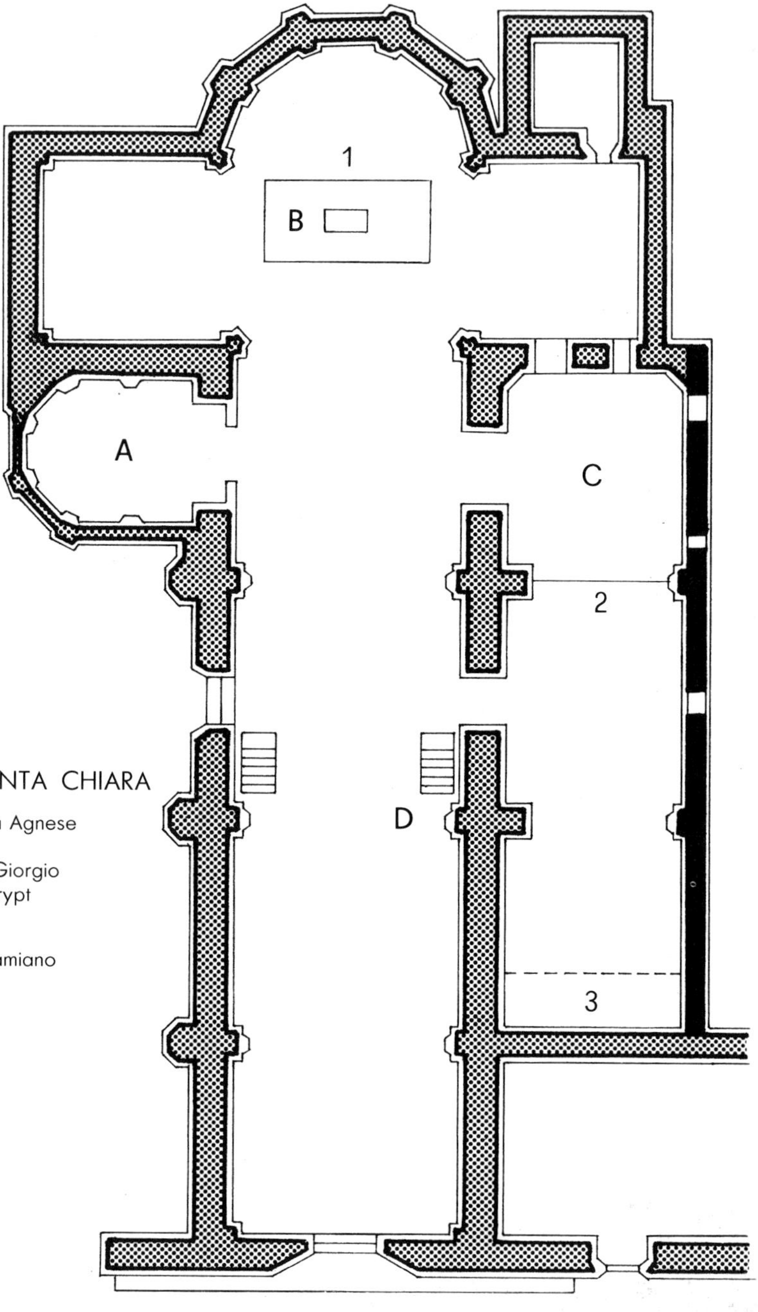

BASILICA OF SANTA CHIARA

A Cappella di Santa Agnese
B Main altar
C Cappella di San Giorgio
D Entrance to the Crypt

1 Crucifix
2 Crucifix of San Damiano
3 Relics

stained glass windows (installed between 1897 and 1925) by Francesco Moretti. The wide walls of the nave were meant to host, for the instruction of the faithful, a detailed legend of St. Clare, of which two episodes remain on the right transept. The illustrations, partly described by Giorgio Vasari in 1568, were covered with a coat of plaster by order of Bishop Marco Palmerini, and suffered further damage due to the disastrous earthquake of 1832. The frescoes of the transept were discovered at the turn of the century by Father Sigismondo Spagnoli. They constitute a unified pictorial cycle, centered on the comparison of Old and New Testament stories with the legend of St. Clare.

The decoration of the nave has been completely lost, except for the votive paintings to the left of the entrance: the *Madonna of Mercy*, a *Saint* and *The Holy Face of Lucca*, 1391, by the Maestro dello Stendardo di San Leonardo.

At the back extremity of the left wall is the 14th century Cappella di Sant'Agnese (A), patterned after the chapels of the Lower Church of San Francesco with pentagonal floor plan and a ribbed vault; the beautiful wrought iron gate is from the same period. Under the altar are the relics of St. Agnes, St. Clare's sister, and the blessed Amata and Benedetta, portrayed by Girolamo Marinelli on the wall. The other figures are by Sigismondo Spagnoli (1914). On the left of the window are *SS. Catherine, Stanislas and Benedetta*; on the right are *SS. Orsola, Anthony of Padua, and Francesco of Assisi*; on the underside of the arch are *SS. Crescenzio, Elizabeth, the Redeemer Conferring His Blessing, Luchesio and Delfina*.

Above the gallery, on two registers of the left transept, are painted the stories of Genesis. The episodes should be viewed from top to bottom, beginning on the right: *Creation of the Animals*; *Creation of Man; Birth of Eve; Original Sin; Expulsion from the Garden of Eden; Construction of the Ark; The Flood; Fall of the Walls of Jericho; Sacrifice of Isaac*. The execution dates from the end of the 13th century and is perhaps by a local painter formed under the influence of the Maestro della Cattura, close to the Maestro del Farneto. In the lower half of the transept is a delightful fresco of the *Nativity* by an anonymous local painter from the mid 14th century, known as Maestro della Natività di Santa Chiara.

Above the altar is an icon with *Madonna with Child* (about 1265), by an Umbrian painter known as the Maestro di Santa Chiara, recently identified as Benvenuto Benveni from Foligno.

On the right transept are painted *Stories from the Infancy of Christ and the Apocalypse*. Above the gallery, on a single register, starting from the left are: *Final Judgement; Annunciation to Joachim; Introduction of the Virgin Mary at the Temple; Wedding of the Virgin Mary*. The stories continue below the gallery with: *Slaughter of the Innocent; the Flight into Egypt; Dispute in the Temple*. In the lower register are two episodes from the life of St. Clare, *Death of St. Clare, and Funeral of the Saint*. These frescoes were done during the first years of the 14th century by a disciple of Giotto who was endowed with great expressive ability and was known as the Maestro Espressionista di Santa Chiara, identified by some as Palmerino di Guido.

Above the altar is a large icon by the Maestro di Santa Chiara, portraying *St. Clare and Stories from Her Life* (1283). From below left are: *Clare Receiving the Palm from Bishop Guido in the Cathedral; Clare Being Welcomed by Francis at the Porzi-*

uncola; Francis Cutting Clare's Hair; The Saint Resisting Her Tutor Who Wants to Draw Her away from the Altar. From above right are: *Agnes Resisting Her Relatives Who Want to Prevent Her from Entering the Convent; Consecration of the Saint; Miracle of the Multiplication of the Loaves; the Virgin Mary Appearing to Clare on Her Deathbed; Funeral of the Saint*.

The decoration of the apse vault was largely redone except for a roundel with *Christ Conferring His Blessing*. In the lower part of the gallery is a fragment of a fresco with a flock of sheep, perhaps part of an *Announcement to the Shepherds*. In the webs of the cross vault above the main altar are painted figures of saints: *Madonna with Child and St. Clare; St. Augustine the Martyr and St. Agnes the Poor Clare; St. Margaret and St. Catherine; St. Lucia and St. Cecilia*. These frescoes were done by the same painter who worked in the right transept at a later date, around 1337.

The modern main altar is protected by a 13th century pergola (B), to a large extent restored, supported by small polygonal pillars with capitals decorated by plant tufts and human heads. A part of the beautiful grating is the original. Behind the altar is a large *Cross* (1), following the model of a *Christus Patiens*, commissioned before 1260 by Abbess Benedetta, who is portrayed in the base together with St. Francis and St. Clare by the Maestro di Santa Chiara.

At the back of the nave, on the right, is the entrance to the **Cappella di San Giorgio** (C), now divided by a glass partition into the Cappella del Santissimo Sacramento and the Oratorio del Crocifisso. The former preserves an important 14th century votive decoration done for private donors. The socle, made of imitation marble by Gaetano Brunacci of Siena, dates from 1900. On the wall behind the altar, from the left are: fragment of a 13th century decoration, wooden panel with *St. Michael the Archangel*; *St. Catherine and Sainted Woman*; *SS. Clare, Francis, and Agnes*, by an anonymous 14th century painter; wooden panel with *St. Clare*. On the lunette of the left wall are *Resurrection, Descent from the Cross*, and *Deposition in the Sepulcher*, by a local disciple of Pietro Lorenzetti (about 1330). Below is a fake polyptych with *Madonna with Child Surrounded by SS. Clare, John the Baptist, Michael the Archangel, and Francis*, masterpiece by Puccio Capanna (about 1340). On the entrance wall are frescoes by Pace di Bartolo (mid 14th century): *Annunciation; St. George and the Dragon; Nativity and Adoration of the Three Magi; St. Lucia*. Behind the glass partition is the *Crucifix* (2) which, according to tradition, addressed St. Francis in the Chiesa di San Damiano: « *Do You not see that my house is falling into ruin? Go, then, and repair it for me* » (*Three Companions*, V). The cross, done by an anonymous master from the mid 12th century, bears the Romanesque iconography of *Christus Triumphans*, with the *Ascension* in the decoration on its top, the *Virgin and St. John the Evangelist* on the side boards, and *Busts of Saints* in the footboard. On the left wall are several mediocre votive frescoes, signed by Francesco Tartaglia and dated 1527: *St. Clare Protecting the Poor Clares; Madonna with Child and St. Anne; St. Jerome; St. Rocco and Stigmata of St. Francis*. On the pillar is portrayed Pope *Urban V*, fresco by Pace di Bartolo.

Behind a grate at the far end of the chapel is a tryptych with doors which bear in the panels a *Madonna with Child and Stories from the Infancy and Passion of Christ*

Basilica di Santa Chiara, right transept, Maestro Espressionista di Santa Chiara, Funerals of St. Clare (beginning of the 14th century)

Basilica di Santa Chiara, Cappella di San Giorgio, Puccio Capanna, St. Michael the Archangel (about 1340)

(about 1270), by Rinaldo di Ranuccio of Spoleto. Next to it are displayed precious Franciscan relics (3): *Breviary Belonging to St. Francis; Tunic of St. Francis; Frock, Hood, and Slipper of St. Francis; Deacon's Alb Embroidered by St. Clare; Frock, Cloak, and Hood of St. Clare; Internal Part of St. Clare's Frock; Grate from the Poor Clares' Parlor at the Church of St. Damian; Chest Containing St. Clare's Hair; The Rule of the Poor Clares Dictated by St. Clare Two Days before Her Death.*
Across the nave a staircase leads to the **Crypt** (D), where the body of St. Clare is now kept, having been transferred from below the main altar when it was found intact on September 23, 1850. The room, designed in neo–Gothic style by Giuseppe Morichelli in 1851 and completed by Marco Rondoni in 1872, was lined with marble and paintings by Francesco Madami and Augusto Malatesta. In the vestibule are two paintings by Nazareno Diotallevi (1912): a copy of the icon of *St. Clare* located in the right transept and *Miracle of St. Clare Putting the Saracens to Flight.* The Monochrome drawings with stories of St. Clare, now replaced by photographic reproductions, are by Alessandro Venanzi. Ascending a staircase one reaches the place where the Saint's body was found, where the original sarcophagus is located.
Next to the church is the monumental **Protomonastero (convent) di Santa Chiara** (cloistered, not open to visitors), built on a slope between Borgo Aretino and Moiano and surrounded by olive trees. The most ancient wing is the one next to the façade. The rest was extended several times between the 14th and the 16th century. Next to the cloister is located the crypt of the ancient Chiesa di San Giorgio. Inside the Monastero are kept numerous reliquaries, among which are: a *Cross* and a tablet decorated with etched glass on a gold background, by Pietro Teutonico (14th century); tryptych with *Crucifixion and Donor, SS. Agnes the Poor Clare, Rufino, and Agnes the Martyr*, by the Maestro Esprerssionista di Santa Chiara, brought from the Cappella di San Giorgio; a banner with *St. George and the Dragon and other Saints*, by Giacomo Giorgetti.

In the direction of the hill, the square is bound by the **Arco di Santa Chiara**, familiarly called Arco dei Pucci for the ancient owners of the building standing next to it. It was built around 1260 by the City to protect the Chiesa di Santa Chiara, but was probably redone after the war against Perugia in 1322. The underside of the arch has a fragmentary fresco attributed to Girolamo Martelli (18th century) with a *Crucifix and Allegoric Figures of Prudence and Faith.* Attached to the arch is a tablet enclosed between two small columns removed from the Duomo Vecchio di Arezzo during the war fought alongside of Perugia against the Tuscan town in 1335. *ISTE SUNT LAPIDES SEU COLUMNAE PRO MEMORIA ADEMPTE DE DOMO ARETINO, CUM ACCEPTUM FUIT PER POPULUM ASISII IN VICTORIOSO EXERCITU PERUSINO CONTRA ARETINOS MCCCXXXV DE MENSE SEPTEMBRIS.*
Beyond the gate begins Via Borgo Aretino and the **Borgo Aretino** town district, realized as an extension of the town following the urban development plan of 1316, when the houses on the hillside of the street were built. Toward the valley is a splendid view of the apse of the Basilica di Santa Chiara, with the bell tower and Convento. At No.37 can be seen a tablet with an engraved circle, in memory of a

Basilica di Santa Chiara, right transept, Maestro di Santa Chiara, St. Clare and Stories of Her Life (1283), detail

prodigious opening throw with which the popular spinning disk game called « Ruzzolone » was begun. Performed by Gregorio Siena on February 12, 1859, the throw sent the disk from Portella di Santa Chiara to this spot. At the end of the street, at No.12, are the buildings which house the Confraternita di Santa Chiara, already in existence in 1329. In a niche on the wall is an *Immaculate Conception between St. Francis and St. Clare*, from the 18th century. In the oratory is a processional banner on which the *Trinity with a Madonna and St. Clare*, by Giacomo Giorgetti is portrayed. To the right, along a street flanking the internal side of the city walls, one can take a restful walk along the edge of the garden of the Monastero di Santa Chiara, and arrive at the Fonti di Moiano.
The town district is closed by the **Porta Nova**, dating from the 14th century. From here, along an unpaved road, one reaches the Franciscan Sanctuary of San Damiano. Returning to Piazza Santa Chiara, and then descending along Via Sant'Agnese, one sees on the right a wall which dates from Roman times and was perhaps part of a system of terraces. Continuing along Via Sant'Antonio one reaches the former **Convento di Sant'Antonio**, built in 1607, as attested on a tablet attached to the façade of the church. The Convento (monastery) once belonged to the Friars of the Franciscan Third Order who took possession of it in 1612 due of the intervention of Bishop Crescenzi. Their emblem appears in the portal of the church. The building, restored in 1990, hosts an elementary school. The church (inquire at the school for visits) has one nave with three chapels on each side. The paintings above the altars have been relocated. On the presbytery arch are the frescoes by Cesare Sermei, *Trinity and Stories of St. Anthony of Padua*.
Where the street widens one finds Palazzo Giampè (17th century), now the seat of the Court. By taking Vicolo Arco di Sant'Antonio one returns to Via Sant'Agnese where, at No.11, the Confraternita di San Biagio, also known as San Crispino's, was once located. It is now a private home. In a shrine above the portal is a *Madonna with Child between SS. Francis and Clare*; on the intrados is *The Mystical Lamb and SS. Biagio and John the Baptist(?)*; on the external side is a poorly preserved *St. Christopher*. All were painted around 1330 by an anonymous disciple of the Maestro Espressionista di Santa Chiara named Maestro di San Crispino. From the oratory were removed several frescoes by the same painter, some of which are now in the Pinacoteca of Assisi and others in the Museum of Fine Arts in Budapest. Also removed were two banners by Niccolò di Liberatore, one of which is at the Pinacoteca of Assisi and the other in the Petit Palais in Avignon.
By descending along a stairway on the left and passing through the Portella di San Crispino, one reaches Porta Moiano (Moiano Gate). This area is named after *Mons Iani* (Mt. Janus), where in Roman times there once stood a small temple dedicated to the god Janus, near which there supposedly was an oracle. Turning to the left one reaches the ancient **Fonti di Moiano**, on record since 1155 and restored in 1294 by Capitano del Popolo Guido di Giacomo da Cortona, as attested on a tablet. The waters of the fountain were known for their health-giving properties, mentioned in two inscriptions, now lost, engraved on the arch wall next to three coats of arms, one of which belonged to the above mentioned Capitano. The final phrases of the inscription once read: *BENEDICITE FONTES DOMINO* and

BIBITE AEGRI ET VALETE. Next to the spring is a washhouse, already in existence in 1491 and reconstructed in 1826. In the Moiano town district once lived a large number of Assisi's shoemakers, who by statute had to clean the washhouse twice a month. From this location one can enjoy a splendid view of the apse of Santa Maria Maggiore and the Monastero di Santa Chiara.

By ascending the steps one reaches, on the left, **Porta Moiano,** one of the gates built in the 14th century walls. It is a rectangular construction with two barrel vaults, supported on the lower side by a scarp. On the keystone of the external arch is the emblem of the city of Assisi. Just outside the gate, on the right, one can see a Roman wall with nine concrete pilasters incorporated into the city wall. It once belonged to a large cistern, one side of which is exposed in the garden of the Vescovado. Farther ahead is the modern Convento delle Suore Svedesi di Santa Brigida (Swedish Nuns of St. Bridget). Opposite, is a small chapel frescoed with a *Madonna with Child and SS. Francis and Rufino*, from the 17th century.

At the bottom of Via Sant'Agnese is the **Piazza del Vescovado**, in the middle of which the Fontana del Leone (Fountain of the Lion) was built in 1559. Originally the water came out of the jaws of a lion, symbol of the City of Assisi. Later the lion was replaced by a small pillar surmounted by a pine cone still present today. On the right (at No.8) stands Palazzo Benzi, with a portal made of ashlars; on the façade is attached the coat of arms of Cardinal Bartolomeo Roverella, governor of Perugia and Assisi in 1449. In the interior can be seen a wall from Roman times. At No.6 is the unique Palazzetto Vannola, with a portal decorated with volutes in manneristic style and a lion in relief. On the architrave is the name of the ancient owner, Ignatio Vannola, governor for the city in 1625. The building once hosted the first hotel of the city, named « del Leone d'Oro » (The Golden Lion). At No.5 is Palazzo Bini, now Casa del Terziario. Next to it, at No.4, was the home of American art historian Frederick Mason Perkins. At No.2, above the entrance of the Parish residence, is a shrine decorated on the underside of the arch with *SS. Rufino and Vittorino* (?) from the 17th century. The *Assumption of the Virgin Mary* was painted by an anonymous Polish painter when the front line of the Second World War was located in the Assisi area in 1944.

The south side of the square is occupied by the **Chiesa di Santa Maria Maggiore** and by the **Palazzo Vescovile** (Bishop's Palace). According to a holy legend, the first cathedral of Assisi was founded in the 4th century by St. Savino, second bishop of Assisi. It was located next to the city walls, on the lower terrace of the Roman town where the Temple of Janus stood. The church was built on a Roman dwelling which was found during archeological excavations begun in 1864 and carried out more extensively in 1954, when a sarcophagus from the 8th century was also found. It is possible to hypothesize that the original building was extended at the end of the 9th century, when the crypt was built. Shortly before 1035 the title of Cattedrale was transferred to the church of San Rufino by Bishop Ugone, who, however, kept his episcopal seat in the church of Santa Maria Maggiore. In 1162 the façade of the church was reconstructed by a master by the name of Giovanni, perhaps the architect Giovanni da Gubbio who designed the church of San Rufino. The apse area was reconstructed in 1216, as mentioned on a tablet where the name of St. Francis appears along with that of Bishop Guido: *INDICTIONE QUARTA ET ANNO DECIMO TEMPORE EPISCOPI GUIDI ET FRATRI FRANCISCI*. The information was repeated in anoth-

Palazzo Vescovile (Bishop's Palace), Giacomo Giorgetti, Prudence (17th century)

er inscription painted in the Tribune: *FR. FRANCISCUS HANC TRIBUNAM FIERI FECIT AN. DNI MCCXVI SANTA MARIA ORA PRO NOBIS*. This was lost during the 1832 earthquake which caused the collapse of the roof and the right aisle. In 1938 the church was reinforced and the façade assumed its present appearance.

The gable façade is partitioned by pilasters and the main portal, rectangular in shape, has as a lunette a marble monolith which is a fragment of the pool from a Roman fountain. The rose window has eight rays and in the middle bears the inscription: *ANN. DNI ML. CT. LXII. IOHS F.* On the sides are two bovine protomes. On the left side rises a bell tower divided into three registers with pairs of two-light windows in the belfry. The semicircular apse is partitioned by four half–columns and by a stringcourse cornice. Above is an order of small arches supported by zoomorphic corbels.
The interior of the church has a nave flanked on each side by the arched walls of its two aisles. The aisles are covered by vaults, whereas the nave has a trussed roof. The presbytery is elevated above the crypt. The decorations along the walls were largely destroyed by the 1832 earthquake. On the left aisle are several fragmentary frescoes from the 14th and 17th centuries, among which is a *Pietà* attributed to Tiberio d'Assisi. On the first pillar on the left in the nave is a *Madonna of Mercy between SS. Biagio and Lucia* (1390), by the Maestro di San Leonardo. In the intrados is a *St. Stephen* (1476) done in the style of Fiorenzo di Lorenzo; below is a portrait of *St. Onofrio* (end of 14th century). On the intrados of the third pillar on the left is a *Madon-*

na with Child by Pace di Bartolo (mid 14th century). On the left side of the presbytery is an *Annunciation* by Pace di Bartolo who is also the author of the decoration on the apse vault, portraying the *Coronation of the Virgin Mary* and the *Visitation and God*, the fragments of which are preserved in the right aisle. Behind the altar is a restored 17th century *Crucifix*. Through a door on the left one enters the sacristy where, in a niche, are frescoed a *Nativity, Christ Conferring His Blessing, and SS. Mary Magdalen, Peter, Rufino, and Catherine*. Once again in the nave, one finds on the second pillar on the right a votive wooden panel inspired by Pintoricchio portraying a *Madonna with Child* (1938) painted by Giustino Cristofani and donated to the church as a vow. At the end of the right aisle is a painting with the *Death of St. Joseph* by Francesco Cilleni Nepis (18th century). In the counterfaçade is an early medieval sarcophagus decorated by a cross enveloped with vines (8th century).

At the end of the nave is a staircase leading to the crypt (not open to visitors) and on the wall is a votive slab with braid motifs (8th century) and a fragmentary fresco of the *Capture of Christ* from the 14th century. The crypt, the foundation of which dates from the 9th century, occupies an irregular space divided by two rows of monolithic columns topped with capitals taken from other buildings, perhaps recovered from the Temple of Janus or from the underlying Roman dwelling.

From the crypt one enters the **Casa Romana** (for visits, inquire at the Soprintendenza Archeologica in Perugia), which includes a cryptoporticus built with *opus vittatum*, decorated on the walls by a *viridarium* and by bands with ornate motifs and small pictures with mythological themes. Still readable are the episodes of *Polyphemus and Galatea* and the *Chariot of Apollo*, described by engraved verses in Greek and Latin. Farther ahead is a room with geometric wall decorations and a floor in mosaic designed on black background in which are included fish, the figures of scorpions, and crabs. Another room has a yellow and pink *opus sectile* floor; still another is without decorations. The house once belonged to someone highly cultured, perhaps to the Assisan poet Sextus Propertius. This is suggested by an epigram in Latin located where an unknown visitor in 367 A.D. is said to « have kissed the house of the Muse », perhaps referring to the poet.

Upon exiting from the church, on the left one finds the **Bishop's Palace** (for visits, inquire at the Diocesan Curia). This building was the scene of a well–known episode from the life of St. Francis, when he renounced his wealth before the Bishop Guido of Assisi.

When Francis had entered into the bishop's room he took off all of his clothes and, having laid his money on them in front of the bishop, his father, and all the bystanders, came out naked and said, « Listen all of you and understand. Until now I have addressed my father as Pietro di Bernardone; but since I have vowed to serve God I am returning to him the money, about which he was concerned, as well as all the clothes I had received from him, for henceforth I wish to say, "Our Father who art in Heaven", and not, "father Pietro di Bernardone" »..

(*Legend of the Three Companions*, 20)

The saint spent the last days of his life inside the building, before being carried to his beloved Porziuncola.

Nothing remains of the medieval building reconstructed by Bishop Marcello Crescenzi in 1612 and enlarged by Cardinal Emilio Rondanini (1653–1668). It suffered very heavy damage from the 1832 earthquake. In the entrance court is a bronze statue of *St. Francis*, copy of an original, sculpted in marble in 1882 by Giovanni Duprè for the square of the Cattedrale of San Rufino for the 7th centennial of the Saint's birth. Through a door on the right one enters the Galleria dei Ritratti (Gallery of Portraits), so named for the potraits of the bishops of Assisi painted on the walls. The vault was frescoed by Giacomo Giorgetti upon a commission by Cardinal Rondanini, with allegoric figures: *Dawn*, the *Storm*, the *Night*, and the *Rainbow*. At the far end of the gallery is a room painted by Giorgetti himself with the *Allegory of the Rondanini Family and Virtue*. In the opposite wing of the building is the Sala del Trono (Throne Room), decorated by Francesco Providoni on commission by Bishop Lodovico Giustiniani (1670–1685), with episodes from St. Francis' life, the *Pardon of Assisi* and the *Gift of the Porziuncola to St. Francis*.

Next to the Palazzo Vescovile begins the steep Via Giovanni di Bonino. At No.5 is the **Monastero delle Clarisse di San Quirico** (Convent of the Poor Clares of St. Quirico). The Monastero was built between 1447 and 1451 for a community of Franciscan Tertiaries subordinate to the Monastero della Beata Angelina da Montegiove in Foligno. Under the building are the ruins of a Roman structure, perhaps a basilica or baths, with a large apse vault, a brick wall, and sections of several columns. Above the entrance of the Monastero is a shrine with *St. Anne and the Sacred Family, God and SS. Quirico and Francis*, painted by Cristoforo di Jacopo of Foligno (about 1460). On the back of the shrine was an *Imago Pietatis* (Image of Mercy), now visible in a room of the Monastero. In the guest quarters (visits upon request) are several frescoes by the Maestro di San Quirico, a mediocre local painter of the 15th century: *Stigmata of St. Francis, Crucifixion and Madonna with Child and Saints*. The church was inaugurated in 1601 and was redecorated in 1899. Above one altar is a beautiful *St. Francis Praying* painted in the style of Caravaggio and attributed in the local literature to Ludovico Cardi, known as « il Cigoli ». Above the other altars are *Immaculate Conception* and *St. Anthony of Padua*, two paintings from the early part of the 19th century by the Venetian Tommaso Bracchi. In the choir is a *Madonna with Child and the Souls of Purgatory*, signed by Cesare Sermei. In the interior of the cloister, in the dining hall, is a fresco by Tiberio d'Assisi portraying an *Enthroned Madonna Surrounded by SS. Francis, Anthony of Padua and Helen*.
Farther on, at No.1 of Via Sant'Apollinare, is the **Monastero delle Benedettine di San Giuseppe** (Convent of the Benedictine Sisters of St. Joseph). The complex is formed by the union of the Monasteri of Sant'Apollinare and San Paolo. The first was founded by a community which originated in the countryside and then transferred to a location near the city walls in 1286. The second once belonged to the Benedictine Sisters of San Paolo delle Abbadesse, formerly located beside the Chiascio River in Bastia where St. Clare found refuge, having fled from her paternal home to follow St. Francis. It was built before 1341, after the settlement of a dispute between the two communities for possession of the site. The communities

were united in 1452 by Pope Nicholas V. After the abolition of the Papal States following Italian unification, the buildings were bought in 1897 by the Benedictine Sisters of San Giacomo (St. James) *de Murorupto*, who then dedicated the complex to St. Joseph.

The two churches are joined at right angles. On the left, the façade of the church of San Paolo has a curtain–wall with rows of white and pink stones and a rectangular portal with a lunette; in a roundel is a portrait of *St. Paul* attributed to Dono Doni. The interior, restructured in modern style by architect Silvio Galizia, is decorated by eight lunettes with stories of saints dating from the early part of the 17th century; in a niche is a *Madonna of the Rosary* (end of the 16th century).

On the right, the façade of the Chiesa di Sant'Apollinare has a portal with a semicircular arch, with above it a rose window with small, twisted, smooth columns. The interior of what was formerly a church (visits on request), is divided into several rooms used as parlors in which important pictorial records of the 14th century are preserved. In the entrance on the right is the *Miracle of the Madonna of the Olive Tree* and a *St. Christopher*, by the Maestro dello Stendardo di San Leonardo. In another room is an *Enthroned St. Apollinaris* and a *St. Michael the Archangel*, in the style of the Maestro delle Vele, and a *St. Onofrio* by a follower of Pace di Bartolo. In the former nuns' choir are: an *Annunciation* and a *Crucifixion*, masterpieces by Puccio Capanna; *Stigmata of St. Francis*, by Pace di Bartolo; and *Madonna and SS. Rufino and Rocco*, from the end of the 15th century.

Pro Civitate Christiana, Galleria d'Arte Sacra Contemporanea (Contemporary Sacred Art Gallery), Georges Rouault, Qui ne se grime pas?, from Miserère et Guerre

Continuing along Via Sant'Apollinare one can see, in a garden on the right, a long stretch of Roman wall. On the left a stairway leads to the 14th century **Porta Sementone,** restored and reopened in 1926. On the opposite side of the street is the complex of **Pro Civitate Christiana**, a group of buildings occupying a large area delineated by Borgo San Pietro, Via Pennacchi, Via del Fosso Cupo, and Via del Pozzo, and also known as La Cittadella. It is the seat of an association for the laity founded in 1939 by Father Giovanni Rossi, which organizes missions, courses, and meetings involving Christian studies. Part of the complex utilizes medieval buildings. Noteworthy for their modern architecture, inserted into the ancient environment of the city, are the dining hall and its various facilities (1962–66) designed by Giovanni Astengo, the Christian Observato-

Porta Sementone (14th century)

ry (1960), the amphitheater (1952), the small chapel (1957), and the roof gardens, designed by Giuseppina Ciampani. The theater was designed by Gaetano Brusa and Giuseppina Ciampani. Within the Observatory scholars have access to a very rich collection of documents concerning Christ in history and the arts, which consists of over 50,000 photographic reproductions of ancient and modern art works, a specialized library with about 60,000 volumes, and a collection of 7,000 records of sacred music. Worth visiting is the **Galleria d'Arte Sacra Contemporanea** (access possible upon request), which includes about 700 works. Among these are: *Resurrection*, stained glass by Aldo Carpi; *Jesus Divine Worker*, by Giorgio De Chirico; *Jesus Calming a Storm*, by Gerardo Dottori; *Jesus Divine Worker*, bronze sculpture by Pericle Fazzini; *Crucifixion*, high relief by Agenore Fabbri; *Jesus Divine Worker*, terra–cotta by Emilio Greco; *Jesus Divine Worker*, by Carlo Mattioli; *Jesus and Lazarus, Pietà, Via Crucis*, bronze sculptures by Francesco Messina; *Crucifixion* by Fausto Pirandello; *The Parish Priest*, by Ottone Rosai; *Miserere et Guerre*, series of 58 *planches* by Georges Rouault; *Nativity*, by Mario Tozzi. In addition, the collection includes a large number of ancient and modern prints.

At No.3 Via Borgo San Pietro is the **Monastero di Santa Colette** (ring for visits) of the French Poor Clares. The church was built in 1910 following the design by Attilio Cangi, which imitates that of the Chiesa di Santa Chiara. In the lunette above the portal is a relief from the same date in neo–15th century style with a *Madonna with Child*. The interior of the church was renovated in 1968 by Franco Maroni; the statue of the *Madonna* is by Chiara Scheridan. Farther along, the buildings on both sides of the street date from the extension of the city planned in 1316. On Via degli Ancajani is the Istituto Ancajani delle Suore Stimmatine (Sisters of the Stigmata), founded in 1855 as an orphanage with a Casa di Lavoro per le fanciulle del popolo (working home for poor young women). The last stretch of Via Borgo San Pietro flanks the Benedictine abbey bearing the same name and offers a view of the lantern and the Romanesque bell tower before ending at the church square of the **Abbazia di San Pietro**. A church located outside of the city and dedicated to St. Peter is on record since 1029. It once belonged to a Benedictine community which around the middle of the 12th century adopted the Cluniac reform, and then embraced that of the Cistercians. The present building dates from the 13th century and was consecrated by Innocent IV in 1253. The upper part of the façade was reconstructed in 1268, when the superior was one Abbot Rustico, as testified by a long inscription on the stringcourse cornice: *PASTOR PETRE GREGIS CHRISTI FIDELISSIME REGIS. HIC FIDEI PURE POPULUS STANS SIT TIBI CURE. HOC OPUS EST ACTUM POST PARTUM VIRGINIS FACTUM. MILLE DUCENTENI SUNT OCTO SEXQUE DENI. TEMPORE ABBATIS RUSTICI.*

The splendid façade is characterized by regular features done in the Spoleto Romanesque style. It is divided into two registers by a cornice formed by small hanging arches, a motif repeated on the exterior of the apse, and into three vertical sections by pilasters. The central portal is decorated by two lions. Its jambs are adorned by a band with racemes extending on the architrave and in the arch, and by thin columns with zoomorphous capitals joined by a stringcourse. Another ar-

Abbazia di San Pietro (St. Peter Abbey, 12th–13th century)

chivolt has animal heads on the impost and at the top. In the upper register, above the portals, are three magnificent rose windows with wide splays; the central one has two orders of columns. The façade once terminated with a tympanum, torn down after heavy damage was caused by the 1832 earthquake.
The interior has a nave flanked on each side by the robust, rectangular pillars which separate it from the aisles. The nave has a ceiling with wooden beams supported by ogival arches; the aisles have barrel vaults. The presbytery is elevated by five steps due to the presence of a crypt (not open to visitors) and is covered by a dome formed by 31 concentric rows of jutting ashlars, probably a motif of Provençal origin. The walls were uncovered during a thorough restoration in 1954, which led to the removal of the Baroque altars. On the left of the entrance is the access to the Cappella del Rosario, for centuries utilized as the seat of the Parish, but now closed for restoration. Above the altar, reconstructed in 1831, is a painting of the *Madonna of the Rosary* (1611). Against the counterfaçade are two tombs which belonged to the Soldani family. On the left is that of Jolo Soldani, dated 1337. Another four tombs of similar style are located at the sides of the presbytery. One of these hosts a ceramic statue of the *Virgin Mary*, done in 1981 by Francesco Vitali. Below the main altar is an early medieval sarcophagus containing the body of St. Vittorino the Martyr, third bishop of Assisi and coprotector of the city. On the left side of the apse is a chapel with a cross vault, the ruins of the ancient *prothesis*. Within are several fragmentary frescoes from the mid 13th century with *Saints*, and a band with hunting scenes reflecting the culture of the times of Frederick II. In the Cappella del Sacramento, on the head of the left transept, are *The Annunciation*, a *Madonna with Child*, a *St. Vittorino* by Pace di Bartolo (mid 14th century), and a detached fresco with *St. Benedict between Two Saints*, repainted during the 17th century. A door on the right of the presbytery is the entrance to the sacristy, which replaces the ancient *diaconicon*.

Exiting from the church, on the right side of the façade is the entrance to the Monastero (visits upon request). The cloister was reconstructed in 1645 by Cardinal Francesco Peretti di Montalto. Beside a staircase is a wooden sculpture from the 14th century, largely repainted, portraying a *Madonna*, brought from the Chiesa di San Masseo. In the monastery chapel the altarpiece with *Madonna with Child between St. Peter and St. Vittorino* is signed by Matteo da Gualdo (1470 c.); next to it is a rare 14th c. wooden *Crucifix* brought from San Masseo. Along the corridor of the dormitory are paintings from the 17th century removed from the altars of the church, among which are a *Miracle of St. Mauro* by Girolamo Martelli, the *Delivery of the Keys* by an anonymous painter from Perugia, and the *Alms of St. Anthony the Abbot*. The square is enclosed by 14th century walls, through which opens the **Porta San Pietro** (St. Peter's Gate), a two–story tower with flat–topped battlements. On the left is Casa Capello (1921), designed by Ugo Tarchi in the neo–medieval style of Franciscan inspiration that was fashionable in Assisi during the 1920's. Ascending along the Piaggia San Pietro one reaches the Basilica di San Francesco. Passing through the gate, one enters the Piazzale Unità d'Italia with its parking facilities and intercity bus stops.

Eighth Itinerary

SURROUNDINGS OF ASSISI.
Convento and Chiesa di San Damiano, Eremo delle Carceri (The Hermitage), Abbazia di San Benedetto al Monte Subasio, Chiesa di San Masseo, Basilica di Santa Maria degli Angeli, Convento e Chiesa di Rivotorto, Rocca Sant'Angelo

At San Damiano
The Convento (monastery) Francescano di San Damiano can be reached by car from the Viale Vittorio Emanuele II, by turning at an intersection located at Santureggio. Nearby, in a pleasant valley shaded by poplars, is the modern **Stabilimento Termale (Spa) di Santo Raggio.** Recent excavations have uncovered the ruins of a nymphaeum (1st century B.C.), which consisted of a wall with squared stones and three outlets for the spring water, the largest of which was decorated with reliefs. Opposite was a catch basin flanked by two low walls. The discovery of votive objects during the excavation suggests that in ancient times the springs were used for cult purposes.
From Porta Nuova one can enjoy a 15 minute walk to the church of San Damiano along an unpaved road, in the midst of olive groves and cypress trees, from which there is a splendid view of the valley and the surrounding hills. Along the way, next to the ruins of a Roman tomb, one finds the small Cappella di San Feliciano, familiarly called San Felicianuccio. It was built to replace a very ancient church which stood on the site where the saint, both bishop and patron of Foligno, bade farewell to his followers before his martyrdom. The altar wall is decorated with wooden panels painted by Mary Berkley portraying in the style of Simone Martini a *Madonna with Child and Franciscan Saints; Annunciation*; and *St. Feliciano and St. Rufino* (1948).
By walking along beside the walls enclosing the cloister, one reaches a widening where, in a garden on the right, there is a statue of *St. Clare with Monstrance* (1912), by the Roman Cesare Aureli, which was formerly located in the church square. The pedestal was decorated with four bronze reliefs by the Florentine Giovanni Giovannetti which have now been moved to the interior of the Convento.

The San Damiano complex is an ancient Benedictine priorate documented from 1030. Early in the 12th century it was given to the church of San Rufino. It is in this church that the conversion of St. Francis took place:
While walking past the Chiesa di San Rufino, he felt inspired to enter it. He then began to pray intensely before the Crucifix, which spoke to him with touching benevolence. « Can you not see, Francis, that my House is falling down? Go, then, and restore it ». Trembling and astonished, the young man replied, « I shall do so gladly, my Lord ». However, he had misunderstood, thinking that he was to fix that very church which because of its antiquity had fallen into ruin. The words of Christ immensely delighted and overjoyed him; he felt that indeed the Crucifix had given him this message ...

Joyful over the vision and the words from the Crucifix, Francis stood up and made the sign of the cross. He then went on horseback to the city of Foligno, carrying with him a package of fabric of different colors. There he sold his horse and goods and returned to San Damiano. He found the priest, who was very poor, and, after devoutly kissing his hands, handed him the money. Then he began telling him the story of his life. The priest, astonished by such a rapid conversion, refused to believe him. Not wishing to appear foolish, he refused the money. Francis insisted, attempting to render his story credible, and implored the priest to accept him in his quarters.
The priest finally gave in to this second request but, fearing the reaction of the young man's parents, did not accept the money. Then Francis, showing sincere contempt for wealth, tossed all the coins on a window sill as if they were but a handful of dust.

(*Legend of The Three Companions*, 13; 16)

This gesture did not please Pietro di Bernardone who, after attempting unsuccessfully to bring his son back to his senses, forced him to return his money. The matter was solved before the bishop of the city, when Francis decided to renounce his father's wealth completely.
Returning from the Chiesa di San Damiano, joyous and enthusiastic, he made himself a hermit's habit and comforted the priest of that church with the same words of encouragement that the bishop had used with him. Then he returned to the town and, deeply inspired, began to walk through the streets and squares praising the Lord. As he finished his laudes, he actively sought the stones needed to restore the church saying, « Whoever gives me one stone will have one reward; for two, two rewards; for three just as many! ».

(*Legend of the Three Companions*, 21)

It is not possible to assess the extent of the restoration carried out by the Saint. The original church had only a nave with an oratory crypt and an elevated presbytery. Perhaps only after the arrival of St. Clare and a Damianite community in 1212 did the building undergo a radical change which consisted in the closing of the crypt and the construction of a dormitory above the nave. Afflicted by a chronic disease, St. Francis stayed there many times. It was there that he wrote the « Canticle of the Creatures » during the winter of 1224–1225. Following the death of St. Clare and her burial in the Chiesa di San Giorgio, the Poor Clares gave the complex of San Damiano to the Chapter at the Cathedral, obtaining in exchange the Chiesa di San Giorgio. A community of friars continued to occupy the Convento. In 1773 it was given to the Osservanti (Observants) of Paoluccio Trinci, who kept it until the abolition of ecclesiastical property in 1860 following the unification of Italy. In 1879 it was purchased by Lord G.F.S. Robinson, Marquis of Ripon and Viceroy of the Indies, who permitted the return of the Observant Minors. The most recent owner, Lord Peter Kerr, Marquis of Lothian, gave it in perpetuity to that religious community in 1983.

The church has a simple gable façade, built with irregular stones, on which there is an off–center circular window. It is bordered on three sides by a portico with segmental arches. In the church square there is a shrine (A) decorated by a local painter of the second quarter of the 14th century (Maestro di San Crispino), portraying a *Madonna with Child between St. Clare and St. Francis Introducing a Pious Man*. In the intrados are *God Conferring His Blessing,* and *St. Rufino and St. Damian*. On the exterior is an *Annunciation*. Under the arcade (B), on the right, are votive figures of *SS. Clare, Francis, Sebastian, and Rocco* (1510), attributed to Francesco Tartaglia.

Convento (Monastery) di San Damiano (13th–16th century)

On the right side of the arcade is the entrance to the Cappella di San Girolamo (C). In the lunette at the far end is a *Madonna with Child and SS. Bernardino, Jerome, Francis, Clare, and Nun in Adoration* (1517), painted by Tiberio d'Assisi on commission by Galeotto de' Bistochi. On the left wall, the same painter painted a *St. Sebastian and St. Rocco* (1522) for Sante di Santorello da Campello. Farther on is the Cappella del Crocifisso (D), built in 1555 and named for a venerated wooden *Crucifix* (1637), sculpted by Brother Innocenzo da Palermo. The work has long touched the faithful due to its tragic realism, although it has not received much attention on the part of art experts. It is said that the expression of the face changes depending on the location of the observer.
The interior of the church (E) has one nave which has an ogival floor plan and is

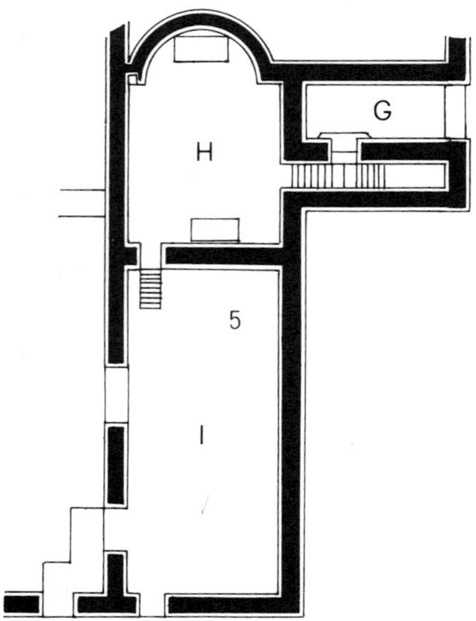

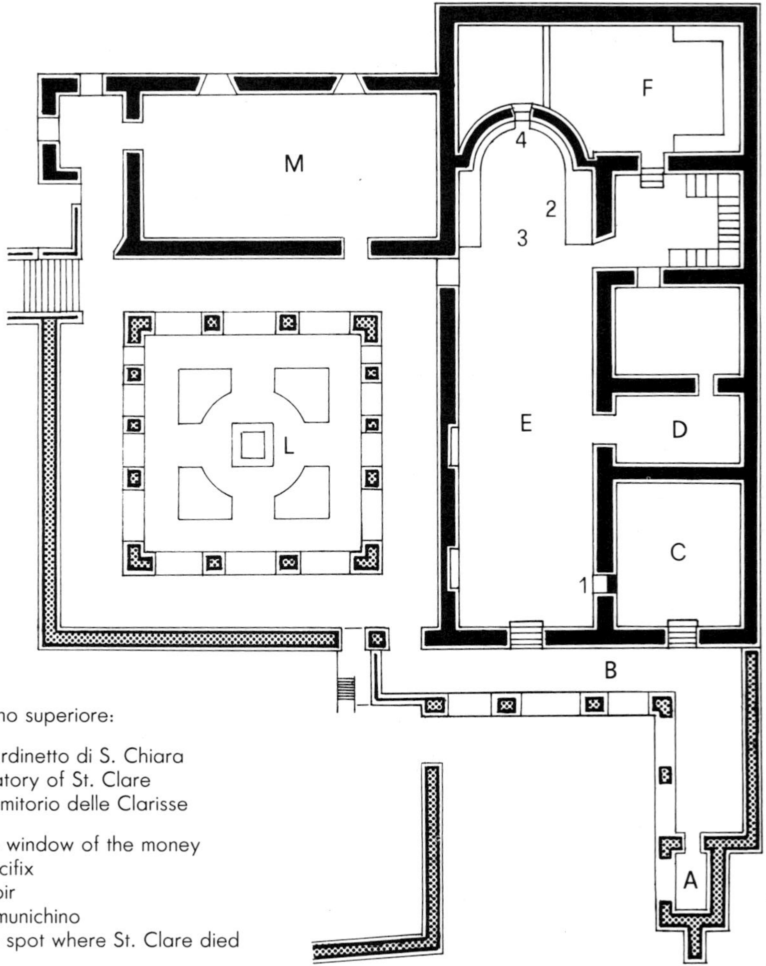

CHIESA DI SAN DAMIANO

A Shrine
B Arcade
C Cappella di San Girolamo
D Cappella del Crocifisso
E Church
F Coretto delle Clarisse
L Cloister
M Refectory

- piano superiore:

G Giardinetto di S. Chiara
H Oratory of St. Clare
I Dormitorio delle Clarisse

1 The window of the money
2 Crucifix
3 Choir
4 Comunichino
5 The spot where St. Clare died

Chiesa di San Damiano, Cappella di San Girolamo, Tiberio di Assisi, Enthroned Madonna and Saints (1517)

covered by a vault. The entrance at the façade is elevated by a few steps. The floor slopes upward toward the choir, which is covered by a vault and terminates with a semicircular apse. This somewhat irregular structure suggests that the floor was lowered to the level of the original crypt and that the elevated presbytery, coinciding with the overlying oratory of St. Clare, was eliminated.
Next to the door, at the beginning of the right wall, is a niche (1) called « the window of the money », where Francis threw his purse containing the money that had been refused by the priest of the Chiesa di San Damiano. The episode is represented on the sides of the niche: *St. Francis Praying before the St. Damian Crucifix; The Saint Throwing the Money before the Priest; Pietro di Bernardone Threatening His Son*. The frescoes are the work of a local painter active at the beginning of the 14th century, also the author of a *St. Agnes*.
Above the arch is a modern replica of the miraculous *Crucifix* which spoke to St. Francis (2) and which is now kept in the Chiesa di Santa Chiara. On the apse vault is a *Madonna with Child between St. Rufino and St. Damian*, repainted, which was discovered in 1927 and is attributed to the Maestro del Farneto.
The wooden choir (3) dates from 1504 and bears an inlaid inscription which reads: *NON VOX SED VOTUM, NON CLAMOR SED AMOR, NON CORDULA SED COR, PSALLIT IN AURE DEI* (Not voice but vow, not clamor but love, not strings but heart, sing to the ear of God). Above the stalls is an opening, called the « comunichino » (4) because it was here that the nuns received the Eucharist. From this location St. Clare bade farewell to the body of St. Francis when it was

brought to Assisi from the Porziuncola. The original grate is kept along with other relics in the Chiesa di Santa Chiara.
Through a small door on the right one enters the Sepolcreto where the first Poor Clares were buried and which leads into the Coretto delle Clarisse (private chapel of the Poor Clares) (F) containing the simple stalls and the lectern from St. Clare's time. On the back wall, built in the 15th century, is a fresco with a *Crucifixion* (1482) by Pierantonio Mezzastris. On the left is a niche where St. Francis once sought refuge when fleeing from his father. This episode is described in a 15th century tablet by the Maestro di San Quirico, stolen recently and replaced by a photographic reproduction.
Ascending along a narrow stairway, one arrives at the Oratorio di Santa Chiara (H). Halfway through there is a small terrace, called the « Giardinetto (small garden) di Santa Chiara » (G), which faces onto the Spoleto Valley. According to tradition, it is on this very spot that St. Francis composed his Canticle of the Creatures, one of the first and highest expressions of Italian poetry. A tablet is attached to the wall with the text of the Canticle and a bronze relief by Vincenzo Rosignoli with *St. Francis Chanting the Canticle of the Creatures*.
The Oratory of St. Clare is a small room with an apse covered by a barrel vault. The pictorial decoration of the vault, largely redone by Leone Bracaloni and following the original design, includes three roundels with a *Madonna with Child, St. Francis* and *St. Clare*. In the triumphal arch is *The Apocalyptic Throne and the Four Evangelists*. The Santissimo Sacramento was kept in a niche on the left of the altar and was worshipped by St. Clare and the Poor Clares who are represented on the adjacent wall.
The relics, formerly displayed in a showcase in the back wall, have been replaced by photographic reproductions and moved into the interior of the Convento.
Climbing up three steps one enters the Dormitorio delle Clarisse (dormitory of the Poor Clares) (I), a large, barren room with trussed roof and brick floor. On the left wall, a cross indicates the spot where St. Clare died on the evening of August 11, 1253 (5). Next to it is a bronze panel with *The Approval of the Rule* (1920) by Giovanni Giovannnetti. On the back wall is a wooden Crucifix from the 17th century. According to tradition, in September 1240 St. Clare stood in a nearby doorway holding a monstrance and thereby put to flight the Saracen troops of Emperor Frederick II who were led by Vitale d'Aversa and were about to attack the city. According to a different tradition, the episode occurred in the refectory.

By Imperial order, ranks of soldiers and swarms of archers as crowded as bees in a nest were stationed nearby, ready to devastate the campsites and to take the city. During an enemy attack on the city of Assisi, a place which is special to the Lord, the army was approaching the gates when the Saracens, the worst possible kind of people, thirsty for Christian blood and capable of any inhuman atrocity, stormed into the vicinity of the church of St. Damian and entered, within the bounds of the convent, indeed inside the cloister itself.
The hearts of those women were terrorized, their voices trembling with fear, and they went to their mother superior weeping. Without a shade of fear in her heart she de-

34.

35.

36.

37.

38.

39.

40.

41.

42.

43.

manded that although seriously ill she be carried to the door and left before the enemy. She was preceded only by the silver case covered with ivory in which, with great devotion, the Body of the Saint of Saints was kept.
Prostrate in prayer before the Lord and in tears, she spoke to Him saying, « Oh, my Lord, do you wish to deliver to the hands of pagans your defenceless servants whom I have raised for the sake of your love? I beg you Lord, protect these your servants whom I alone cannot save ». Immediately a child–like voice resounded in her ears from the new ark of grace saying, « I shall protect you always! » « My Lord », she added, « also protect, if you would, this city which maintains us for the sake of your love ». And Christ replied, « It must withstand hardships, but it will be defended through My protection ».
Then the virgin, raising her face dampened with tears, comforted her weeping sisters. « I assure you, my children, that you will come to no harm. Only have faith in the Lord ». Immediately, the boldness of those brutes was checked and replaced by fear. Fleeing hurriedly the walls they had climbed, they were defeated by the strength of a nun's prayer.

(Tommaso da Celano, *Legend of St. Clare*, 21–22)

Attached to the church is a pleasant **cloister** from the 16th century (L) which is normally filled with flowers and birds. To the right of the entrance is a bronze panel with *St. Francis Repairing the Chiesa di San Damiano* (1920) by Giovanni Giovannetti. On the corner wall are painted an *Annunciation* and *Stigmata of St. Francis* (1507), by Eusebio da San Giorgio of Perugia, on commission by the city Priors. On one side of the cloister is the **Refettorio** (refectory) (M), a dark, rectangular room covered by low cross vaults which contains simple tables and the original benches. A flower vase and a cross indicate the seat which was once occupied by the Saint. The frescoes at the top of the opposite walls, done by disciples of Cesare Sermei, are entitled: *Crucifixion with St. Francis in Adoration and Angels with the Instruments of the Passion; St. Clare Blessing the Loaves in the Presence of Gregory IX, by Engraving them with the Sign of the Cross.*
In the Convento's cloister are kept a 14th century wooden panel by the Maestro del Farneto, formerly in the Coretto delle Clarisse, which portrays a *Madonna with Child and the Blessed Corrado da Offida* and two bronze panels by Giovanni Giovannetti portraying *St. Clare Blessing the Loaves* and *St. Francis Composing the Canticle of the Creatures* (1920). Also present are important relics brought from the Oratorio di Santa Chiara: an ivory ciborium with silver crescent (12th century), utilized by St. Clare to put the Saracens to flight; a silver cup (13th century); a small bronze bell, used by St. Clare to call the nuns; an alabaster monstrance; a breviary written by Brother Leo for St. Clare; a pectoral silver cross (13th century) belonging to St. Bonaventure.

At the Carceri (The Hermitage)
Through Porta Cappuccini a well–kept road climbs the hill of St. Rufino. After about four kilometers, one arrives at the Eremo delle Carceri (The Hermitage). At first the road gradually ascends through olive groves. As the slope becomes steep-

er, the cultivated fields give way to the thick vegetation of small bay oaks, holm oaks, and hornbeams, decorated in the spring by bright yellow broom flowers. At the foot of the mountain is the Spoleto Valley with the towns of Bastia, Santa Maria degli Angeli, Cannara and, farther east, Foligno. Many locations along the road offer beautiful views of the Rocca.

The Eremo delle Carceri is hidden in a deep gorge amongst oaks and holm oaks at an elevation of about 800 meters, and is enclosed by the cloister walls. There is access to the woods through an arch decorated by a *Madonna with Child between St. Francis and St. Clare*, by Carlo Gino Venanzi. Beyond this is the beginning of an unpaved road flanked by low walls and which leads to the gate of the monastery.

During the early Christian period, this mountain was a shelter for hermits who initiated solitary meditation in its grottos near a small chapel called *Santa Maria Carcerum* or *ad Carceres* (of the prisons), a reference to the habit of living removed from the rest of the world. This solitary spot was special to St. Francis and he spent time here in contemplation with his early companions. In the early 14th century this became the shelter for friars who were protected from the anger of John XXII by the Comune of Assisi until they were expelled in 1340 by Minister General Gerardo degli Oddi. In 1373 it was given to Paoluccio Trinci, founder of the Obser-

Eremo delle Carceri (Hermitage), Chiostrino (small cloister, 15th century)

vants, who had the first cells built. The present Convento is the result of an enlargement realized by St. Bernardino of Siena in 1426.

By passing through a large vault one enters a charming terrace with a triangular floor plan, called the « Chiostrino dei Frati » (friars' small cloister). This is located on a wall overlooking the « Fosso (ravine) delle Carceri », a steep cliff at the top of which was built the Conventino, a complex consisting of two wings at right angles to each other. A monogram of St. Bernardino is attached above the door of the Convento. In the interior (not open to visitors) is the refectory with its simple 15th century tables and a fresco of *The Last Supper* (1595). On the upper floor is the dormitory with the friars' cells located against the bedrock. In the cloister are two wells. In a wing on the right side a chapel was built (1970) for the liturgical services. Under a low roof is the entrance to the **Cappella di San Bernardino**. In the extrados is an apocryphal inscription which reads: *SANTO FRANCESCO PUOSE A QUESTA CAPELLA EL NOME DI SANTA MARIA* (St. Francis gave this chapel the name of St. Mary). The small room, covered by a vault, is decorated with a *Crucifixion and St. Francis* (beginning of 15th century), in the style of Giovanni di Corraduccio. On the altar front is painted the emblem of the Monti di Pietà (pawnshops). There is one French stained glass window from the end of the 13th century, with a *Madonna with Child* brought from the region around Lyons about a decade ago. Farther ahead is the simple **Cappella di Santa Maria delle Carceri**, a very small room partly dug into the bedrock. At the altar is a *Madonna with Child and St. Francis*, (1506) by Tiberio d'Assisi, frescoed over a *Crucifixion* from the end of the 13th century. Nearby is the coretto (small choir) of the friars (not open to visitors). Its wooden stalls are from the time of St. Bernardino. Descending a steep stairway, one can see on a lunette an *Imago Pietatis* (Pietà) from the 15th century. Further down is the **Grotto** of St. Francis, now divided into two rooms. In the first is the bed carved in the bedrock on which the Saint used to rest, using a log as a pillow; the second is the part of the grotto in which he meditated. Outside, above the entrance to the chapel, is a poorly preserved fresco of the *Sermon to the Birds*, interpreted as an allegory of the Franciscan mission and inscribed with the words: *RICEVUTA CHE EBRO LA BENEDITIONE DA SANTO FRANCISCHO, DIVISENSI IN QUATRO PARTE E PRESERO LE QUATRO PARTE DEL MONDO, INDECHANDO LORO CHE ESO SANTO FRANCISCHO DOVIVA PIARA TUTO EL MONDO* (Having received the blessing of St. Francis they divided into four groups and departed for the four corners of the world announcing that the influence of St. Francis would be felt in every part of the world). On the floor is a slab with a hole through which one can see the bottom of the ravine which was opened by the devil when he was driven away by Brother Rufino, as the engraved inscription testifies. This episode is described in the « Fioretti di San Francesco » (*Little Flowers of St. Francis*, XXIX).

The devil, having taken the form of a Crucifix, appeared many times to Brother Rufino, telling him that he was wasting his time doing good deeds, for he was not among

those destined to eternal life. St. Francis learned of this by Divine revelation and let Brother Rufino understand that he had made a mistake believing it.
Brother Rufino again returned to his cell in the woods and while he was praying with tears in his eyes, the enemy again approached him in the semblance of Christ saying to him, « Brother Rufino, did I not say that you should not believe the son of Pietro Bernardone and spend your time in prayer and tears, for you are damned? What is the use of tormenting yourself while you live, if you will be damned when you die? » And immediately Brother Rufino replied, « Open your mouth so I may defecate in it ». At this, the devil immediately fled in anger causing such a storm and jumble of stones from the overhanging Mount Subasio that the mass of rocks spread over a wide area; and the rocks struck with such force as they fell that they caused huge sparks in the valley. As a result of the terrible noise, St. Francis and his companions, greatly astonished, came out of their chapel to see what was happening. Today one can still see that huge mass of stones.

The path is protected by a small wall built by Cardinal Alessandro Peretti di Montalto in 1609. A legend relates how the underlying ravine was dried by St. Francis, so that the babbling sound of the water would not disturb the friars' prayers, and how the water reappears in times of calamity. In the river bed is a holm oak where, according to tradition, birds listened to the Saint's words. This episode, according to Franciscan sources, occurred at Pian d'Arca, near Bevagna. Ascending a short stairway on the left, one reaches the Cappella della Maddalena where Holy Barnaba Manassei, founder of the Monti di Pietà (The Pawnshops), is buried. In the woods above are the grottos of Blessed Rufino and Blessed Masseo. On the other side of a bridge, within an enclosure, is a bronze statue by Vincenzo Rosignoli, *St. Francis Freeing the Doves* (1882), a small scale reproduction of the group preserved in the Santuario della Verna. Here begins the so-called Viale di San Francesco, a charming path through the green holm oaks, where one has the impression of reliving the ideal of Franciscan simplicity and the mystic rapture evoked in the Fioretti. In a natural open–air theater is an altar made of two large stones which is used for liturgical services for the pilgrims. By descending a steep path, one reaches the grotto of Brother Leone. On the slope on the opposite side of the ravine are the other grottos once used by the first companions of the Saint: Antonio da Stroncone, Bernardo da Quintavalle, Egidio, Silvestro and Andrea da Spello.

At the Abbazia (Abbey) di San Benedetto al Monte Subasio Proceeding from Porta Nuova in the direction of Foligno, after about 800 meters one takes Via Panzo to the left. Having passed on the left the sports complex of **Stadio degli Olivi,** the road ascends the mountainside for about 6 km until it reaches the **Abbazia di San Benedetto al Monte Subasio** (about 700m above sea level).

The date of the foundation of the abbey is uncertain. The oldest date on record goes back to 1051 when it appears as a part of the powerful Latium abbey of Farfa. The wealth of the monastic center reached its peak in the 13th century, when dependent upon it were a hospital, ten churches and twenty–three chapels in the territory between Assisi and Foligno. At the end of the 14th century, the Monastero was abandoned by the monks and due

Abbazia di San Benedetto al Monte Subasio (11th century)

to its strategic location became a refuge for the exiled citizens under the leadership of the Fiumi family. In 1391 the abbey was stormed by the Perugian troops, allies of the Nepis. In 1399 the Comune of Assisi demolished the abbey, desiring to thus free itself of the problem of the rebels. In 1405 the abbey was given « in commendam », and so remained until 1834 when it passed to the Congregazione di Propaganda Fide. With the abolition of ecclesiastical property in 1860 it passed into private hands. It was re–acquired by the Benedictines of San Pietro sul Monte Subasio in 1945, who saw to its restoration with the financial assistance of the Italian government.

Of the abbey complex there now remain only the ruins of the surrounding outer walls. The church is from the second half of the 11th century. It has a floor plan in the form of an Egyptian cross, with a single nave without a covering, a raised presbytery, and a crypt divided into five small aisles having eight columns with leaved capitals. In another part of the complex there is an older crypt which is evidence of an older settlement. It is supported by three columns and is perhaps from the 7th or 8th century, analogous with that of San Silvestro di Collepino on Monte Subasio.

At San Masseo

By traveling from the complex of San Damiano for about 15 minutes along an unpaved road through cultivated fields, one arrives at the Romanesque Chiesa di San Masseo, now part of a homestead. The Benedictine priorate of San Masseo, or San Matteo *de plathea*, was founded in 1059, according to some sources in 1091, by

Lupone di Monaldo Count of Postignano and Gaifana. In 1130 the son of Lupone, Bonconte, gave the church to the Abbazia di Sassovivo di Foligno, which kept it until 1503. It was then incorporated, along with its goods, into the Abbazia di San Pietro di Assisi, to which it still belongs.
Of the original structure, ruined by the earthquake of 1832, there remains only the semicircular apse divided by half–columns with small, suspended arches, and cut off at the top by the slope of the roof. Through a small door on the valley side, one enters the crypt, a small room with one nave and two aisles covered by cross vaults which are supported by six spoil columns with rough–hewn Romanesque capitals. In a corner is an early Christian sarcophagus.

At Santa Maria degli Angeli
Indispensable for the completion of one's knowledge of the city is a visit to the Santuario di Santa Maria degli Angeli, located 4.3 km from Assisi, in which there are many sites important to the story of the Franciscan movement. Those who cannot arrive by car may easily make use of public transportation, which connects Assisi with the train station and stops at the side of the Basilica.
Upon leaving Porta San Pietro, one takes Viale Marconi which passes alongside the city wall. A tablet is attached to it in memory of Colonel Valentin Müller, medical officer and commander of the German garrison in Assisi during the Second World War, who was instrumental in having Assisi declared a hospital city, thus saving its art treasures from destruction. Arriving at a crossroad, one takes the road descending on the right, which passes by the Istituto Serafico per sordomuti e per ciechi (Seraphic Institute for Deaf–Mutes and the Blind), built in 1935–40 by architect Ugo Tarchi. Just ahead on the left, is an unpaved road leading to the Pontificio Seminario Regionale Umbro (Umbrian Regional Pontifical Seminary), designed by architect Giuseppe Momo in 1930 in the neo–Romanesque style, which was at its peak in Assisi just after the First World War. Beside this is the Chiesa di San Niccolò dell'Orto, seat of a community of Poor Clares since 1342. Within is a frescoed *Crucifixion* from the beginning of the 17th century.

The road descends through an olive grove, passing below the Convento di San Francesco. At the bottom of the descent is **Casa Gualdi**, the ancient Ospedale di San Salvatore delle Pareti, already in existence in 1193 along Via Francigena and run by the Ordine dei Crociferi (Order of Crossbearers). In 1560 it was given to the Augustines of Perugia, who kept it until the abolition of ecclesiastical property in 1860. In the chapel, now used for secular purposes, is a fresco by Dono Doni, representing an *Enthroned St. Augustine and Saints*. On the façade, restored in neo–Renaissance style, is attached a relief depicting *St. Francis Dying and Blessing the City* (1910), by Colombo Graziani. The episode is narrated in the Fioretti (*Little Flowers of St. Francis*).

And arriving at a hospital that was on the way, Saint Francis said to those who were carrying him, « Put me on the ground facing the city ». And placed facing Assisi, he blessed the city with many benedictions saying, « May you be blessed by God, Holy

City, for because of you many souls will be saved, and within you many servants of God will live, and from you many will be chosen for the Kingdom of Eternal Life ». And having said these words, he was then taken onward to Santa Maria degli Angeli.

The road continues straight across the Umbrian plain, through cultivated fields and past the occasional residence, in the direction of the Sanctuary of the Porziuncola, the high dome of which can be seen against the horizon. Turning in the opposite direction, one can see a magnificent panorama of the city of Assisi, extend ing along the western flank of the Asio Hill. The view is particularly impressive at sunset, when the sunlight accentuates the rose color of the Subasian stone in which the city is built. This was the view seen through the train windows by the Danish poet Johannes Jorgensen (1911):
A few moments later, an entire city appears like a white band next to Monte Subasio, and it happens that for the third time I have arrived at Assisi.
I cannot take my eyes off her. The train goes around Mt. Subasio. I see the gorge of the Carceri and, in the midst of green vineyards, the little church of Rivotorto with its cusped façade and pointed bell tower. I also pass near the Basilica with its square tower, where St. Francis is buried and the majestic Convento dei Frati Minori built next to her, which is connected, down in the valley, with the barbicans of its walls.
One after another, I recognize all the towers of Assisi. Above, near the dome, is the

View of Santa Maria degli Angeli

tower of the cathedral; in the center is the tower in the square; below are the other smaller towers of Santa Maria del Vescovado, of the Chiesa Nuova, of San Pietro. The sky, which has almost completely cleared, is a beautiful blue above the city. Soon we are near the station, and I see rising on the right, the Dome by Vignola which covers the little church of the Porziuncola. How well I recognize all of these!

(*The Pilgrim's Book*)

The road to the Porziuncola was paved with bricks around the middle of the 15th century for the processions which were held for the Festa del Perdono (Feast of the Pardon), in which thousands of pilgrims participated. In 1667 two rows of elms were planted on the sides of the street to give relief from the August sun. Cut down in 1743 by the Spanish troops, they were replaced by mulberry trees. Halfway down on the right is the **Cappellina della Madonna delle Grazie,** built in 1561 close to a venerated image. It was completely redone in 1877 after a disastrous earthquake. At the altar is a roundel with the *Madonna of the Graces*. Further ahead, in a verdant park, is Villa Carlini, formerly Fiumi–Roncalli, built in the 16th century.

To the left of the residential area is the train station, located on the Terontola–Foligno Railway and in service since 1866. The present structure was built in 1926. The modern suburb of Santa Maria degli Angeli began with the arrival of the railroad and the construction of the first hotels for travelers. Previously, next to the Santuario there was nothing but a post office and the building where the Capitano della Festa del Perdono took up lodging. The first homes were built after the unification of Italy, when a Papal brief forbidding the construction of private homes within a radius of 60 canes (about 150 m) of the sanctuary was repealed. The first public housing came after the opening of a plant by the Unione Italiana (1907), later taken over by Montecatini, for the production of chemical fertilizers. Then, in the 1920's the opening of the Costanzi flour mill and several brickwork factories offered jobs to a growing number of workers arriving from the countryside. After the Second World War, with the transformation from a predominantly agricultural economy to that of the industrial boom of the 1960's, the town grew very rapidly. At present, Santa Maria degli Angeli is the largest suburb within the Municipality of Assisi.

One enters town from Assisi by means of Viale Patrono d'Italia. The buildings on the right belong to the Suore Francescane Missionarie di Gesù Bambino (Franciscan Missionary Nuns of the Infant Jesus), founded by Sister Maria Giuseppa Micarelli. On the corner with Via Protomartiri Francescani is the entrance to the **Casa Nostra Signora delle Rose** of the Suore Francescane Missionarie di Maria (Franciscan Missionary Nuns of Mary).
In 1896 Sister Maria della Passione, formerly Helene de Chappolin de Neuville, acquired a farmhouse near the railway and established a community. Soon another piece of property was acquired near the apse of the Basilica, which for a long time hosted an artisan laboratory for young women. The church and the Convento were inaugurated on October 3, 1926, to celebrate the 7th centennial of the death of St. Francis. Proceeding along a cypress–lined road, one arrives at the church in Assisan stone. The interior, an imitation of the Lower Church of San Francesco, was decorated by the painter Gina Baldracchini of Florence with paint-

ings inspired by the mosaics of Ravenna (1926). In the apse vault is *Christ the King with St. Francis, St. Clare and Two Angels*. On the walls is *Sainted and Blessed Women in Procession, Wearing the Franciscan Missionary Habit*. By the same painter are the cartoons for the stained glass windows. The *Annunciation* and a copy of the *Cross of St. Damian* on the entrance wall were done by members of the religious community.
The road continues along the apse and the left side of the large Basilica, attached to which is the *Fountain of the Twenty–six Spouts*, rebuilt in 1610 by the Medici family of Florence, to which belongs the coats of arms. Cosimo il Vecchio (de' Medici) had already built an aqueduct for use by the friars which was renovated by his grandson Lorenzo il Magnifico in 1486. On the opposite side of the road is the second fountain, no longer in use, called the *Fountain of the Three Spouts*, built by order of Pope Clement VII Medici in 1526. In Piazza Garibaldi is the **Palazzo dei Capitani del Perdono**, popularly called « Palazzetto Mediceo », which hosted the magistrates charged with organizing the great fair held annually for the Festa del Perdono. The Palazzetto, two stories high with a columned portico and a loggia, was built between 1615 and 1620.

Basilica Patriarcale di Santa Maria degli Angeli

Located on the site occupied by the small chapels attached to the Porziuncola, around which a small Convento had risen, the Renaissance Basilica was decided upon at the conclusion of the Tridentine Council convened by Pope Pius V, in the same manner as the Santa Casa di Loreto, with the purpose of giving new momentum to the Franciscan Order and to further the practice of the indulgences of the Pardon which could be obtained at the site. Every year, during the first days of August, thousands of pilgrims arrived at the Porziuncola seeking refuge in the Convento and creating great inconvenience for the religious community. The Perugian Galeazzo Alessi, the most famous Umbrian architect at that time, was charged with drawing up a model, already finished on March 15, 1568, which received the approval of the pontifical architect Giacomo Vignola. Pius V permitted the use of the « malefici », the proceeds from fines collected in the Spoleto Valley, for the construction work. On March 25, 1569 the first stone was laid by the Bishop of Assisi, Filippo Geri. Due to the shortage of funds and the hostility of the friars, who with great anguish saw the locations frequented by the Saint and his first companions fall under the pickaxe, the work proceeded slowly for more than a century, beginning with the nave and the pillars of the dome. In 1638 work was still being carried out on a pillar of the dome, which was not finished until 1679 when a copper ball was placed upon the lantern. In 1685 one of the two planned bell towers was completed; the other was never built. The earthquakes of 1832 caused the façade and the nave vaults to collapse, but fortunately the dome resisted the tremors and the Porziuncola was saved. The nave was soon rebuilt in its original form by Luigi Poletti. The façade received temporary repairs until the present structure was erected between 1925 and 1930, following a design by Cesare Bazzani.

Despite the lengthy period of time required for its construction, its appearance conforms with the original model by Alessi. The outside is in the shape of a parallelepiped, scanned by Doric order pilasters, with a non–protruding transept and a semicircular apse. The elegant dome, 75 m high, rises on an octagonal drum in

which there are large windows with alternating lunettes and tympanums divided by Corinthian pillars and terminating in a lantern. To the right of the apse is a three–ordered bell tower, with barrel vaults in the belfry.
The façade of travertine and bricks is decorated by massive *Angels* designed by Guglielmo Colasanti. In two niches on the sides are the statues of *St. Francis* and *St. Clare*, done by Ernesto Vighi. On the tympanum is a colossal, gold–plated, bronze statue of the *Madonna* (1930), by Guglielmo Colasanti. In 1948 this statue was said to have moved, thus attracting to Assisi huge crowds of pilgrims and curiosity seekers. Below the arcade, next to the central portal, is a bronze relief by F. Biasia, dedicated to the visit by Pope John Paul II and the heads of the most important religions in the world to the Porziuncola, on October 27, 1986.
The interior, 115 m long, has one nave flanked by Doric pillars with semicircular arches which separate it from the two aisles; the nave is covered by a barrel vault, the aisles by cross vaults. The aisles host five chapels on each side, all with square floor plans. The dome rests on four huge pillars with triangular bases. At the far end of the nave is a short transept with lateral chapels and a deep choir with semicircular apse. In the large area under the dome, the small chapel of the **Porziuncola** (A) is lovingly preserved.

According to tradition, but without any documentary support, the small church dedicated

Basilica Patriarcale di Santa Maria degli Angeli

to the Virgin Mary was founded in the 4th century by hermits from Palestine. In 576 St. Benedict presumably took possession of it for his monks. At the time of St. Francis the chapel was subordinate to the Monastero di San Benedetto al Subasio and was isolated in the midst of the thick, oak woods. The Saint arrived there between 1205 and 1206 and, as it appeared run down, he restored it.

Then he moved on to a place called the Porziuncola where there stood an ancient church dedicated to The Blessed Virgin, Mother of God, and, which had been neglected and abandoned. He saw it in such a poor state that he was moved to compassion, especially since he felt great devotion for the Mother of all goodness. The Saint took up his abode there and completed the repair work during the third year of his conversion.

The habit he wore was similar to that of the hermits. He wore a leather belt, carried a walking stick in his hand, and wore sandals on his feet. But one day, while a passage from the Gospel was being read in the church concerning the order given to the Apostles to preach, the Saint, who had perceived only its general sense, asked the priest after the mass to explain the passage to him. The priest explained it to him in detail. Francis, upon hearing that Christ's disciples « must possess neither gold, nor silver, nor money, nor must they carry a haversack, or bread, or a walking stick, or have shoes, or two robes, but only preach the Kingdom of God and penance », immediately rejoiced in the Holy Spirit and exclaimed, « This I desire, this I request, this I long to do with all my heart! ».

(Tommaso da Celano, *Vita* I, 21–22)

Having obtained the approval of the Rule by Innocent III, and after a short stay at Rivotorto, the Saint asked the Abbot of the Monastery of San Benedetto, Teobaldo, for the use of the Porziuncola. He then settled there with a small group of companions. The friars lived in poverty next to the chapel, in huts made of branches.

Here began the Order of the Minors, and their noble organization rose as large and harmonious as if it were truly resting on solid foundations. The Saint loved this place more than any other, and ordered his brothers to love it with special devotion. He wanted it to be guarded always as a symbol of the humility and utmost poverty of the Order. He left its ownership to others, while keeping for himself and his followers only its use.

(Tommaso da Celano, *Vita* II, 19)

The general chapters of the friars used to be held on the plain of Santa Maria degli Angeli. The most famous is the Chapter of the Mats of May 1217 or 1219, in which over five thousand friars participated, lodged in huts made of leaf branches. According to tradition, the Saint obtained plenary indulgence from the Virgin Mary for those who went to the Porziunola to pray, thus initiating the Festa del Perdono (Feast of the Pardon) of Assisi, celebrated on August 1st and 2nd every year.

The Porziuncola is a simple rectangular construction made of Mt. Subasio stone, with a gable roof and a portal with semicircular arch. The interior has the form of an apsed room covered with a stonework vault with an ogival cross section, perhaps dating from the restoration by St. Francis. The neo–Gothic shrine on its top, which replaces a small, rib–vaulted bell tower, was built after the 1832 earthquake. On the façade is a fresco by the German painter Johann Friedrich Overbeck, a member of the Nazarene group. Returning to models from the Umbrian Renaissance, the painter re–proposed the traditional iconography of the Perdono di Assisi (1829). The work replaces a fresco by Girolamo Martelli (1639) which had been superimposed on an earlier one by Niccolò di Liberatore (1492), mentioned by Vasari and reproduced in the stories of the Perdono of the Cappellina delle

Rose. At the bottom are the words of St. Francis: *HAEC EST PORTA VITAE ETERNAE*, referring to the Porziuncola. On the threshold is written *HIC LOCUS SANCTUS EST*. On the arched lintel of the portal the plenary indulgence of the Perdono is recalled by the words: *PETITIONEM TUAM FRANCISCE ADMITTO*. The carved wooden door is from the mid 15th century.
The interior, barren and undecorated, was restored to its original Franciscan simplicity and is an invitation to concentration and prayer. The altar wall is entirely covered with a majestic, painted wooden panel, commissioned by Francesco da Sangemini to Prete Ilario da Viterbo in 1393, as can be read in an inscription on the frame: *ISTAM TABULAM FECIT FIERI FRATER FRANCISCUS DE SANCTO GEMINO DE HELEMOSYNIS PROCURATIS. ANNO DOMINI MCCCLXXXXIII. INCEPTA DE MENSE AUGUSTI COMPLETA DE MENSE NOVEMBRIS. IN ISTIS PARTIBUS DURANTE GUERRA ET CARISTIA. PRESBYTER YLARIUS DE VITERBO PINXIT*. In the lunette is *Granting of Pardon to St. Francis*; in the center is *Annunciation*; on the right, from above are *St. Francis Being Tempted by the Devil* and *The Saint Being Taken to the Porziuncola by Two Angels*; on the left, from above are *Honorius III Granting Indulgence to the Saint* and *St. Francis Proclaiming the Indulgence Together with the Seven Bishops of Umbria;* in the ledge is *Miracles by St. Francis and the Virgin Mary*; on the frame is *Figures of Saints and Donors*.
The overhanging arch is decorated by two frescoed bands with the *Evangelists*, attributed to Ilario da Viterbo. On the left wall is an *Imago Pietatis* from the same period.
One exits the chapel through a lateral door on the right. On the exterior side of the wall is a tablet placed above the tomb of Pietro Cattani, second companion of St. Francis and first Vicar of the Order who died at the Porziuncola in 1221. On the same wall are two incomplete frescoes which decorated the altars next to the chapel. On the left is a *Maestà between St. Francis and St. Bernardino*, noteworthy work by a Perugian master from the mid 15th century, influenced by Beato Angelico. On the right is a fragmentary *St. Bernardino*, attributed to Matteo da Gualdo. The apse wall preserves the left side of a *Crucifixion* (1486), a masterpiece autographed by Pietro Perugino. It was repainted to a large extent and completed by Luigi Castelletti in 1830, after it had been rediscovered under a coat of plaster. It used to occupy the whole bottom wall of the friars' choir, which had been built behind the Porziuncola in 1485 and was torn down in 1569 to leave room for the Basilica by Alessi.
Beside one of the large piers supporting the dome on the right is the **Cappella del Transito** (B), the ancient infirmary of the Convento near which St. Francis died in the evening of Saturday, October 3, 1226. The chapel was intentionally preserved by Alessi in his project to erect the Basilica.
Here, in the last days of his life, the Saint composed the last stanza of the Canticle of the Creatures, dedicated to « Sister Death ». Sensing that the end was near, and awaiting it joyfully, he sent for Donna Jacopa de' Settesoli, writing to her:
If you wish to find me still alive, as soon as you see this letter rush to Santa Maria degli Angeli. If you do not come before Saturday, you will not find me alive. And bring along both a light grey canvas in which you may wrap my body, and the candles for my

Basilica di Santa Maria degli Angeli, the Porziuncola (13th century)

burial. I beg you to also bring me those sweets that you used to give me when I was ill in Rome.

(Francesco d'Assisi, *Lettera a Donna Giacomina*)

The Saint's death was thus described by biographer Tommaso da Celano:
When he felt that his last days were near, when ephemeral light would be followed by eternal light, he showed with the example of his virtue that he had nothing in common with the world. Exhausted by a severe illness, which was about to put an end to all his suffering, he had himself placed naked on the barren ground. In this manner he prepared himself for that critical moment, when the enemy could still release his rage, to fight naked against a naked opponent. In reality he was fearlessly awaiting his triumph and with hands joined he was tightly holding the crown of justice. Placed thus on the ground and without his canvass, he turned his face toward the sky as he usually did. With his look directed to the glory of God, he covered the wound on his right side with his left hand, not to let it be seen. He then told the friars, « I have done my duty; may the Lord show you what you are to do! »

(Tommaso da Celano, *Vita* II, 214)

The chapel stands against an ancient wall which is part of the Basilica wall. On the exterior is a fresco by Domenico Bruschi portraying *Death and the Funeral of St. Francis* (1886). The interior, closed by a wrought iron gate surmounted by a plaque held by small angels, preserves a shrine with St. Francis' *cingulum*. In a niche is a melancholic *St. Francis* in enameled terra–cotta (about 1490), by Andrea della Robbia. On the walls is *The Early Companions of St. Francis and Franciscan Saints* (about 1514), by Giovanni di Pietro, called « lo Spagna ».

Crossing (C)
The tapered dome rests on four large pillars. The pendentives are decorated with frescoes by Francesco Appiani, inspired by episodes which occurred at the Porziuncola: *The Renunciation of Possessions; The Benedictines Donate the Porziuncola to St. Francis; St. Clare Taking the Habit; St. Bonaventure Writing the Life of St. Francis and Visited by St. Thomas Aquinas* (1757). On the pillars are four stucco reliefs by Gioacchino Grampini da Foligno portraying the Cardinal Virtues of *Prudence, Justice, Strength,* and *Temperance*; and four colossal statues of the prophets *Ezekiel, David, Isaiah, Jeremiah*. The paintings below are by Stefano Montanari da Rimini and portray stories of the Pardon: *St. Francis Visited by Two Angels; St. Francis Obtains the Indulgence of Pardon; St. Francis Asks Honorius III for the Approval of the Indulgence; Announcement of Indulgence to the Crowds Convened at the Porziuncola* (1829). Opposite the Porziuncola, at the pier on the right is the *Monument to the Genoese Noblewoman Teresa Grilli Pamphili* (1762), by the Roman Tommaso Grilli; at the opposite pier is the *Monument to Antonio Folch da Cordona*.
Following the construction of the 16th century Basilica, numerous small private chapels surrounding the Porziuncola and connected with the Convento by arcades were torn down. Various distinguished noble families from Assisi and the surrounding cities, as well as local brotherhoods, became involved in decorating and

Basilica di Santa Maria degli Angeli, Cappella del Transito, lo Spagna, First Companions of St. Francis (about 1514)

maintaining the chapels found along the aisles. Although they were built during the Counter–Reformation, a historic period which has not been particularly appreciated in the past, they host the largest collection of late manneristic painting in Umbria. The chapels were once dedicated to the main mysteries of the Virgin Mary, to which St. Francis was particularly devoted.
It is convenient to begin the visit from the **left aisle.**
Cappella di San Diego d'Alcalà (1). At the altar is *St. Diego Healing the Sick* (Brother Ippolito da Coceto, 1710); on the left wall is *St. Francis Announcing to the People the Indulgence of the Pardon* (Benedetto and Giovanni Cavallucci, 18th century); on the right wall is *St. Francis Obtaining the Confirmation of the Pardon by Honorius III* (Baldassarre Orsini, 1787); in the vault is *Glory of St. Diego* and *Allegories of the Cardinal Virtues* (Anton Maria Garbi, 1773).
Cappella delle Stimmate (2). Built under the patronage of the Franciscan Third Order, it was decorated in 1630 by the Assisan painters Cesare Sermei and Giacomo Giorgetti. At the altar is *Stigmata of St. Francis* (Giorgetti); on the left wall is *The Verification of the Stigmata* (Giorgetti); on the right wall is *St. Clare Bids Farewell to the Body of St. Francis* (Sermei); in the center of the vault is *St. Francis Welcomed in Heaven* (Sermei); to the left is *The Tertiaries Taking the Habit* (Giorgetti); to the right is *Approval of the Rule* (Sermei).
Cappella della Deposizione del Signore (3). Built under the patronage of the Vigilanti family of Assisi, it was decorated around 1602 by Ventura Salimbeni of Siena and Baldassarre Croce of Bologna. The paintings on the side walls are by Piergi-

BASILICA OF SANTA MARIA DEGLI ANGELI

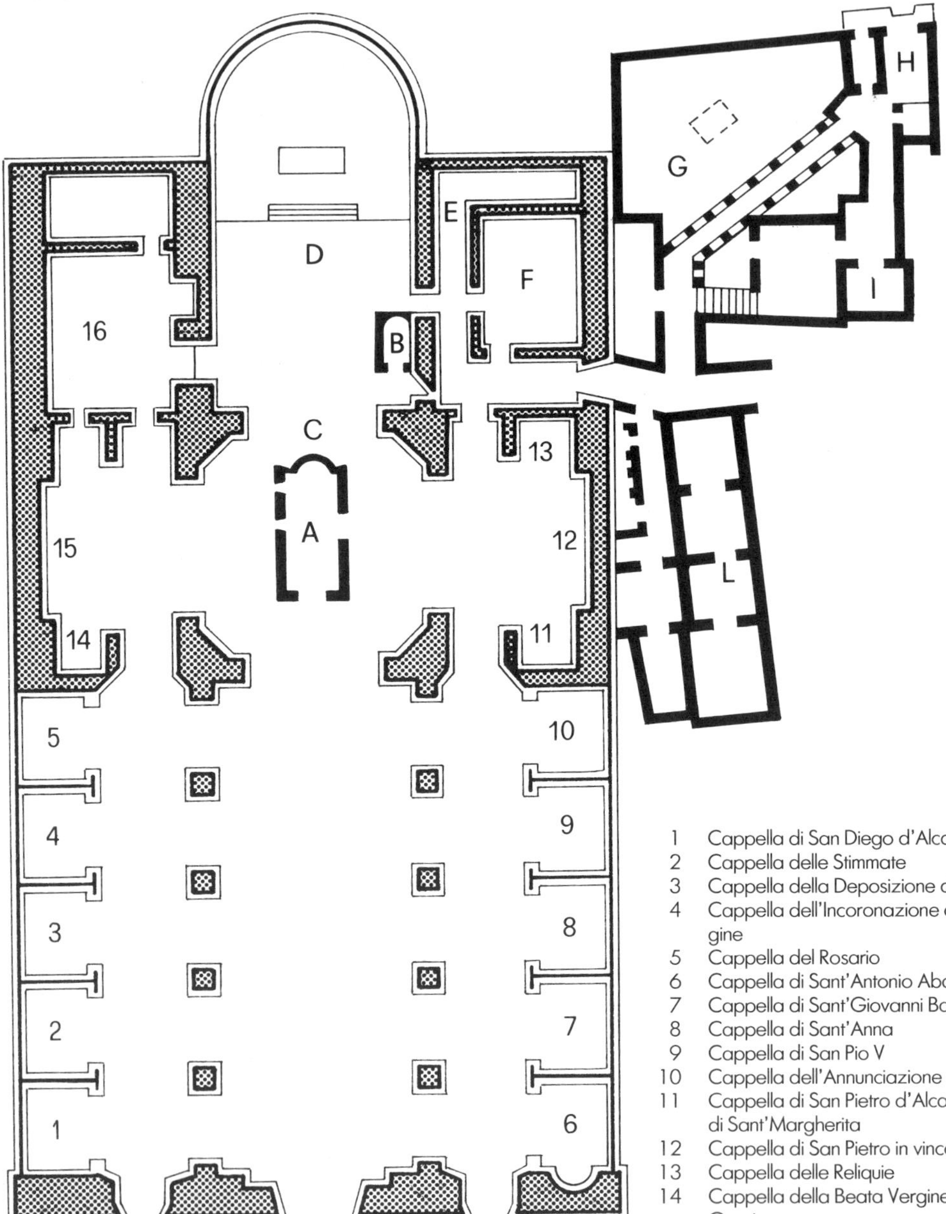

1 Cappella di San Diego d'Alcalà
2 Cappella delle Stimmate
3 Cappella della Deposizione del Signor
4 Cappella dell'Incoronazione della Vergine
5 Cappella del Rosario
6 Cappella di Sant'Antonio Abate
7 Cappella di Sant'Giovanni Battista
8 Cappella di Sant'Anna
9 Cappella di San Pio V
10 Cappella dell'Annunciazione
11 Cappella di San Pietro d'Alcantara e di Sant'Margherita
12 Cappella di San Pietro in vincoli
13 Cappella delle Reliquie
14 Cappella della Beata Vergine delle Grazie
15 Cappella di Sant'Antonio da Padova
16 Oratorio del Sacramento

A Porziuncola
B Cappella del transito
C Crossing
D Presbytery
E Entrance to the Crypt
F Sacristy
G Rose Garden
H Cappella delle Rose
I Cappella del Pianto
L Museum

rolamo Crispolti. At the altar is *Deposition of the Cross* (Croce); on the left wall is *Christ Taking Leave from the Madonna* (Crispolti); on the right wall is a *Resurrected Christ Introducing to the Madonna the Souls Released from Limbo* (Crispolti); in the center of the vault is *Resurrection of Christ* (Salimbeni); to the left is *St. Clare Taking the Habit* (Croce); to the right is *Dying St. Clare Visited by the Pope* (Salimbeni).

Cappella dell'Incoronazione della Vergine (4). Built under the patronage of the Veglia family of Perugia, it was decorated in 1603 by the Perugian Simeone Ciburri. At the altar is *Coronation of the Virgin Mary*; on the left wall are *The Mystic Supper of St. Francis and St. Clare at the Porziuncola*; on the right wall is *St. Diego Healing the Son of the King of Spain*; in the vault is *God in Glory Amidst Angels and Saints.*

Cappella del Rosario (5). Built under the patronage of the City of Perugia, it was decorated by the Assisan painter Carlo Morelli due to the initiative taken by Ottavio Spader, Bishop of Assisi from 1695 to 1715. At the altar is *Madonna of the Rosary and Saints* (Domenico Maria Muratori); on the left wall is *Martyrdom of St. Rufino* (Morelli); on the right wall is *Galeazzo Alessi Submitting the Project for the Basilica to Pius V* (Baldassarre Orsini). In the center of the vault is *Triumph of St. Rufino* (Morelli); to the left are *St. Clare Driving Back the Saracens and St. Benedict Restoring the Porziuncola* (Morelli); to the right are *Alms by St. Elizabeth of Hungary and Encounter between St. Dominic and St. Francis* (Morelli).

Right aisle

Cappella di Sant'Antonio Abate (6). The chapel was inaugurated in 1664 by the Confraternita di Sant'Antonio Abate. At the altar is *St. Anthony the Abbot* (Giacomo Giorgetti, 1670); on the left wall is *Miracle of St. Anthony the Abbot* (Anton Maria Garbi, 1773); on the right wall is *Baptism of Christ* (Michelangelo da Monticelli). In the vault are *Glory of St. Anthony the Abbot*, and, in roundels, *Prudence, Justice, Strength, Temperance* (Francesco Appiani, 1756). The baptismal font is by Father Leonardo da Casoli.

Cappella di San Giovanni Battista (7). The chapel was built under the patronage of the Locatelli family, which had it decorated after 1602 by Cesare Sermei. At the altar is *Baptism of Christ*; on the left wall are *Birth of the Baptist, Presentation and Visitation at the Temple*; on the right wall are *The Baptist before Herod, The Miraculous Catch of Fish* and *Dance by Salome*; in the vault are *Heaven, Sermon of the Baptist*, and *Beheading of the Baptist*. The bronze statue of *St. John the Baptist* is by Vincenzo Gemito.

Cappella di Sant'Anna (8). The chapel was built under the patronage of the Fiumi–Roncalli family. The altar painting with the *Nativity of the Virgin* is by Cristoforo Roncalli, known as « il Pomarancio ». The frescoes on the walls are by Antonio Circignani (about 1602–1603). On the left wall is *Wedding of the Virgin*; on the right wall is *Introduction of Mary in the Temple*. In the center of the vault is *Pentecost*; to the left is *Jesus Amidst the Doctors*; to the right is *Wedding in Cana*.

Cappella di San Pio V (9). The chapel was decorated by Baldassarre Croce of Bologna (about 1602–1603). At the altar is *Ecstasy of St. Pius V* (18th century); on the left wall are *St. Francis Welcoming Men and Women into the Third Order of Penance, Miracle of the Boy with Dropsy*; on the right wall are *St. Francis Obtaining the*

Basilica di Santa Maria degli Angeli, Cappella delle Stimmate, Giacomo Giorgetti, The Taking of the Habit by the Tertiaries (1630)

Pardon of Assisi, Proclamation of the Pardon. In the center of the vault is *Immaculate Conception*; to the left is *Visitation*; to the right is *Introduction of Mary in the Temple*.

Cappella dell'Annunciazione (10). The chapel was entrusted in 1591 to the Perugian noblewoman Laura Pontani Coli, who commissioned Federico Barocci of Urbino for the altarpiece and Perugian painters for the decoration of the walls. At the altar is *Nativity* (Domenico Paci, about 1830); on the left wall is *Procession of the Sacred Veil* (Silla Piccinini); on the right wall is *Donation of Mt. Verna to St. Francis* (Silla Piccinini); in the vault are *The Pardon of Assisi* and *Allegories and Stories of St. Francis* (Giovan Battista Lombardelli).

Right Transept

Cappella di San Pietro d'Alcántara e di Santa Margherita da Cortona (11). Above the altar is a statue of the *Nursing Madonna*, possibly from the very early 15th century and in late Gothic style, which was removed from the tabernacle on the façade of the Porziuncola. The painting with *Christ Adored by St. Pietro di Alcántara and St. Margherita da Cortona* (1760) is by Francesco Appiani.

Cappella di San Pietro in Vincoli (12), popularly called Cappella di Santa Giuliana for the saint whose relics are preserved in an urn. The grandiose Baroque altar was inaugurated by Pietro Giuliani da Foligno in 1675. The stuccos are by the Frenchman Jean Regnaud, known as Giovanni di Champagne, pupil of Bernini. Above the altar is *St. Peter Released from Prison*; to the left is *Statue of St. Feliciano*; to the right is *St. Bonaventure*. The roundel in the cyma, with the *Glory of St. Peter*, is by Gian Domenico Mattei.

Cappella delle Reliquie (13). Above the altar is a cupboard for relics. On the walls are decorations by Brother Luigi d'Amatrice (1888) and the two paintings from the 17th century, *Christ at the Pillar* and *St. Francis*.

Left Transept

Cappella della Beata Vergine delle Grazie (14). The chapel was formerly dedicated to St. Joseph. The bronze altar–front with *Stories of the Virgin Mary* (1977), by Tommaso Gismondi da Anagni, contains a Byzantine icon from Mount Phileremo, in Rhodes. On the sides are a wooden statue of *San Pasquale Baylon* (Gioacchino Grampini) and of *St. Anthony of Padua*.

Cappella di Sant'Antonio da Padova (15). The chapel was founded in 1718 by the Municipality of Perugia. At the altar is a magnificent wooden, polychrome *Crucifix* carved in the early part of the 16th century by an artist of Nordic background. The *God* in the cyma is by Brozzini. In a roundel on the left is *San Giovanni della Marca and San Leonardo da Porto San Maurizio*; on the right is *San Salvador da Horta, San Pietro Regalato and Santa Margherita da Cortona*, by Ippolito da Coceto.

Oratorio del Sacramento (16). The Oratory was reconstructed in 1984 within the Coretto d'Inverno dei Frati (winter private chapel of the friars). The opening of an entrance to the Oratory caused the demolition of the Cappella del Crocifisso, and the Cappella di San Pasquale Baylon and San Giovanni da Capestrano, where a painting by Francesco Providoni was located. On the entrance wall is the painting by Brozzini, *St. Anthony Receiving the Infant Jesus from the Hands of the Virgin Mary* (1718); on the right wall is *St. Pietro di Alcántara*, by Giacomo Giorgetti; at the altar wall is a large, gilded wooden tabernacle brought from the Monastero di Santa Chiara; on the sides are *The Virgin* and the *Angel of the Annunciation*, frescoes by Pietro Perugino, largely retouched by Luigi Castelletti in 1830 and removed from the exterior of the apse of the Porziuncola.

The deep **Presbytery** (D) was raised and modified in 1970 to adapt it to the liturgical reform of Vatican Council II. On the left wall is *Assumption of the Virgin Mary* (1885), by Brother Luigi d'Amatrice. Next to this is a wooden pulpit decorated with *Episodes from the Story of the Pardon* (17th century), by Brother Giacomo da Borgo San Sepolcro. The design of the altar is by architect Bruno Apollonj–Ghetti, with bas–reliefs by Enrico Manfrini representing *Christ the Master and Franciscan Saints*. The two bronze ambos with *Stories of St. Francis* are by Toni Fiedler (1970). The Papal Throne on the left was designed by architect Aristide Leonori when the church was promoted to Patriarchal Basilica with Papal Chapel (1909). The wooden choir, elaborately carved, was built between 1689 and 1700 by Franciscan artisans under the guidance of Brother Luigi da Selci. The stained glass of the three apse windows, portraying *The Assumption of the Virgin Mary into Heaven* (1897), and *Saints and Patriarchs* (1911), are the work of Francesco Moretti and Ludovico Caselli.

In the right transept is the entrance to a corridor which leads to the crypt (E), to the sacristy, and to the museum. Above the door is a painting by Federico Barocci of Urbino portraying the *Annunciation* (1596), brought from the chapel bearing

the same name located in the right aisle, and a lunette with *The Death of St. Francesco Saverio* (18th century).
The **crypt** was constructed under the new presbytery in 1968 based on a project by Bruno Apollonj–Ghetti. It was built in order to display the ruins of a building constructed by the City of Assisi during the celebration of the Chapters of 1220, an important episode in the life of St. Francis.

What follows happened when it was nearly time for one of the Chapters. In those days, they were celebrated every year at Santa Maria della Porziuncola. The people of Assisi had seen that by the grace of God there was a multitude of friars and their number was increasing day by day. They also noticed that when the Chapters convened the friars had but a poor and small dwelling covered with straw, with walls made of wicker and mud. It was the hut that had been built by the friars when they had settled in that location.
Having decided by resolution of the assembly, the Assisans, with great haste and devotion, built within the period of a few days a large building made of stone and plaster. They did so, however, without the consent of St. Francis, who was absent. When he returned from a different province to participate in the Chapter and saw the building, he was astonished. He feared that with the excuse of this construction the friars would build or would have built for them similar dwellings in the places they were occupying or would occupy later. Since, however, it was his desire that the Porziunola remain a model and an example for the Brotherhood, one day before the end of the Chapter, he climbed onto the roof of that construction and ordered the friars to join him. Then, with their help, he began throwing down the tiles with the intention of tearing the building down.
Some squires and other citizens of Assisi were present representing the City in order to protect the area from laymen and strangers arriving from everywhere and crowding outside to see the friars' assembly. Noticing that Francis and the other friars intended to tear down the building, they came forward and told the Saint, « Brother, this building is the property of the City of Assisi and we are here representing it. We order you, therefore, not to destroy our building ».
Francis replied, « As you wish. If this building belongs to you, I do not wish to tear it down ». And he descended immediately from the roof, followed by the friars who had climbed up with him.

(Perugian Legend, 11)

Before the entrance is a ceramic with *St. Francis Tearing Down the Building Belonging to the City of Assisi* (1970) by Italo Costantini. Behind the altar, sculpted by Franco Prosperi, is an altar–front made of glazed terra–cotta (about 1490) by Andrea della Robbia, brought from the chapel built after 1458 near the Porziuncola by Braccio II Baglioni. It portrays *The Crowning of the Virgin, Stigmata of St. Francis, and Penance of St. Jerome*. On the predella, from the left, are *Annunciation, Nativity and Adoration of the Magi*. The modern stained glass windows (1970) were done by Father Alberto Farina di Cangi.

The Sacrestia (Sacristy) (F) is a large room covered by a cloister vault. In the twelve lunettes are frescoes by Girolamo Martelli, with *Franciscan Saints and Stories of St. Francis. The Immaculate Conception* painted in the center of the vault, which fell during the 1832 earthquake, was replaced in 1940 by temperas by Elpidio Petrignani. The walls are covered by cupboards and kneeling–stools (1671) carved by Brother Giacomo da Borgo San Sepolcro. Noteworthy is a tablet with the *Redeemer*, attributed to Berto di Giovanni. Outside the sacristy, a corridor leads to the interior of the Convento. Turning to the left, one can see a statue of St. Francis holding a nest containing turtledoves. Further on, one passes under an arcade into a garden, which is what remains of the original woods where St. Francis and his early companions once lived. A group in bronze with *St. Francis and the small Sheep* (1916), by Vincenzo Rosignoli, recalls an episode from the life of the Saint, described by St. Bonaventure. Nearby is the famous thornless **roseto** (rose garden) (G).

A holy legend, described by Francesco di Bartolo in his *Treatise on the Indulgence of the Porziuncola*, tells how the Saint, tempted by the devil, rolled naked in the brambles. Miraculously the thorns of the brambles turned into fragrant roses, and drops of his blood stained the leaves. Then angels came to him and, after covering him with a white robe, led

Basilica di Santa Maria degli Angeli, Cappella delle Rose, Tiberio d'Assisi, St. Francis Proclaiming the Indulgence at the Porziuncola (1516)

him to the Porziuncola. Here Francis had a vision of Christ and the Madonna, who asked him what he wanted as a reward for his faith. Immediately Francis replied, « *That all those who, following confession and penance, enter this church, be forgiven for all their sins* ». At that time, Pope Honorius III was in Perugia with his court. Francis appeared at an audience carrying with him a garland of roses and put forward his request: « *If this meets with the favor of Your Holiness, owing to the grace that God has given to this place, I wish that whoever is penitent, has confessed and, if need be, is absolved by a priest, upon entering this church, be free both in heaven and on earth of the punishment and guilt for that which he has committed from the day he was baptized to the day and the hour in which he enters this church, and that from then on he not be submitted to any punishment* ». The Pope then granted plenary indulgence, the Pardon of Assisi, extended only one day of the year.

Next to the rose garden is the **Cappella delle Rose** (H). It consists of two sections. The section in the back was built by St. Bonaventure on the spot where the hut inhabited by St. Francis stood, and which was enlarged or reconstructed in 1344. The oratory in the front was built at the time of St. Bernardino da Siena, during the first decades of the 15th century. In the interior are represented *Stories of the Pardon* (1516), by Tiberio d'Assisi: *St. Francis Throwing Himself into the Brambles; St. Francis Led by Two Angels to the Porziuncola; St. Francis Asking Christ and the Virgin for the Indulgence of Pardon; St. Francis Obtaining the Confirmation of the Indulgence from Honorius III; the Saint Proclaiming the Indulgence at the Porziuncola*. The latter episode faithfully represents the Porziuncola, showing the façade decorated by Niccolò di Liberatore (l'Alunno), the friars' choir, and other chapels no longer in existence. The same painter did the frescoes in the internal, small chapel. Above the altar is *St. Francis and His Early Companions*; on the left wall are *St. Bonaventure and St. Bernardino da Siena* and *St. Ludwig of Toulouse and St. Anthony of Padua*; on the right wall is *St. Clare and St. Elizabeth*; in the vault is *God*. In the crypt below are preserved two beams which belonged to the pulpit from which St. Francis and the seven bishops of Umbria proclaimed the indulgence of Pardon. Through a lateral door one exits from the chapel into a small garden where a fig tree was planted in remembrance of the episode of St. Francis and the cicada. From here one enters the **Cappella del Pianto** (Wailing Chapel) (I), restored in 1926. Above the altar is a majolica (1931) by Amerigo Lunghi, inspired by a painting of Weeping St. Francis kept in the Sanctuary Greccio. From here, through a 15th century cloister, one returns to the church. Along the way, the ruins of the ancient Convento are visible. This was built in 1230 and enlarged in 1288 by Nicholas IV. In a court is the well of St. Francis. According to tradition, the Saint performed a miracle causing water to gush from this well. On the walls are attached various archaeological fragments, among which is a balustrade (9th–10th century) once used as an antependium for the altar of the Porziuncola. On the ground floor of the small Convento, in the refectory of Pope Nicholas IV, is a museum.
The **Museum** (L) hosts objects of sacred art, paintings, archaeological objects, and an ethnological collection. One enters through the **Sala dei Parati** (Adornments Room), where there are displayed in three cupboards valuable cloth and liturgical vestments from the 16th–18th century, along with numerous reliquaries and pieces of jewelery. In a glass showcase in the middle of the room is a *reliquary cross* with

Basilica di Santa Maria degli Angeli, Museo, Giunta Pisano, Crucifix (about 1236), detail

engraved glass; and a bone, bronze, and engraved glass polygonal *reliquary* (beginning of the 14th century), attributed to Pietro Teutonico. On the far wall is a fresco by Pierantonio Mezzastris, *Madonna with Child and Angels*, removed from the Refettorio dei Morti (Refectory of the Dead).
In the **Second Room,** known as the Sala delle Pitture (Paintings Room) are *Crucifix* on a wooden panel (about 1236), a rare work by Giunta Pisano; and *St. Francis* (about 1250), by the Maestro di San Francesco, so named for this painting which was done on the board used to wash the body of the Saint. This is referred to in the inscription in the book represented: *HIC MICHI VIVENTI LECTUS FUIT ET MORENTI*. Also in the room are *St. Francis*, attributed to Cimabue, but more likely a later copy of the Saint's portrait painted by Cimabue in Assisi; and *Pair of Angels*, formerly part of a Crucifixion, attributed to Lattanzio di Niccolò.
In the **Third Room** are the frescoes by Ugolino di Gisberto of Foligno, *Madonna of Loreto, St. Sebastian and St. Rocco*, brought from a shrine in Foligno; and *Sermon to the Birds*, bas–relief by Libero Andreotti. Embroidered lace and linen are displayed in glass showcases.
In the **Fourth Room** are paintings from the 17th and 18th century, largely mediocre copies of famous paintings. In a showcase is *Madonna with Child*, by Sano di Pietro (15th century).
In the **Fifth Room** are silverware and an interesting collection of archaeological, ethnographical, and folkloric objects brought from the Franciscan missions in Rhodes and Latin America. On the upper floor is the small, medieval Convento, restored in 1923. It consists of a kitchen and seventeen small, austere cells assigned to the saints and the blessed who lived at the Porziuncola. In these are kept prints and pieces of furniture. At the end of the corridor is a *Christ in Mercy* (1508) painted by Tiberio d'Assisi.

Next to the Basilica is the **Convento dei Frati Minori,** consisting of a large quadrilateral around a wooded cloister. It was begun in 1493 by the Blessed Bernardino da Feltre, who had the wing built facing Assisi. In 1527 a second body was added facing the east, and in 1559 the Refettorio Grande (large refectory) was built facing the south. The fourth wing, attached to the Basilica and with a Refettorio Piccolo (smaller refectory), was completed in 1606. At the center of the cloister is a well–curb (1620) with a large cistern. The lunettes of the cloister are decorated with *Stories of St. Francis* (1666) by Francesco Providoni; the lunettes in the wing toward Assisi were redone by Elpidio Petrignani in 1939. *The Wedding in Cana* (1668), frescoed in the anteroom of the large refectory, is also by Providoni. At the far end of the large room is a *Calvary* (1561), by Dono Doni, commissioned by Donna Finalteria di Meneco da Bevagna. In the Refettorio Piccolo is a *Last Supper* (1606), by Marcantonio Grecchi. On the walls are the paintings by Cesare Sermei, *Visitation,* and *Rest in Egypt*.
The large square in front of the Basilica was designed by architect Giuseppe Nicolosi in 1950 and built by the firm Esmeraldo Lunghi and Sons.

At Santa Maria di Rivotorto

Not far from the Chiesa di San Damiano, on the edge of the valley crossed by the

Santa Maria di Rivotorto, Cesare Sermei, St. Francis Inviting His Companions to Pray (about 1640)

old Route 75 leading from Santa Maria degli Angeli to Spello, is the Convento Francescano of Santa Maria di Rivotorto. The area takes its name from a stream which originates on Mt. Subasio and runs beside the church. On this spot once existed a hovel which St. Francis turned into his first home around 1208 together with Bernardo da Quintavalle and Pietro Cattani.

The happy Father, with his children, was still at a place near Assisi called Rivotorto, where there was a hovel once abandoned by everyone. The hovel was so small that one could barely sit or sleep in it. Often not having even bread, they would eat only turnips, for which they would beg here and there in their poverty.
The man of God wrote the names of the friars on the beams of the hovel so that each one, wishing to sit or pray, would know his place, and no noise could disturb their peace of mind in such a small and unimportant site.

(*Legend of the Three Companions,* 55)

When the community increased in size, Francis went to Rome from Rivotorto to ask the Pope for the approval of a Rule of Life. Having obtained it, the friars were forced to look for another home.
One day, while the friars were inside, a peasant arrived with his donkey, wishing to rest in the hovel with it. In order not to be sent away by the friars, he entered with the donkey and said to it, « Enter, we will do some good to this place ». As the holy Father heard that, he understood the intention of the peasant and became somewhat upset with him. The peasant had created confusion with his donkey, disturbing the friars who were silently gathered in prayer. Then the man of God told the friars, « Come brothers, let us leave, for God did not call upon me to arrange shelter for the donkey, nor to be in the company of people, but to show mankind the way

to safety by praying and giving useful advice. We must dedicate ourselves mainly to prayer and to giving thanks to God ». So they left the hovel to be used by the poor lepers and moved to the Church of Santa Maria della Porziuncola, near which they had already once lived in a hut, before they received permission to use the church.

(*Legend of the Three Companions,* 55)

The primitive hut was turned into a chapel by Brother Francesco Saccardo in 1455, who built around it a church dedicated to the Madonna. Finally, in 1586 Pope Sixtus V promoted the construction of a larger church, which was begun only in 1600 by Brother Filippo Gesualdo da Castrovillari and was completed around 1640. Following the 1853 earthquake, the church was reconstructed in the neo–Gothic style following a design by Brother Bernardo Tini.

The church has a gable façade in pink Mt. Subasio stone, and repeats the design of the Cattedrale di San Rufino with its three portals, the circular windows, and the large niche in the tympanum. The latter is decorated by a mosaic portraying two episodes which occurred in Rivotorto, *The Vision of the Fiery Chariot*, and *The Passage of Emperor Otto IV* (1955). Over the portal is the inscription: *HIC PRIMORDIA FRATRUM MINORUM*. Above this is the papal emblem and a tablet with the papal bull by Benedict XIV proclaiming the church Basilica and Papal Chapel. The flanks, reinforced by buttresses, and the shape of the bell tower, imitate those of the Basilica di Santa Chiara. The interior has a polygonal apse and a nave flanked by the pillars which divide it from the two aisles. In the nave is the **Tugurio** (hovel) of *Somma umilitate*, returned to its 14th century appearance by a restoration in 1926. It consists of three small compartments: the so–called *Bed of St. Francis*, where a wooden statue indicates the cell of the Saint; a small chapel with a 15th century altar top, above which is a *Madonna of Consolation*, votive offering from the 18th century left by a Polish pilgrim; and the kitchen or fire room.
Nineteenth century pictorial decorations simulating marble were removed from the church during a restoration campaign which is still underway. A number of paintings by Cesare Sermei (about 1640), inspired by episodes lived by the early Franciscan community, are still preserved, with the exception of the four which were lost during the 1853 earthquake. Those preserved are: *St. Francis Sending a Friar to Otto IV, to Remind Him of the Brevity of Glory in This World; The Miraculous Healing of Morico; His Companions Seeing Him on a Fiery Chariot; Francis Healing a Friar by Giving Him a Bunch of Grapes to Eat; Innocent III Orally Approving the Rule; Supper with a Friar Starved by Excessive Penance; Francis Abandoning the Hovel for the Porziuncola; Francis Inviting His Companions to Prayer; Francis Living and Fasting in Prayer with His Companions at Rivotorto in Prayer; Francis Receiving Egidio in the Hovel; Francis Listening to the Gospels and Choosing to Live in Poverty; Francis Followed by Bernardo da Quintavalle after Reading the Gospel.*
On the counterfaçade is a painting by Gian Domenico Mattei, portraying *St. Michael the Archangel* (second half of the 17th century). The stained glass windows with Franciscan episodes are by Father Alberto Farina (1990).

At Rocca Sant'Angelo
Leaving Porta San Pietro in the direction of the road to Perugia, one takes a de-

Rocca Sant'Angelo, Chiesa di Santa Maria della Rocchicciola, lo Spagna, Maestà (about 1514)

viation shortly after Ponte San Vittorino in the direction of Palazzo to arrive at the cemetery of Petrignano. From this point one travels for 3 km on a country road which runs alongside the Chiascio River to the village of Rocca Sant'Angelo, a medieval–looking castle in a scenic position facing the Perugian hills on a slope in the Chiascio valley. On the hilltop, outside he castle walls, is the Convento di **Santa Maria della Rocchicciola,** improperly called « di Santa Maria in Arce ». It was founded in the second half of the 13th century and is mentioned for the first time in a document in 1300. In 1380 it was given to Paoluccio Trinci for the Friars of the Osservanza (Observance). Before 1464 it was returned to the community of the Convento.

The small church found near the Convento largely preserves its original decoration which consists mostly of votive frescoes from the 14th–16th century. The most ancient are the frescoes in the apse vault, the *Presentation in the Temple, Christ among the Doctors,* and *Flight into Egypt* (about 1340), by the Maestro della Natività di Santa Chiara. On the right wall are *The Stigmata of St. Francis* (about 1315) by the Maestro di Figline; and a *Maestà between St. Francis and St. Clare* (about 1320) by the Maestro Espressionista di Santa Chiara. The *Crucifix* on a wooden panel (about 1470) is by Matteo da Gualdo. The *Madonna with Child between SS. Jerome and Anthony of Padua*(1487) in the counterfaçade, and the Saints *Mary Magdalen and Anthony the Abbot* are by the Perugian Bartolomeo Caporali. At the lateral altars are a *Crucifixion* and a *Madonna with Child and SS. Sebastian and Lucia* (1502) by Orlando Merlini. Above the altar is a *Maestà between SS. Francis and Anthony of Padua* (about 1514), by Giovanni Spagna.

THE CANTICLE OF THE CREATURES

Most high omnipotent good Lord, to Thee
praise, glory, honour, and every benediction.

To Thee alone Most High do they belong.
And no man is worthy to pronounce Thy Name.

Praise be to Thee my Lord with all Thy creatures.
Especially for Master Brother Sun who illuminates
the day for us,
and Thee Most High he manifests.

Praise be to Thee my Lord for Sister Moon and
for the stars, in Heaven Thou hast formed them,
shining, precious, fair.

Praise be to Thee my Lord for Brother Wind,
for air and clouds, clear sky and all the weathers
through which Thou sustainest all Thy creatures.

Praise be to Thee my Lord for Sister Water,
she is useful and humble, precious and pure.

Praise be to Thee my Lord for Brother Fire,
through him our night Thou dost enlighten,
and he is fair and merry, boisterous and strong.

Praise be to Thee my Lord for our sister Mother Earth,
who nourishes and sustains us all, bringing
forth diverse fruits and many–coloured flowers,
and herbs.

Praise be to Thee my Lord for those who pardon
grant for love of Thee and bear infirmity and tribulation,
Blessed be those who live in peace, for by Thee
Most High they shall be crowned.

Praise be to Thee my Lord for our Sister Bodily Death
from whom no living man can flee; woe to them
who die in mortal sin but blessed they
who shall be found in Thy most holy Will;
to them the second death can do no harm.

O bless and praise my Lord all creatures, and
thank and serve Him in deep humility.

San Francesco

Bibliography

This bibliography offers a selected list of documents and books consulted; it has been divided into thematic sections and put in alphabetic order.

General works

AA.VV., *Aspetti di vita benedettina nella storia di Assisi,* Assisi 1981; AA.VV., *Le fraternite medievali di Assisi, linee storiche e testi statutari,* Assisi 1989; Astengo G., *Assisi. Piano generale e piani particolareggiati di primo intervento*, Torino s.d. (ma 1958); Brufani S., *La vita religiosa in Assisi dal 1316 al 1367*, Città di Castello 1982; Bracaloni L., *Assisi medievale. Studio storico–topografico*, in AFH, 7 (1914), pp. 3–19; Canonici L., *Santa Maria degli Angeli: nascita e sviluppo di un paese,* Assisi s.d.; Cenci C., *Documentazione di vita assisana 1300–1530,* 3 voll. Grottaferrata 1974–1976; Cristofani A., *Le storie di Assisi,* Assisi 1866; De Giovanni C., *L'ampliamento di Assisi nel 1316,* in DBSPU, (1975), pp. 1–78; Duff Gordon L., *The Story of Assisi*, London 1913; Fortini A., *Assisi nel Medioevo, leggende, avventure, battaglie*, Roma 1940; Fortini A., *La lauda in Assisi e le origini del teatro italiano*, Assisi 1961; Frondini F.A., *Notizie storiche delle famiglie nobili e cittadine della città di Assisi* (sec. XIX), ms. Archivio della Cattedrale di S. Rufino; Giacanella U., *Rivotorto e il suo territorio*, Assisi 1983; Grohmann A., *Le città nella storia d'Italia. Assisi*, Bari 1989; Tini A., *Appunti storici sulle chiese d'Assisi* (sec. XIX), ms. Archivio della Cattedrale di S. Rufino.

Saint Francis and the Franciscan Order

AA.VV., *La questione francescana dal Sabatier ad oggi*, Atti del I convegno SISF, Assisi 1974; AA.VV., *La povertà del secolo XII e Francesco d'Assisi*, Atti del II convegno SISF, Assisi 1975; AA.VV., *Che erano gli Spirituali*, Atti del III convegno SISF, Assisi 1976; AA.VV., *Francesco d'Assisi e il francescanesimo dal 1216 al 1226*, Atti del IV convegno SISF, Assisi 1977; AA.VV., *Assisi al tempo di San Francesco,* Atti del V convegno SISF, Assisi 1978; AA.VV., *Espansione del francescanesimo tra occidente e oriente nel secolo XIII*, Atti del VI convegno SISF, Assisi 1979; AA.VV., *Movimento religioso femminile e francescanesimo nel secolo XIII*, Atti del VII convegno SISF, Assisi 1980; AA.VV., *Francescanesimo e vita religiosa dei laici nel '200*, Atti del VIII convegno SISF, Assisi 1981; AA.VV., *L'immagine di Francesco nella storiografia dell'Umanesimo all'Ottocento*, Atti del IX convegno SISF, Assisi 1983; AA.VV., *Diffusione del francescanesimo nelle Americhe*, Atti del X convegno SISF, Assisi 1984; AA.VV., *Il rinnovamento del francescanesimo. L'Osservanza,* Atti dell'XI convegno SISF, Assisi 1985; AA.VV., *I frati minori tra '400 e '500,* Atti del XII convegno SISF, Assisi 1986; AA.VV., *I Francescani in Europa tra riforma e controriforma, Atti del XIII convegno SISF,* Assisi 1987; AA.VV., *I Francescani nel Trecento*, Atti del XIV convegno SISF, Assisi 1988; *AA.VV., Santi e Santità nel secolo XIV*, Atti del XV convegno SISF, Assisi 1989; Esser K., *Origini e inizi del movimento e dell'Ordine francescano,* Milano 1975; *Fonti Francescane*, Padova 1978; Fortini A., *Nova Vita di San Francesco*, Assisi 1959; Manselli R., *San Francesco d'Assisi*, Roma 1953; Manselli R., *Nos qui cum eo fuimus. Contributo alla questione francescana*, Roma 1980; Miccioli G., *La storia religiosa*, in *Storia d'Italia*, II, Torino 1974; Sabatier P., *Vie de Saint François d'Assise*, Paris 1898; Stanislao da Campagnola, *Le fonti francescane come problema storiografico*, Perugia 1979; Stanislao da Campagnola, *Francesco d'Assisi nei suoi scritti e nelle sue biografie dei secoli XIII–XIV*, Assisi 1981.

Guide Books

Bellucci G., *Assisi cuore del mondo*, Bergamo 1989; Chierichetti S., *Assisi guida artistica illustrata*, Assisi s.d.; Cristofani A., *Vita breve del patriarca S. Francesco seguita dalle illustrazioni dei monumenti d'arte in Assisi*, Assisi 1859; Cristofani A., *Guida d'Assisi e suoi dintorni per Antonio Cristofani, condot-*

ta a fine da Leonello Leonelli, Assisi 1884; Desbonnets T., *Sulle strade di San Francesco. Guida spirituale ai "luoghi" francescani*, Milano 1986; *Guida de' pellegrini che bramano visitare i luoghi santi della serafica città d'Assisi...*, Assisi 1618; Lunghi E., *Assisi*, in "Città da scoprire. Guida ai centri minori", T.C.I., Milano 1984; Scarpellini P., *Assisi*, Novara 1973; *Umbria*, a cura del T.C.I., Milano 1978; Zimmermanns K., *Umbrien*, Koln 1987; Zocca E., *Assisi e dintorni*, Roma 1949.

Archeology

Antolini G., *Il tempio di Minerva in Assisi*, Milano 1828; Brizi A., *Tracce umbro–romane in Assisi*, in AAPS, II (1908), pp. 405–434; Forni G. (a cura), *Epigrafi lapidarie e romane di Assisi*, Perugia 1987; AA.VV., *Umbria–Marche. Guide archeologiche Laterza*, Roma–Bari 1980; Giorgetti D., *Umbria. Itinerari archeologici*, Roma 1984; Guarducci M., *Domus Musae. Epigrafi greche e latine in un'antica casa di Assisi*, in "Memorie dell'Accademia Nazionale dei Lincei", XXIII (1979), pp. 269–297; Manca M.L., *Osservazioni sulle mura di Asisium*, in "Annali Facoltà di Lettere di Perugia. Studi classici", XV, (1978), pp. 98–123; Strazzulla M.J., *Assisi romana*, in AAPS, 10 (1985); Temperini L., *Assisi romana e medievale*, Tivoli 1985.

Museum Catalogues

AA.VV., *Gesù nell'arte contemporanea. Catalogo della Galleria d'arte sacra della Pro Civitate Christiana*, in Assisi 1964; AA.VV., *Il Tersoro della Basilica di San Francesco ad Assisi*, Assisi 1980; AA.VV., *La Biblioteca del Sacro Convento di Assisi I. I libri miniati di età romanica e gotica*, Assisi 1988; Lunghi E. *Il Museo della Cattedrale di San Rufino ad Assisi*, Assisi 1987; Palumbo G., *collezione Federico Mason Perkins. Assisi*, 1973; Todini F., Zanardi B., *La Pinacoteca Comunale di Assisi*, Firenze 1980; Zeri F., *La Collezione Federico Mason Perkins*, Torino 1988; Zocca E., *Assisi. Catalogo delle cose d'arte e di antichità d'Italia*, Roma 1936.

Art and Architecture

AA.VV., *Giotto e i giotteschi in Assisi*, Roma 1969; AA.VV., *Pittura in Umbria tra il 1480 e il 1540*, Milano 1983; AA.VV., *Puccio Capanna*, Assisi 1989; Barroero L., Casale V., Falcidia G., Pansecchi F., Toscano B., *Pittura del Seicento e del Settecento. Ricerche in Umbria 2*, Treviso 1980; Boskovits M., *Pittura umbra e marchigiana tra medioevo e rinascimento*, Firenze 1973; Lunghi E., *Osservazioni su Dono Doni*, in *Arte e Musica in Umbria tra Cinquecento e Seicento*, Spoleto 1981, pp. 93–101; Lunghi E., *Affreschi del "Maestro della Santa Chiara" (e la primitiva decorazione del Duomo di Giovanni da Gubbio)*, in "Paragone", 381 (1981), pp. 58–65; Lunghi E., *Pittori del Quattrocento ad Assisi*, in AAPS, 6 (1982), pp. 49–63; Longhi R., *La pittura umbra della prima metà del Trecento*, in "Paragone", 281–283 (1973), pp. 3–44; Todini F., *Pittura del Duecento e del Trecento in Umbria e il cantiere di Assisi*, in *La Pittura in Italia. Le Origini*, Milano 1985, pp. 317–355; Todini F., *La Pittura Umbra. Dal Duecento al Primo Cinquecento*, Milano 1989; Vignoli F., *L'Alessi in Assisi*, in AAPS, 13 (1986), pp. 197–243.

Basilica di San Francesco

AA.VV. *Il Sacro Convento di Assisi*, Bari 1989; Bellosi L., *La pecora di Giotto*, Torino 1985; Belting H., *Die Oberkirche von San Francesco in Assisi*, Berlin 1977; Iacovelli A., *La Basilica di San Francesco ad Assisi*, in "San Francesco patrono d'Italia", 1967–1973; Kleinschimdt B., *Die Basilica S. Francesco in Assisi*, Berlin 1915–1928; Ludovico da Pietralunga (fra'), *Descrizione della Basilica di S. Francesco e di altri Santuari di Assisi* (1570 c.), ed. a cura di P. Scarpellini, Treviso 1982; Marchini G., *Le vetrate dell'Umbria*, Roma 1973; Nessi S., *La Basilica di S. Francesco in Assisi e la sua documentazione storica*, Assisi 1982; Poeschke J., *Die Kirke San Francesco in Assisi und ihre Wandmalereien,* Munchen 1985;

Previtali G., *Giotto e la sua bottega*, Milano 1967; Rocchi G., *La Basilica di San Francesco ad Assisi*, Firenze 1982; Romanini A.M. (a cura di), *Roma anno 1300*, Roma 1983; Ruf G., *Giotto in Assisi*, Assisi 1974; Zaccaria G., *Diario storico della Basilica e Sacro Convento di S. Francesco in Assisi (1220–1927)*, in MF (1963–1964).

History of civil and religious buildings

AA.VV., *La basilica di S. Maria degli Angeli 1. Storia e architettura*, Perugia 1989; Abate G., *Nuovi studi sull'ubicazione della casa paterna di S. Chiara d'Assisi*, in BDSPU, L (1953), pp. 111–144; Abate G., *La medievale "Piazza Grande" di Assisi* (a cura di F. Santucci), Assisi 1986; Bigaroni M., *S. Damiano – Assisi. La chiesa prima di San Francesco*, in AAPS, 7 (1983), pp. 49–97; Bigaroni M., *La chiesa di S. Giorgio in Assisi*, in AFH, 83 1990; Brizi A., *Della Rocca di Assisi*, Assisi 1896; Cardelli E., *Tentativo di ripristino ideale della chiesa di S. Rufino in Assisi*, Assisi 1969; Casolini F. *Il protomonastero di S. Chiara in Assisi. Storia e cronaca (1253–1950)*, Milano 1950; Guasti C., *La basilica di S. Maria degli Angeli presso Assisi*, Firenze 1882; Lunghi, *La decorazione della Chiesa di S. Maria in Arce a Rocca S. Angelo*, in AAPS, 7 (1983), pp. 113–141; Santucci F., *La "strada mattonata" da Assisi a S. Maria degli Angeli (secc. XV–XVIII)*, in AAPS, 16 (1988), pp. 79–108.

Environment

Battistella R., *Il Subasio. Paesaggio, ambiente ed economia*, Bologna 1967; Piccolpasso C., *Le piante e i ritratti delle città e delle terre dell'Umbria, sottoposte al governo di Perugia* (1578–92), ed. a cura di G. Cecchini, Roma 1963; Rambotti F. (a cura di), *Il parco del Monte Subasio – Ambiente fisico e umano*, Assisi 1986; Vetturini E., *I "mortai" e gli altri fenomeni carsici del Subasio*, in AAPS, (1989), pp. 93–130; Vetturini E., *Evoluzione del paesaggio agrario e naturale nel comprensorio di Assisi durante gli ultimi decenni. Uso del territorio*, in AAPS, 13 (1986), pp. 165–196; Vetturini A., *Settanta anni di rimboschimento del Subasio*, in AAPS, 17 (1989), pp. 72–203.

Abbreviations

A.A.P.S. = Atti dell'Accademia Proprerziana del Subasio; AA.VV. = Autori vari; A.F.H. = Archivium Franciscanum Historicum; B.D.S.P.U. = Bollettino della Deputazione di Storia Patria per l'Umbria; M.F. = Miscellanea Francescana; S.I.S.F. = Società Internazionale di Studi Francescani

INDEX OF PLACES

INDEX OF NAMES

Abbreviations:

A = architect; Bish. = bishop; Capt. = captain; Card. = cardinal; doc. = documented; Emp. = emperor; Engr. = Engraver; G = goldsmith; Gen. = general; Gov. = governor; P = painter; S = sculptor; W = woodworker

COLOR PLATES

Printed by
Arti Grafiche Antica Porziuncola – Cannara (Pg)
September 2005